P9-DTC-587

everything must change

WHEN THE WORLD'S BIGGEST PROBLEMS
AND JESUS' GOOD NEWS COLLIDE

BRIAN D. McLAREN

THOMAS NELSON
Since 1798

NASHVILLE   DALLAS   MEXICO CITY   RIO DE JANEIRO   BEIJING

© 2007 by Brian D. McLaren

All rights reserved. No portion of this book may be reproduced, stored in a
retrieval system, or transmitted in any form or by any means—electronic, mechanical,
photocopy, recording, or any other—except for brief quotation in printed reviews,
without the prior written permission of the publisher.

Published in Nashville, Tennessee, by Thomas Nelson. Thomas Nelson is a registered
trademark of Thomas Nelson, Inc.

Published in association with Kathryn A. Helmers, Helmers Literary Agency, PO Box 50737,
Colorado Springs CO 80949-0737.

Thomas Nelson, Inc., titles may be purchased in bulk for educational, business,
fund-raising, or sales promotional use. For information, please e-mail
SpecialMarkets@ThomasNelson.com.

All Scripture quotations, unless otherwise indicated, are taken from the HOLY BIBLE,
TODAY'S NEW INTERNATIONAL VERSION®. Copyright © 2001, 2005 by
International Bible Society. Used by permission of Zondervan. All rights reserved.

ISBN: 978-1-4002-8029-2 (tradepaper)

Library of Congress Cataloging-in-Publication Data

McLaren, Brian D., 1956–
  Everything must change : Jesus, global crises, and a revolution of hope / Brian D. McLaren.
    p. cm.
  Summary: "What do the life and teaching of Jesus have to say about the most
critical global problems in our world today?"—Provided by publisher.
  Includes bibliographical references.
  ISBN: 978-0-8499-0183-6 (hardcover)
  ISBN: 978-0-7852-8936-4 (IE)
  1. Christianity—Philosophy. 2. Christian life. 3. Church and social problems—Biblical
teaching. 4. Jesus Christ—Teachings. 5. Jesus Christ—Biography. I. Title.
  BR100.M34 2007
  261—dc22   2007025312

Printed in the United States of America
09 10 11 12 QW 6 5 4 3 2 1

This book is printed on paper containing 30% post-consumer waste.

Contents

Acknowledgments   v

1. Hope Happens   1

PART 1: TWO PREOCCUPYING QUESTIONS

2. The *Amahoro* Flowing Between Us   11
3. Everything Must Change   18
4. Not What Jesus Intended   25
5. Second Thoughts Had Come to Stay   32

PART 2: SUICIDAL SYSTEM

6. Simmering on the Back Burner of My Mind   43
7. Three Interlocking Systems   52
8. That Could Never Happen to Us   59
9. The Stories We Tell Ourselves   65

PART 3: REFRAMING JESUS

10. How Much More Ironic   77
11. Switching Jigsaw Lids   87
12. No Junk DNA   93
13. Jamming the Accelerator, Slamming the Brakes   101
14. Or So It Appeared   109

PART 4: REINTRODUCING JESUS

15. Peace Through Domination   119
16. Occupying Regime, Equity Gap, Excrement Factory   128
17. How Different It Would Be   134
18. Which Jesus?   141

PART 5: THE SECURITY SYSTEM

19. Joining the Peace Insurgency   151

20. Whose Side Are We On?   161
21. Layers and Layers More   170
22. Joining Warriors Anonymous   176

PART 6: THE PROSPERITY SYSTEM

23. Capitalism as God   189
24. Obligations to Nonexistent Future People   200
25. Quick Bliss Through Footwear, Palate Grease,   206
    and Skin Paint
26. Collaboration for Co-liberation   216

PART 7: THE EQUITY SYSTEM

27. On the Side of the Rebel Jesus   227
28. Beyond Blame and Shame   237
29. A New Kind of Question   248
30. Organized Religion or Religion Organizing   256
    for the Common Good?

PART 8: A REVOLUTION OF HOPE

31. The Most Radical Thing We Can Do   269
32. An Unfolding, Emergent, Spiraling Process   275
33. Exposing the Covert Curriculum   283
34. Moving Mountains   294

Notes   302

Acknowledgments

Thanks to several friends who read and commented on an early draft of this manuscript: Mark Buckingham, Linnea Nilsen Capshaw, and Keith Kranker. Their insights regarding economics, theology, and politics helped me avoid several mistakes and also allowed me to risk making other mistakes less naively and more knowledgeably. Special thanks to my editors, Greg Daniel, Brian Hampton, and Bryan Norman; and my agent, Kathryn Helmers, for helping break a bucking bronco of untamed ideas into a herd of chapters people will want to saddle up and take for a ride.

Thanks to Dr. Leonard Sweet for providing the term *suicide machine,* which is so important in these pages, and thanks for so much insight and inspiration through the years. Thanks to Jim Wallis and the Sojourners/Call to Renewal community; to Tony, Peggy, and Bart Campolo and the Red-Letter Christians; to Tony Jones and Doug Pagitt and the people of emergentvillage.com; to Claude Nikondeha and the people of amahoro-africa.org; to Tomas Yaccino and Rene Padilla and the people of lareddelcamino.net, and to Matthew and Lisa Dyer, Melanie Griffin, Chris and Elaine Hill, Bill and Shobha Duncan, and the people of crcc.org—people with whom I am able to think and dream and believe.

Thanks especially to all the people I met in my travels whose lives and words teach and inspire me, especially friends in Latin America, Africa, Asia, and Europe. Your influence is strong in these pages.

Hope Happens

If you're like some people (including my wife and a few friends who have been nervous about this book since they heard what I was writing about), you may already feel a little skeptical and suspicious, having only read the title and subtitle of this book.

You've surmised that the statement "everything must change" is hyperbole. Whatever your reaction to the subtitle's mention of "Jesus" and "revolution of hope," you've judged "global crises" to be totally depressing and overwhelming. You've determined that people who talk about global crises aren't life-of-the-party types; instead, they score high in the categories of being boring, humorless, and guilt-inducing.

If we're going to get anywhere, I have to convince you—and fast—of at least four things. First, that I'm not another blah-blah-blah person ranting about how bad the world is and how guilty you should feel for taking up space in it. Second, that I can help you understand some highly complex material and make it not only accessible but maybe even interesting and inspiring. Third, that when you're done with this book, you'll not only better understand the world and your place in it, but you'll also know how you can make a difference. (You'll also be able to engage in dialogue and further research through the book's website—www.brianmclaren.net.) And fourth, I must

1

convince you that making a difference is not another dreary duty for an already overburdened person, but rather that making a difference is downright joyful—fulfilling, rewarding, good.

You also may be wondering who I am and why I'm writing on the subjects of Jesus, global crises, and hope. I'm not an economist, politician, or certified expert on anything really. But I am a normal person like you who cares and wants to do the right thing. I started my career as a college English teacher and then became a pastor for twenty-four years. In the mid-1990s, while I was a pastor, I started writing books, a few of which have been best sellers. I serve on a number of nonprofit boards and travel extensively as a public speaker and networker. I've been on national news shows as a spokesperson for "the emerging church" and "progressive evangelical Christianity" and other such oxymorons (some would say), and you can Google my name and find websites and blogs from fundamentalist groups who consider me the son of Satan or on the wrong side of both the "culture war" and "truth war."

More personally, I'm a rather ordinary person. I care about my young adult kids and the kids they may someday have. I care about my friends, neighbors, and fellow citizens and our common future on this beautiful, imperiled planet. I care about the billions of people I've never met and never will meet, including people who might be called my nation's enemies. I also care about our fellow creatures—brown trout and blue herons, raccoons and gopher tortoises, red dragonflies and royal palms, barrel cactus and woodland ferns. I care about all of these for a lot of reasons, especially because I am a committed follower of Christ, and people with this commitment, it seems to me, can't help but care about all these things.

As a follower of God in the way of Jesus, I've been involved in a profoundly interesting and enjoyable conversation for the last ten years or so. It's a conversation about what it means to be "a new kind of Christian"—not an angry and reactionary fundamentalist, not a stuffy traditionalist, not a blasé nominalist, not a wishy-washy liberal, not a New Agey religious hipster, not a crusading religious imperialist, and not an overly enthused Bible-waving fanatic—but something fresh and authentic and challenging and adventurous. Around the world, millions of people have gotten involved in this conversation, and more are getting involved each day. (One reason we keep calling it a *conversation* is that we can't find a short way of describing it yet.)

The couple hundred thousand people who have read my previous books seem to find in them some hope and resonance with things they've already been thinking and feeling, including a suspicion that the religious status quo is broken and a desire to translate their faith into a way of life that makes a positive difference in the world. They share my belief that the versions of Christianity we inherited are largely flattened, watered down, tamed . . . offering us a ticket to heaven after death, but not challenging us to address the issues that threaten life on earth. Together we've begun to seek a fresh understanding of what Christianity is for, what a church can be and do, and most exciting, we're finding out that a lot of what we need most is already hidden in a trunk in our attic. Which is good news.

So this is a religious book, but in a worldly and unconventional and ultimately positive way, a way some nonreligious people would probably call "spiritual but not religious."

UNCONVENTIONAL QUESTIONS

I've always had a propensity to think a few degrees askew from most people, especially about religion. And not only am I often unsatisfied with conventional answers, but even worse, I've consistently been unsatisfied with conventional questions.

For instance, when I was a pastor, people often asked my opinion on hot-button issues like evolution, abortion, and homosexuality. The problem was that after discussing those issues in all of their importance and intensity, I couldn't help asking other questions: Why do we need to have singular and firm opinions on the protection of the unborn, but not about how to help poor people and how to avoid killing people labeled *enemies* who are already born? Or why are we so concerned about the legitimacy of homosexual marriage but not about the legitimacy of fossil fuels or the proliferation of weapons of mass destruction (and in particular, *our weapons* as opposed to *theirs*)? Or why are so many religious people arguing about the origin of species but so few concerned about the extinction of species? Then I'd wonder, If we religious people have exclusively seized on a couple of hot-button questions, what other questions should we be thinking about that nobody's asking? That's the kind of wonderment that can turn into a book like the one you're holding.

Part of what it means to be "a new kind of Christian" is to discover or rediscover what the essential message of Jesus is about. As I explained in some detail in *The Secret Message of Jesus*,[1] more and more of us are realizing something our best theologians have been saying for quite a while: Jesus' message is not actually about escaping this troubled world for heaven's blissful shores, as is popularly assumed, but instead is about God's will being done on this troubled earth as it is in heaven. So people interested in being a new kind of Christian will inevitably begin to care more and more about this world, and they'll want to better understand its most significant problems, and they'll want to find out how they can fit in with God's dreams actually coming true down here more often.

Which is why I wanted to write this book: because when I started caring about these things, I didn't know where to begin. I started reading books and websites and talking to knowledgeable people, but I soon felt my naïveté being replaced by an overwhelming complexity. I kept looking for a way to tame the complexity in a big picture or metaphor, and when the big picture began to come into focus, I felt I had discovered something worth sharing.

The Leverage Point—A Better Framing Story

To make preliminary sense of the crises that surround us, I can briefly introduce a few metaphors or word pictures that we'll consider later in more detail. For example, I can speak of a perfect storm of global crises brewing like an undetected hurricane out at sea, sending preliminary rain bands ashore that aren't themselves the problem but are signs of the problem that approaches. I can develop a disease metaphor, comparing our global crises to varied symptoms of a single as-yet undiagnosed autoimmune disease. Or I can explore the ways our society has become an addict.

In particular, I can use the image of a *suicide machine* that co-opts the main mechanisms of our civilization—our economic, political, and military systems—and reprograms them to destroy those they should serve. It's not coincidental that the image of a machine that turns on its creators has recently become popular in movies from *The Matrix* to *I, Robot*. In this book, I suggest that the image is true.

Whatever metaphors I employ—an undetected storm, an undiagnosed disease, an unacknowledged addiction, or a machine that has gone destructive—I'll suggest that our plethora of critical global crises can be traced to four deep dysfunctions, the fourth of which is the lynchpin or leverage point through which we can reverse the first three:

1. Environmental breakdown caused by our unsustainable global economy, an economy that fails to respect environmental limits even as it succeeds in producing great wealth for about one-third of the world's population. We'll call this the *prosperity crisis*.

2. The growing gap between the ultra-rich and the extremely poor, which prompts the poor majority to envy, resent, and even hate the rich minority—which in turn elicits fear and anger in the rich. We'll call this the *equity crisis*.

3. The danger of cataclysmic war arising from the intensifying resentment and fear among various groups at opposite ends of the economic spectrum. We'll call this the *security crisis*.

4. The failure of the world's religions, especially its two largest religions, to provide a framing story capable of healing or reducing the three previous crises. We'll call this the *spirituality crisis*.

By *framing story*, I mean a story that gives people direction, values, vision, and inspiration by providing a framework for their lives.

It tells them who they are, where they come from, where they are, what's going on, where things are going, and what they should do.

In searching for a better framing story than we currently proclaim, Christians like myself can discover a fresh vision of our religion's founder and his message, a potentially revolutionary vision that could change everything for us and for the world we inhabit. We can rediscover what it can mean to call Jesus Savior and Lord when we raise the question of what exactly he intended to save us from. (His angry Father? The logical consequences of our actions? Our tendency to act in ways that produce undesirable logical consequences? Global self-destruction?) The popular and domesticated Jesus, who has become little more than a chrome-plated hood ornament on the guzzling Hummer of Western civilization, can thus be replaced with a more radical, saving, and, I believe, *real* Jesus.

THE HOPE THAT CAN CHANGE EVERYTHING

As I worked on this book—grappling to understand our world's top problems and to see them in relation to the life and message of Jesus—I was struck as never before with the one simple, available, yet surprisingly powerful response called for by Jesus, a response that can begin to foment a revolution of hope among us, a hope that can change everything. That hope may happen to you as you read, without you even noticing it. If it happens in enough of us, we will face and overcome the global crises that threaten us, and we will sow the seeds of a better future.

I spent 2006 and early 2007 writing and editing this book. It brings to fruition thought processes that go back for several decades. This book took shape in a variety of places around the world, over twenty countries in all: Fiji, Australia, New Zealand, South Africa, Canada, England, Wales, Ireland, Switzerland, Norway, Denmark, Sweden, Mexico, Honduras, El Salvador, Guatemala, Costa Rica, Chile, Argentina, Malaysia, Kenya, Uganda, and the United States. It was written in slums, in airports and trains, in hotels, in homes, in seminary dormitories, in places of great natural beauty, in places of great human ugliness, and some of it (thankfully) in my own home in Maryland, in the good company of my wife and life companion, Grace. It was written under the musical influence of Bob Dylan and Bruce Cockburn, Afro Celt Sound System, the Putumayo Mali collection, Steve Bell, U2, Harp 46, Carrie Newcomer, David Wilcox, Eva Cassidy, Mozart, Vivaldi, Bach, and Keith Jarrett. These many influences, plus the ongoing wars in Afghanistan and Iraq, the invasion of Lebanon, the deteriorating conditions in Darfur, and the slow, sad burn of the Congo . . . all of these have marked and flavored this book in some way, making it, of all of my books so far, the most "worldly."

The book is a first visit to a new way of seeing the world and hearing the message of Jesus. Many things I have understated in the interest of gentleness; they could have been expressed in much stronger language, but that more passionate language would have been off-putting for uninformed readers (just as the understatement may be off-putting for informed readers, which shows my bias). Everything here also could have been explored in much greater detail. That's why in the back of this book, you'll find extensive notes that cite resources to help you go deeper in areas that grip you. You'll find much additional background in *The Secret Message of Jesus*, and although it is the prequel to this book, you can read either book first.

Having finished writing the book, I am eager for you to read it—slowly and thoughtfully, I hope, and with some friends if possible—and I'm eager for all of us to get to work. There is much to dismantle, much to overturn, much to rebuild, much to imagine and create, and there are many seeds to be sown and grown.

GROUP DIALOGUE QUESTIONS

1. As you begin this book, what are you most excited about? Confused or curious about? Eager to learn more about? What feelings has this chapter elicited in you?

2. What are your impressions of the author? Is he winning your confidence, or do you feel some of the skepticism he identified in the opening paragraphs of this chapter?

3. How do you react to the summary of global crises in this chapter—environmental breakdown (the prosperity crisis), the growing gap between rich and poor (the equity crisis), the danger of cataclysmic war (the security crisis), and the failure of the world's religions to address the first three crises (the spirituality crisis)? Think of issues you've seen in the headlines lately. How do they fit under these four categories?

4. This chapter introduces the subject of hope. How would you describe your level of hope about global crises as you begin this book?

5. What would you like other people in your discussion group to know about you as your group begins?

6. Are there some traditions or patterns you would like to observe when you gather (whether you gather in person, by conference call, or online)? For example, would you like to begin an end with the Lord's Prayer or one of the prayers attributed to St. Francis? Would you like to take a collection each week and use the proceeds to help someone in need? Would you like to sing or a play a theme song to conclude your meeting? If some of you are writers or poets or artists of other sorts, would you like to share things you're inspired to create as you read?

7. You can find links to other group resources at the book's website: everythingmustchange.org. Discuss with other group members some of the resources you discovered on the website.

PART 1

TWO PREOCCUPYING QUESTIONS

The *Amahoro* Flowing
Between Us

A person's life is shaped by many things—among the most important are the questions she or he can't help but ask. This book explores two of the shaping questions of my life. I began asking myself these two questions when I was in my twenties, and they've been simmering in my mind ever since.

Two Preoccupying Questions

You may criticize my two questions for their lack of modesty, or you may feel I have no business asking questions of this magnitude. But then again, you may find yourself as intrigued by them as I have been. For people who share a commitment to ethics or faith or both, not asking these questions seems unthinkable—once you think of them.

Question #1: What Are the Biggest Problems in the World?

The first question I asked was this: *what are the biggest problems in the world?* By *biggest*, I mean problems that cause the most suffering in the present, that pose the greatest threat to our future, that cause most of the other problems, that lie at the root of what's wrong with the world—and therefore at the root of what must be done to set the world on a better course.

When I asked myself this question in my twenties, and then when it resurfaced in my forties, what disturbed me most was that I couldn't remember ever hearing anyone address it. Instead, I had heard a long list of un-integrated crusades against or for this or that, with little rationale as to why the crusade was worthwhile. Through all the commotion, I had seen too little progress on any front.

Question #2: What Does Jesus Have to Say About These Global Problems?

The second question flowed naturally from the first question and from my faith, my chosen path as a follower of God in the way of Jesus—which you may or may not share and still find this book of interest: *what do the life and teachings of Jesus have to say about the most critical global problems in our world today?* Believing, as I do, that Jesus was (among many other things) unique and brilliant and wise, I had reason to believe that if I could determine the top global problems, I would find some relevant wisdom in the life and teachings of Jesus. And, in turn, I reasoned, my view of Jesus would be deepened and enriched by seeing him in light of today's global problems.

But most of what I had heard religious people say about Jesus related to (a) how some individuals could go to heaven after death, or (b) in the meantime, how some individuals could be more personally happy and successful through God and the Bible. Jesus, as someone focused on individuals and the afterlife, seemed to have little to offer regarding pressing global matters. This common assumption, I hope to show, is false.

Additional questions flowed from the tension between the original two: *Why hasn't the Christian religion made a difference commensurate with its message, size, and resources? What would need to happen for followers of Jesus to become a greater force for good in relation to the world's top problems? How could we make a positive difference?*

All these questions may sound too religious for your taste already. If you have no religious commitment, and even if you have a strong anti-religious commitment, I certainly sympathize. Those of us who are deeply involved in the religious community see abundant reasons to be cynical about religion. Though we see many signs of hope, goodness, and resurrection, the truth is that we often keep faith in spite of religion, not because of it. But whatever your background, I think you'll agree on the most pragmatic level: if the problems are as big as they seem to be, we'll need all the help we can muster to address them, including the help of the religious community.[1]

In addition, since the Christian religion is the biggest religion in the world (with about 2 billion adherents, or 33 percent of the world's population),[2] whatever constructive things Jesus might have to say about our top global problems could be important in determining our world's future.[3] This would be the case at the very least because solutions in sync with Jesus' life and teachings might get more buy-in among his professed followers. Add to that the fact that Islam is the world's second biggest religion (1.3 billion adherents, or 21 percent of the world's population) and that Muslims revere Jesus as a great prophet, and you discover even more practical value in seeing Jesus' teachings in relation to today's global problems.

Beyond the Christian and Islamic religions, which together account for more than half of the world's people, and which together share a high regard for Jesus, we could add that many Hindus (14 percent of the world's population), Buddhists (6 percent), Jews (0.22 percent), and even nonreligious people (16 percent) admire Jesus—even though they may be less enthusiastic about the religion that bears his name.[4]

THE JOURNEY TOWARD ANSWERS

These two questions—what are the world's top problems, and what do the life and message of Jesus have to say about them—have been my preoccupation, or perhaps *obsession* is the better word, over recent years. Seeking for answers has led me to some interesting and even dangerous places. For example, a few years ago, I found myself standing in a dilapidated airport in Bujumbura, Burundi, East Africa, staring at bullet holes in a dirty skylight, their cracks spreading outward from small impact craters, reaching like silvery spider legs across the blue African sky.

My journey to Bujumbura began with a phone call about a year earlier: "Hi, Brian. My name is Claude Nikondeha. I have read some of your books, and I think what you write about is relevant to my country. Would you like to talk?"

Claude was from Burundi in East Africa, the world's third poorest country and the twin-sister country of Rwanda.[5] Like most Americans, I'm embarrassed to say, I couldn't have found either one on a map without some work.

Both countries, it turns out, were about the same size as my home state, Maryland, with a population of about seven million each, a million more than my state. Rwanda, of course, was the more famous of the two, or perhaps *infamous* is the better word. It became an icon of genocide in 1994 when some eight hundred thousand people were killed in one hundred days—not with guns or bombs, but with machetes and hammers and garden tools; and not by soldiers in uniforms, but by neighbors, friends, even relatives who happened to be identified with the other tribe. The 2004 film *Hotel Rwanda* eventually exposed the world to the tragic story, but Claude's call came before the movie released, so the relevant history and geography weren't yet clear in my mind.

Claude and I met for breakfast some time later when he was visiting my home city, Washington, DC. By our last cup of coffee, an important friendship had started. Before we paid our bill, Claude extended an invitation to me: "Brian, would you be willing to come to Burundi and meet with about fifty young leaders I know from the region? I would like to expose them to your thinking. I think it would help us." I gave him a firm "I'll think about it" and told him that if I came, I didn't want to simply speak or teach. I wanted to come to listen, to learn, to try to understand what life was like for these people whom now, through Claude, I was beginning to feel somehow connected to.

Before I gave him my final answer, I went on the Internet and did some research. The US State Department strongly urged Americans not to visit Burundi because it had been torn by civil war for a decade and by outbreaks of genocide for more than four decades. The animosity between Hutu and Tutsi tribes that had possessed Rwanda like a nightmarish demon had taken even more lives in Burundi than in Rwanda. Armed rebel groups still showed their power through random killings. You never knew when a grenade would be tossed in a window or when gunfire would rip through your car door. Not only that, but tropical diseases were a real danger in Burundi as well because during the civil war, the healthcare system deteriorated, along with all social structures. Even so, somehow I felt I should go.

I mentioned this to my cousin and his wife, world travelers who do relief and development work and are no strangers to dangerous situations. They both seemed a bit surprised that I would consider going, even more so when they learned that I was considering taking my seventeen-year-old daughter, the youngest of our four children. "The hatred there runs deep and the violence has been brutal," they cautioned. "And the conflict is nowhere near over."

When our kids were still preteens, I promised them that before they graduated high school, I would take each of them on a trip, just the two of us, somewhere out of the US. Rachel had accompanied me to Italy, France, and Spain; Brett had joined me on an adventure in Costa Rica; and Trevor and I went to the Galapagos Islands. Somehow, I felt that this trip to Burundi would be the right one for Jodi to experience. And somehow, I felt that this trip would help me in my search for answers to my two preoccupying questions.

I shared my safety concerns with Claude. "It's true, it would be a little dangerous for you to go alone. But I know the situation, and I know people there, and if you're with me, you'll be safe." So I said yes.

A BUMPY RIDE TOWARD PEACE

In some ways, I could not *not* go on this trip. As a follower of Jesus, and as a pastor for over two decades, I knew that in the Bible God shows a special concern for the poor, the vulnerable, the forgotten, the oppressed. I knew that Jesus said, "Whatever you did for one of the least of these . . . you did for me" (Matthew 25:40).

But I also knew that most churchgoers, including myself, either didn't share that concern for the poor or didn't know how to turn concern and good intentions into constructive action. Even though we believed that the poor should be helped—that poverty should be fought—we didn't know how. We had heard liberal and conservative arguments blaming poverty on everything from capitalism to communism, from corruption to bad trade policies, and from debt, to the selfishness of the West, racism, family breakdown, the irresponsibility or immorality of the poor, government regulation of business, and badly administered charity. We seemed polarized by our ideological diagnoses of the causes and cures of poverty, and even worse, we were paralyzed by our polarization, and so the poor continued to suffer—trapped by their poverty and our polarizing, paralyzing arguments about poverty.

I was forty-eight years old, and if I was ever going to do something about poverty and injustice, it seemed like high time for me to get more firsthand experience.

Jodi and I got the necessary immunizations, and, after promising my wife in every way possible that we would return home safely, my daughter and I walked down a jetway to a plane bound for Africa. We passed through Amsterdam and Nairobi, and then we finally landed at the Bujumbura airport, artistically designed in a beehive style, reflecting indigenous African architecture, African culture and African pride. But that pride had clearly suffered a major setback. A few old, dilapidated planes sat unused on the cracked tarmac, relics of a national airline that had long been bankrupt. Grass and vines were encroaching on the pavement. In many of the airport's windows and skylights—long in need of a good wash—those bullet holes glinted in the African sun, a kind of three-dimensional graffiti made by the random gunfire of Burundi's rebel factions.

Claude and his wife, Kelley, welcomed us. On our bumpy ride from the airport to the home of Claude's parents—swerving around countless craters made by grenades, weaving between barefoot or sandaled pedestrians and herds of skinny cows and goats—Claude explained to us how to properly greet his mom and dad when we arrived. "First, shake my father's hand with two hands, your left hand grasping your right forearm. Then kiss my mother on one cheek and then the other, several times, and each time, whisper into her ear the word *amahoro*," he explained. "The word means peace. She'll be welcoming you into the peace of our home, and you'll be offering your peace to her. After all we've been through, *amahoro* is a very precious word to us."

"Exactly how many times should we do this?" I asked.

"We basically do it again and again, until we feel the *amahoro* flowing between us."

GROUP DIALOGUE QUESTIONS

1. How do you respond to the author's two preoccupying questions? Have you ever asked them? Have you ever heard others ask them?

2. Have you heard debates about the causes of poverty? In your current understanding, what are the primary causes of poverty?

3. How do you think most Christians today respond to the issue of poverty? Does their faith make them care about it more or less than the average person? What has been your experience with the issue of poverty as it relates to your faith?

4. Have you ever visited a foreign country? If so, share a vivid memory or two. If not, where would you like to visit, and why?

5. As a group, consider watching and discussing *Hotel Rwanda, Tsotsi, City of God, Blood Diamond, Beat the Drum,* or another film that relates to themes in this chapter.

Everything Must Change

It was May 2004. My daughter and I joined a group of fifty-five young *amahoro*-hungry leaders at a conference center near Bujumbura. Most were from Tutsi and Hutu tribes from Rwanda and Burundi, and there were even a few Twa (also known as pygmies—one of the most ill-treated people groups on the planet). As well, there were several guests from Uganda and eastern Congo. Their homelands were a random sample of the most violent, poverty-stricken, and dangerous countries in the world.[1]

At our first gathering, I remember looking through the windows as Claude began to speak, the mountains east of Bujumbura rising hazy and brown in the midmorning light. He spoke in his native tongue, Kirundi, which was translated into French for the Congolese participants and whispered in English to my daughter and me. My two questions were sizzling beneath the surface of everything he said.

"Friends, most of you know me. You know that I am the son of a preacher, and as a result, I grew up going to church all the time, maybe five times a week. What may surprise you, though, is to learn that in all of my childhood, in all the church services I attended, I only heard one sermon." At this, eyes got larger and people seemed curious, maybe confused. *One sermon in all those years?*

He continued, "That sermon went like this: 'You are a sinner and you are going to hell. You need to repent and believe in Jesus. Jesus might come back today, and if he does and you are not ready, you will burn forever in hell.'"

At that, almost everyone began to laugh. They weren't laughing at the idea of going to hell or the idea of believing in Jesus; they were laughing in recognition that *this was the only sermon they had ever heard too.* Sunday after Sunday, year after year, different words, different Bible verses, but the same point.

Then Claude got serious. "When I got older, I realized that my entire life had been lived against the backdrop of genocide and violence, poverty and corruption. Over a million people died in my country in a series of genocides starting in 1959, and nearly a million in Rwanda, and in spite of huge amounts of foreign aid, our people remain poor, and many of them, hungry. This is the experience we all have shared." Around the room, people leaned forward, their heads nodding.

"So much death, so much hatred and distrust between tribes, so much poverty, suffering, corruption, and injustice, and nothing ever really changed. Eventually I realized something. I had never heard a sermon that addressed these realities. Did God only care about our souls going to heaven after we died? Were our hungry bellies unimportant to God? Was God unconcerned about our crying sons and frightened daughters, our mothers hiding under beds, our fathers crouching by windows, unable to sleep because of gunfire? Or did God send Jesus to teach us how to avoid genocide by learning to love each other, how to overcome tribalism and poverty by following his path, how to deal with injustice and corruption, how to make a better life here on earth—here in East Africa?"

Claude walked a few steps closer to the center of the group, seated around long tables arranged in a semicircle. "Let me ask you a question. How many of you from Burundi and Rwanda have ever heard even one sermon telling Tutsi people to love and reconcile with Hutu people, or Hutu people to love and reconcile with Tutsi—or telling both Tutsi and Hutu to love the Twa as their neighbors and brothers and sisters?"

Two hands went up. Both, it turns out, were Anglican priests—and they had preached those sermons themselves in the aftermath of the genocide in Rwanda. But nobody else had ever heard a sermon addressing the most pressing issue of their lifetimes, before or since the Rwandan genocide.

Claude continued, "Over the years, I have come to realize that something is wrong with the way we understand Jesus and the good news. Something is missing in the version of the Christian religion we received from the missionaries, which is the message we now preach ourselves. They told us how to go to heaven. But they left out an important detail. They didn't tell us how the will of God could be done on earth. We need to learn what the message of Jesus says to our situation here in East Africa. And that is why we have come together."

NOT JUST AN AFRICAN PROBLEM

As he spoke, I thought, *This is not just an African problem*. The same has been true here in the Americas where I live, as it has been in Australia, New Zealand, Europe, and Asia. Did North American church leaders teach the early colonists to treat the Native Peoples with love and respect? Did they consistently and with one voice oppose slavery because it was an assault on the dignity of fellow human beings? Later in our history, did they express outrage over the exploitation of factory workers or the second-class status of women? Did they stand up for refugees and immigrants?[2] Did they oppose white privilege, segregation, anti-Semitism, stereotyping of Muslims, and other forms of ethnic prejudice? Did they see the environment as God's sacred creation that deserves to be cherished and conserved?

"Well," you might say, "some got it right." But you would have to agree: too few, and too late. Most were preoccupied with other matters—arguments about religious esoterica, fights over arcane biblical interpretations, fanciful escapes into theological speculation, heat and fury over drinking or gambling or playing cards or using tobacco, controversies over whether guitars and drums can be used in worship gatherings or whether only pianos and organs produce holy music, and other matters that—in comparison to racism, genocide, carelessness toward the poor and various minorities, exploitation of the environment, and unjust war—seem shamefully trivial, weapons of mass distraction.

I knew it would be an interesting few days for my daughter and me in Burundi. I knew I was on the scent of answers to my two simmering questions.

REVISITING THE ESSENTIAL MESSAGE OF JESUS

Later that day, our group talked in depth about the essential message of Jesus. We talked in particular about the metaphor Jesus used again and again to convey his essential message: *the kingdom of God.* We considered how this message of the kingdom—contrary to popular belief—was not focused on how to escape this world and its problems by going to heaven after death, but instead was focused on how God's will could be done on earth, in history, during this life. We described God's kingdom in terms of God's dreams coming true for this earth, of God's justice and peace replacing earth's injustice and disharmony.[3]

We talked about how nations engaged in colonialism would find it hard to face the full dimensions of Jesus' essential message, since it would, if they saw it, call into question the whole colonial project. We talked about how the time had come—for blacks like them, as descendants of the colonized, and for whites like me and my daughter, descendants of the colonizers—to tell the painful stories of our past, not to stir up anger and revenge, but to face the truth together in a spirit of grace and reflection, and to discover together what to do now, where to go next, how to move forward.

Using an old blackboard and white chalk, Claude and I created a chart with two columns: *colonial* and *postcolonial.* It also had two rows: *colonizers* and *colonized.*

We asked, "How did the colonizers feel during the colonial times?

And how do they feel now, in postcolonial times?" The answers were predictable: during colonialism, they felt powerful, clean, knowledgeable, superior, capable, and civilized. But now, looking back on colonialism, they must be feeling ashamed, humbled, repentant, uncertain, conciliatory, regretful.

The next question: "How did the colonized feel during both eras?" Under colonialism, they said, they felt dirty, ashamed, grateful, dependent, incompetent, incapable, uneducated, unintelligent, resentful, abused, and afraid. But now, with colonialism decades behind them, and for many of them, nothing more than a fading memory of their parents and grandparents, they felt competent, capable, hopeful, confident, and empowered.

Then under the *colonial* column, we wrote, "The gospel of avoiding hell," or something to that effect, and under the *postcolonial* column, we wrote, "The gospel of the kingdom of God." The time had come, we said, to center our lives on the essential message of Jesus, the message of the kingdom of God—not just a message *about* Jesus that focused on the afterlife, but rather the core message *of* Jesus that focused on personal, social, and global transformation in this life. This message *of* Jesus could help us imagine what the world could be if Jesus was right in his proclamation of the kingdom of God. I think we all felt that this imagining had to be a shared project for us. Because—again, I think we all felt this—the message of the kingdom of God had been nearly invisible to all of us, even as we—descendants of the colonial evangelizers and the evangelized—had spoken and sung and preached and prayed the name of Jesus, Jesus, Jesus, for so many Sundays, so many years.

IF IT'S TRUE, THEN EVERYTHING MUST CHANGE

The second day of our gathering in Bujumbura came to an end. As the group dispersed for some free time before dinner, I noticed Justine, a Burundian currently living in Rwanda, sitting alone at a table. Her head was on the table, sheltered in her arms, and she was completely motionless. At first I wondered if she was asleep or maybe sick. I asked another woman who could translate to come with me to see if she was okay. The woman put her hand on Justine's shoulder, and Justine slowly raised her head. "Are you okay?" we asked.

She replied, "I'm okay, but I'm shaken up. I don't know if anyone else here sees it, but I do. I see it. Today, for the first time, I see what Jesus meant by the kingdom of God. I see that it's about changing this world, not just escaping it and retreating into our churches. If Jesus' message of the kingdom of God is true, then everything must change. Everything must change."

Justine realized that the kingdom of God is not simply a new belief or doctrine that can be patched into an old way of life; it is, rather, a new way of life that changes everything. Her words still echo in my heart. They found their way into the subtitle of *The Secret Message of Jesus* and the title of this book. Her simple declaration—*if Jesus' message of the kingdom of God is true, then everything must change*—continually challenges me to rethink my thirty-five years as a follower of Christ, along with my whole understanding of theology, church history, and ministry in today's world. Justine's simple sentence elegantly combines my two questions into one: *what could change if we applied the message of Jesus—the good news of the kingdom of God—to the world's greatest problems?*

Of course, it raises additional questions as well. If professed adherents to the Christian religion in Burundi and Rwanda could celebrate Jesus in thousands of local churches for a half-century, and all the while miss what Jesus said to their most pressing social, political, and economic issues, what are we in the West missing today? If adherents to the Christian religion in Europe and America could experience revivals and write theological masterpieces and send missionaries by the shiploads around the world, but remain in naive, unconscious, or willful denial about the injustices inherent in their way of life, what are we missing now?

All of these questions, with all their implicit urgency, again pressed down on me one day in 2006, during another trip to Africa.

GROUP DIALOGUE QUESTIONS

1. How did you respond to Claude's talk? Was his experience of hearing one basic sermon in his childhood similar to or different from your own?
2. Try to define or describe "the kingdom of God" in your own terms. See if you as a group can come up with a good definition.
3. Could you relate to Justine's response to the conversation about the kingdom of God?
4. What in the history of your country resonates with the history of colonialism in Africa?
5. What questions are raised for you at this point in your reading? What does your reading so far have you thinking about? Is there anything that bothers you, concerns you, or especially interests you?

Not What Jesus Intended

In a modest church building in a township near Capetown, South Africa, twenty-some local Pentecostal, charismatic, and Baptist pastors were seated in a circle. Two guests of paler hue were present as well: my local host, Johannes, and me. We had paper plates on our laps and coffee cups on the floor beside each chair. The group had gathered at my request, as part of my search for answers to the two shaping questions that gave rise to this book. We were discussing ministry in the postcolonial, post-apartheid world.

One fellow, a handsome dark-skinned man in his early thirties (I'd guess), had been strangely silent so far in our conversation. He made eye contact with me, and as he did, I noticed how his brow was furrowed and his jaw tense. Was he afraid of something, perhaps angry?

"Do you want to say something?" I asked him.

"Yes, I have something I . . . *need* to say," he began. He moved forward to the edge of his chair, elbows resting on knees. Slowly, his hands stretched open, and they remained extended like this until he was well into his impromptu speech. "Brothers, I am not a pastor. I am a healthcare worker. I do HIV/AIDS work in Khayelitsha." At this everyone nodded. Known as an informal settlement to some, a squatter area to others, Khayelitsha [pronounced "ka-yeh-LEET-sha"] is the third-largest township in South Africa. Its shacks made of scavenged building supplies stretch along the nearby airport road as far as the eye can see, providing substandard shelter for immigrants from villages across the eastern half of the country. Around half a million black and colored people had landed there seeking a better life after the fall of apartheid, but now they suffered from the predictable problems associated with migration, poverty, and unemployment: substance abuse, domestic violence, and HIV infection. Many of these pastors were working in Khayelitsha, setting up tents to conduct services there Sunday by Sunday.

The young man continued, "You pastors are . . ." He hesitated as he raised one outstretched hand toward heaven. "You are causing such destruction in Khayelitsha. It reaches to the skies. I know you mean well, but you don't realize that you cause devastation in the lives of the people among whom I work."

Eyes widened, pastors shifted in their seats, and the young man continued, "You come to Khayelitsha every Sunday and set up your tents, which is good, but I have listened to your preaching, and you are preoccupied with three things, and three things only. First, you constantly talk about healing. You tell people they can be healed of HIV, and some of them believe you, so they stop taking their medication. When they stop, they develop new resistant strains of the disease that don't respond as well to the medications, and they spread these tougher infections to other people, leaving them much sicker than they were before. Then you're always telling the people they need to be born again, but after they're born again on Sunday, they're still unemployed on Monday. They may be born again, but what good is that if their problems are the same as before? You know as well as I do that if they're unemployed, they're going to be caught in the poverty web of substance abuse, crime and gangs, domestic violence, and HIV. What good is that? All this born-again talk is nothing but nonsense."

At this, I could see some of the pastors bristling. I wondered if a shouting match would erupt, but the healthcare worker leaned a little farther forward, and the pastors constrained themselves a little longer.

"Then what do you do? After telling these desperately poor people to get born again and healed, then you tell them to tithe. You tell them to 'sow financial seed' into your ministries and they will receive a hundredfold return. But you're the only ones getting a return on their investment. You could be helping so much. You could motivate people to learn employable skills, you could teach them and help them in so many ways, but it's always the same thing: healing, getting born again, and tithing.

"Even the religious organizations that try to help people with HIV—most of them get US aid money, which only allows them to talk about abstinence and fidelity. They can't even mention condoms, and as a result, a lot of people die. And most of you—you won't talk about abstinence and fidelity, because the subject of sex is taboo among us. And so more people die.

"You know your problem? You Pentecostals and you evangelicals specialized. You specialized in healing, in getting people born again, in creating financially successful churches—but you need to go beyond that. It's time to get a better message—something bigger than just those things. If you stop there, all your preaching is nonsense."

Nonsense was the verbal grenade, lobbed a second time now, unleashing the pastors' vigorous response. For the next twenty or thirty minutes, one pastor after another replied with impassioned speeches, testimonies, sermonettes. Some were fatherly; some were brotherly; some were stern; some were gentle. But each defended the fact that being born again and getting healed were *biblical*, which means they weren't nonsense. We never got to the subject of tithing.

The young man listened. As the older pastors spoke, he respectfully gave them his full attention and didn't defend himself when they used words like "heresy" and "false doctrine" to discredit his words. When there was a lull in the conversation, he responded in a quiet but firm tone: "Brothers, I am not your enemy. I am your friend. I believe in Jesus. I am born again myself. I even speak in tongues, so I'm Pentecostal like most of you. I'm sorry I offended you by the word *nonsense*. But if you would simply teach them some practical things that relate to their daily lives, that could make such a big difference."

After the gathering, I found this young man and told him how much I respected his courage. Seeing that I was sympathetic, he poured out his heart.

"Brian," he said, "these pastors are so needed. They could make such a difference. Who else loves the poor and forgotten people in Khayelitsha? Their lives, maybe even the future of our nation, depend in large part on these pastors. Yet they think that HIV is a matter of sex, and they can't talk about sex because of our cultural taboos. But in Khayelitsha, HIV isn't just about sex; it's more about unemployment and boredom. If you have hundreds of thousands of unemployed people packed together in a small space, with nothing productive to do—and I mean nothing, absolutely nothing, day after day—what's going to happen? Of course they're going to have sex. It feels good. It breaks the boredom.

"So two people might just be friends, and there's no sexual attraction at all, but they find themselves having sex. The pastors could teach them how to be friends without having sex, and they could talk frankly about the problems of sex outside of marriage, and they could help them find things to do—maybe get some sports equipment or organize some activities—it could be music even, which churches like, or maybe gardening, or weightlifting and exercise. And you know what would really help? They could teach them job skills, even just the necessity of getting up and showing up somewhere in the morning, of keeping your word, of working hard, of being honest. Then they could work through their denominations and other networks to start businesses so the people could get jobs. These are the kinds of things pastors could do.

"The opportunity that's being missed, the incredible cost as they keep up the routines of their various forms of the Christian religion, that's what makes me so passionate. That's what makes me speak out, even though they try to make me look ridiculous by quoting the Bible to me about being born again, as if that negates all the truth I told them. I love God. I love Jesus. That's why I'm in Khayelitsha trying to help and serve. But I can't stomach what goes on there in the name of God. I see what's going on—all the shouting and singing and raising money—and I know: this is not what Jesus intended. By talking only about individuals being born again, they keep Khayelitsha and our whole nation from being born again in a fuller sense of the term."[1]

At that moment, I realized this man saw clearly what I had begun to see: that religion, even the religion we are committed to and in which we have found God and purpose and meaning and truth, can become captive to a colossal distortion. It can become a benign and passive chaplaincy to a failing and dysfunctional culture, the religious public relations department for an inadequate and destructive ideology. It can forego being a force of liberation and transformation and instead become a source of domestication, resignation, pacification, and distraction.

A right understanding of God and faith can train people to hold their heads high, to doubt the lies of a dysfunctional society and to work for its transformation. But a misguided understanding can be an opiate that keeps their heads down in submission or desperation so they continue to serve the societal system that is destroying them, believing its lies, performing according to its self-destructive script.

JOINING IN THE CONVERSATION

In my travels, I have discovered that our conversation in South Africa is echoed in a thousand places, especially across the global South. The young healthcare worker represents a turning tide. For example, in Zambia, a young female theology student violates taboo and speaks openly about female initiation rites, calling on her fellow students in the name of the gospel to liberate women from these traditions in the name of justice and mercy. As we've seen already, in Rwanda and Burundi, young Christian leaders are beginning to tell the truth about their history and the failure of Christian missionaries to preach a gospel that called for justice and reconciliation among tribes.[2] Across Latin America, groups like La Red del Camino and the Latin American Theological Fellowship stimulate similar conversations. They explore the role of Christian faith and Christian institutions in relation to human suffering and social injustice. They try to develop an integral understanding of faith so that our track record in the future will be better than it has been in the past.

As younger generations of Christian leaders honestly face our shared history, they can begin to imagine a different role for our churches in the future, in hopes of creating a different path for their nations, a different world for their children. This shared dissatisfaction, together with this shared imagination and hope, combine to form an emerging consensus that is spreading across the global South.

For example, in the Dominican Republic, a Pentecostal pastor develops a healthcare program; one of his colleagues reaches out to glue-sniffing street kids, installing a shower in the church basement so the kids can get clean; they're developing a free "Life University" so those kids can get a nontraditional education on Saturdays. Across town, another pastor opens local gyms in poor neighborhoods so unemployed or underemployed young men and women can do something constructive to develop themselves physically—and in that context, he helps them consider their spiritual, emotional, and character development as well.

In Costa Rica, a local church unites its community to address pollution and unemployment.[3] In the Philippines, middle-class suburban churches organize to help poor people in the squatter areas develop small businesses. In India, courageous followers of Jesus confront the caste system and say that the time has come for it to die. These emerging Christian leaders realize that if their message isn't good news for the poor, a message of liberation for the oppressed, it isn't the same message Jesus proclaimed.

This consensus is spreading, not only in the global South among the formerly colonized but also among the descendants of the colonizers, among emerging leaders in North America and Europe, and among white South Africans and Australians and New Zealanders. As the consensus spreads, our two preoccupying questions take on more and more significance.

GROUP DIALOGUE QUESTIONS

1. Imagine you were one of the pastors present in the discussion about Khayelitsha. How would you have reacted to the young healthcare worker's statement? How do you react now? Were his thoughts new to you, or familiar?
2. Have you heard people express the "emerging consensus" described in the last part of the chapter? Where and when?
3. What might the healthcare worker say about churches in your city, state, or nation? Could you have problems similar to the ones he described?
4. What emotions did this chapter stir in you? What can you learn from your emotional responses?
5. If you were to give a speech like the healthcare worker's, trying to encourage church leaders in your city, state, or nation to take action about something, what would you say?
6. What sentence stood out to you most in this chapter? Why was it important to you?

Second Thoughts Had
Come to Stay

In spite of the problems identified by the young healthcare worker in South Africa, the Christian religion continues to explode in the global South, as Philip Jenkins makes clear in *The Next Christendom*.[1] Meanwhile, in the global North, especially in Europe and especially among the young and highly educated, the Christian faith seems in many ways to be evaporating. Even in the United States, where church attendance figures are comparatively strong, church leaders can't help but notice the rapid decline in local church involvement among younger generations and wonder what to do about it. Church leaders often begin by criticizing the young people: "What's wrong with them?" But eventually, some leaders ask a more productive question: "What's wrong with us?" Typically, they proceed on a rather superficial level, talking about cosmetics: musical styles, ambience and lighting, digital projection, dress codes, various ways of getting "cooler" or "hipper." These are of some importance perhaps, but certainly not the whole story. Then some thoughtful leaders go a little deeper, addressing the need to be relevant to culture and to contextualize their ministry for today's world. But they're still barely dipping below the surface.

Eventually some leaders begin to realize that many young and alienated ex-churched people originally dropped out of their churches after attending college (or getting out on their own where they could think for themselves) and learning about the dark side of the Christian religion's track record . . . the Crusades, witch burnings, colonialism, slavery, the Holocaust, apartheid, environmental irresponsibility, mistreatment of women.

These young people started caring about these issues, but they didn't find their fellow adherents to the Christian religion very concerned. Too often, they realized, Christians through history have played on the wrong side of these issues. And even when Christians in recent decades concerned themselves with contemporary issues, they focused primarily on personal and sexual matters, simultaneously neglecting larger societal and systemic injustices that caused unimagined suffering. And even in regard to their narrow range of "moral issues," they were consistently effective in generating heat and conflict but consistently less effective in making a lasting, constructive difference. In so doing, they created an image of the typical Christian believer as tense, judgmental, imbalanced, reactionary, negative, and hypocritical.[2]

A FAILED RELIGION?

More and more reflective Christian leaders are beginning to realize that for the millions of young adults who dropped out of their churches in the late twentieth and early twenty-first centuries, the Christian religion appears to be a failed religion. And for a reason not unlike the one expressed by the young healthcare worker from Khayelitsha: it has specialized in dealing with "spiritual needs" to the exclusion of physical and social needs. It has specialized in people's destination in the afterlife but has failed to address significant social injustices in this life. It has focused on "me" and "my soul" and "my spiritual life" and "my eternal destiny," but it has failed to address the dominant societal and global realities of their lifetime: systemic injustice, systemic poverty, systemic ecological crisis, systemic dysfunctions of many kinds.

When young adults from churchgoing backgrounds lose confidence in this version of the Christian religion to address the pressing issues of our world, their faith becomes more and more privatized and personalized and therefore diminished. They may or may not continue to practice it, but they will almost certainly become less enthusiastic about sharing it with others. As a result, those on the outside of the Christian religion find fewer and fewer enthusiastic proponents, and there seems to be less and less reason to accept or even consider it—apart from threats of hell, which lose their effect when those making the threats seem a little defensive, deranged, out of touch, manic, or embarrassed about their faith.

Before long, those remaining in local churches and those outside of them share the same sense of doubt: *a message purporting to be the best news in the world should be doing better than this.* The religion's results are not commensurate with the bold claims it makes. Truly good news, they feel, would confront systemic injustice, target significant global dysfunctions, and provide hope and resources for making a better world—along with helping individuals experience a full life. If only they could find a faith community with good news like that . . .

At that point, these global Northerners find themselves wishing for exactly what the healthcare worker in the South African township wished for: a vibrant form of Christian faith that is holistic, integral, and balanced—one that offers good news for both the living and the dying, that speaks of God's grace at work both in this life and the life to come, that speaks to individuals and to societies and to the planet as a whole.

THE STORY OF THE WORD *POSTMODERN*

I have just described the journey of thousands, maybe millions, of people in the West, and I am one of them. For many of us grappling with these issues, just as the word *postcolonial* was helping our counterparts in the global South name and interpret their reality, the word *postmodern* was helping us.

I originally encountered the term *postmodern* in graduate school in the 1970s, in a seminal essay by novelist Walker Percy.[3] I rediscovered the term in the mid-1990s when it became a helpful tool in my search to identify what seemed wrong with the modern American Christian religion of which I was part. Just as an Eskimo can distinguish between many types of snow because he has names for them at his disposal, the term *postmodern* helped give me a range of names—including *modern* and *premodern*—so that I could distinguish between versions of the Christian religion. In this way, I found the freedom to articulate dissatisfaction and concern about a version of the Christian religion—the modern Western version, or the modern colonial version—without rejecting Jesus and the Christian faith as a whole.

If you've listened to some popular religious broadcasters in recent years, you've probably heard simplistic caricatures of the word *postmodern*. For defenders of the modern Western, colonial version of the Christian religion, the word has become the latest in a series of epithets like *secular humanist* or *New Age* or *liberal*, meaning morally bankrupt, relativistic, nihilistic, cast adrift from deep and solid commitments, and so on. These defenders don't realize that if it weren't for the term *postmodern* (and its cousins *modern, nonmodern,* and *premodern*), many of us may have, because of our disillusionment with sleet, rejected snow altogether. We don't want to reject whatever is good and true in the Christian faith. But to hold our faith in good conscience, we needed to debug it from the viruses (modern, Western, colonial, imperial, rationalist, reductionist, and other types of viruses) that seem to have invaded its software. We needed the freedom to seek and articulate a debugged version of the Christian faith that we can hold with confidence, honesty, and hope.[4]

Because of the ways that the word *postmodern* has been abused— by fans and foes alike—I am often tempted to dump it altogether. But one of the best ways to better understand something is to learn its story, and the story of the term *postmodern* is worth understanding and relevant to our conversation, especially as it relates to the word *postcolonial.*

In the aftermath of World War II, many European intellectuals (eventually joined by Americans and many others) were forced to ask this question: how could this have happened? *This* referred to two world wars, and especially to the Holocaust. After 1945, intellectuals around the world began asking how Germany in particular—the epicenter of the Enlightenment with its rationality and its scientific mind-set—could sink into the barbarism of Nazism and all it entailed. They were simultaneously assessing even greater atrocities in the former Soviet Union under Stalin (1922–1953).

The diagnosis that emerged may be faulty, but one must at least applaud the diagnosticians for asking what went wrong and what should be done about it.[5] The diagnosticians could have identified the Christian religion itself as the problem. After all, Hitler was a Catholic in good standing, and Germany was ostensibly a Christian country dually resourced by Roman Catholicism and the Reformation heritage of Martin Luther, both of which contributed significantly to the anti-Semitism that energized Nazism. But these European intellectuals instead identified a disease shared by the Christian religion and European civilization at large: they diagnosed the sickness that had befallen Western civilization in general and "Christian" Germany in particular to be *excessive confidence.*[6]

In other words, just as cancer is an excessive growth of cells—both *cells* and *growth* normally being good things—the intellectuals realized that Nazism was an excessive growth of confidence—confidence in their national ethos, in their rational and interpretive powers, in their scientific prowess, and so on. When this confidence grew out of proportion, it became malignant, giving the "us" of Germany a kind of manic hyperconfidence to claim racial superiority and global dominance, even if that meant extermination of those who were determined to be "other," "them," or "not us"—Jews, homosexuals, Jehovah's Witnesses, gypsies, the mentally handicapped, and so on.

Just as this kind of reflective diagnostic work was being done in the aftermath of World War II regarding Germany, other European colonial powers were releasing their remaining colonial holdings. In some cases they were motivated by what we would today call terrorism and violent revolution, and in other cases motivated by nonviolent campaigns for freedom. For example, during these postwar years, the United Kingdom released India and Pakistan (1947), Burma and Ceylon (1948), Iraq (1958), Tanzania, Sierra Leone, Kuwait, and South Africa (1961), and Uganda (1962). France released Laos (1949), Cambodia (1953), Vietnam (1954), and Algeria (1962). Belgium gave up its remaining colonies (including Burundi and Rwanda in 1963), as did the Netherlands (including Indonesia in 1949). As they did so, they were forced to realize that their colonial projects were the hosts of the same cancer of excessive confidence. That excessive confidence cost millions of people their lives and millions more their dignity, leaving a legacy of social, economic, political, and environmental consequences that would play out for decades, if not centuries.

And during these very same postwar decades, the Civil Rights movement was born in the United States. From the Montgomery bus boycott to the Selma bridge to the steps of the Lincoln Memorial, the brutality with which blacks were treated in their struggle for freedom in the United States—and soon, in South Africa—would raise still more troubling questions: why were white people so confident that they deserved to be "more equal" than blacks? For the first time, millions of white people around the world had to look back and face how their ancestors had treated nonwhite people, not in shame and secrecy, but openly, *confidently*, without a second thought. Now they were having to entertain those second thoughts, questioning not only the racism masked behind centuries of white privilege, but also the rationale by which they and their ancestors could be so confidently wrong for so horribly long.

That led to even more second thoughts about how Native Americans had been treated. As a boy in the 1950s and 1960s watching cowboy and Indian movies on TV, I never considered the settlers to be participants in land theft or genocide, the Janjaweed and death squads of US history. But when I read the 1974 classic *Bury My Heart at Wounded Knee*,[7] I, like thousands of other white Americans, got a glimpse of history from "the other's" point of view for the first time. My confidence was shaken; second thoughts had come to stay.[8]

In those same turbulent years, with the daily news dominated by the war in Vietnam and the broader Cold War, along with continual tension between Israelis and Palestinians and eventually the atrocities of the Khmer Rouge in Cambodia, more and more second thoughts coalesced into an unsettling question: what gives some people the confidence that they have the right to kill others, sometimes by the millions?

During these same turbulent years after World War II, more and more people became aware of what we now call the environmental crisis—the extinction of species, the pollution of water and air, and the threat of human-induced global climate change (the fear then being nuclear winter rather than the greenhouse effect). Again, an excessive confidence seemed to be at the root of the problem: modern Industrial-era people had an industrial-strength confidence that motivated them to dam any river, fill any wetland, catch and can any school of fish, strip-mine any mountain, pollute any breeze, pave any meadow, and otherwise exercise and express their dominance—with confidence.

THE ROOTS OF CERTAINTY

Having diagnosed the disease in this way, thoughtful people in the last half of the twentieth century addressed the next natural question: what was the source of this cancer of excessive confidence? The answer came in two parts.

First, many thinkers traced excessive confidence back to an intellectual methodology designed by Rene Descartes, explained in his great work *A Discourse on Method*.[9] Descartes' method, known to us today as foundationalism, sought to establish universally accessible first principles—incapable of being doubted or debated because of their pristine and universal logical clarity.[10] Building on that foundation using reason alone (with no appeal to religion), practitioners of foundationalism erected an intellectual framework that promised absolute, objective, universally accessible certainty from the ground up. That kind of certainty produced amazing positive results, but as critics of foundationalism began to realize in the 1950s, '60s, and '70s, it also produced a dangerous, malignant confidence that is willing to exploit or even kill millions of people—not to mention nonhuman living things—to achieve its ends.

Second, certain philosophers surmised that this intellectual method of foundationalism alone wasn't the only source of modern Western overconfidence. They began to speak of *metanarratives*—framing stories that weave together memories of grievances that need to be avenged, stories of dangers that need to be avoided, or stories of superiority that explain why one group should be advantaged to dominate over others. Driven by these fearful, vengeful, or dominating framing stories, and bolstered by a feeling of bottom-up, invulnerable certainty, nations or civilizations could easily become vicious, genocidal, and perhaps even suicidal—capable of bringing down the whole planet.

CONNECTING THE TWO QUESTIONS

Thinking along these lines, I became convinced that, yes, many of our world's worst atrocities were indeed the result of overconfidence. And yes, overconfidence was indeed resourced by foundationalism. And yes, deeper still, destructive framing stories fueled the hatred and fear and greed that perpetuated so much human suffering—whether in Africa, Latin America, or my own nation.

I took the next natural step from these conclusions. I returned to my two original questions and began wondering: Is it possible that at the heart of the life and message of Jesus was an attempt to expose, challenge, confront, transform, and replace the unhealthy framing stories of his day? And could there be a resonance between the unhealthy framing stories of his day and their counterparts in our day?

At that moment, I felt some new electricity beginning to flow between my two original questions.

GROUP DIALOGUE QUESTIONS

1. Have you noticed a decline in church attendance among younger generations, as this chapter suggests? What do you think are the factors that contribute to this trend?
2. Discuss this statement from this chapter: "The Christian religion appears to be a failed religion."
3. The author speaks of colonialism in this chapter. As a group, define the term and give examples of it from history.
4. How do you respond to the discussion of excessive confidence as a cancer in Western civilization? Where do you see examples of excessive confidence?
5. Give an example of a framing story that has helped one group of people harm another group of people.
6. What do you think the author might mean when he suggests Jesus was confronting a set of framing stories in his day and seeking to replace them with another framing story?

Part 2

SUICIDAL
SYSTEM

Simmering on the Back Burner of My Mind

When I left my career as a college English instructor to become a pastor, I never expected to get into these profoundly broad, complex, interdisciplinary questions about global injustice, genocide, or societal suicide. I was interested in other less lofty, more practical questions like how to help people become sincere followers of Christ, how to grow an effective local church, how to lead worship gatherings and preach decent sermons, how to help couples stay married and build healthy families, how to deal with congregational conflict and pay the bills, and how to be sure we had enough volunteers to cover the nursery this Sunday. Frankly, I felt (and still feel) unprepared for huge global questions, and I would still be avoiding them if I could. But I couldn't, and can't.

Even before people like Claude and Justine and the healthcare worker in Khayelitsa pushed me out of the comfortable nest of my conventional thinking, I was already grappling with what I perceived to be a deep shift in context—from what many of us now call a modern to a postmodern culture, from a hyperconfident Western culture to a culture full of second thoughts and profound suspicions. This shift repeatedly intruded upon my work as a pastor, so I couldn't avoid it. Sincere spiritual seekers would attend my church, and they asked me questions I didn't have answers for—at least not satisfying answers. In my first several books, I grappled with this shift, describing "a new kind of Christian," namely a Christian who wasn't functioning within the assumptions and values of modern, Western, hyperconfident—some might say *arrogant* —culture.[1]

Many people have received these books with enthusiasm, sometimes even tears of relief. The most common feedback I receive runs along these lines: "You've said exactly what I've been thinking for years, but I couldn't put it into words. I'm so relieved to know I'm not crazy, or at least I'm not the only one who is crazy." Meanwhile, just as *Time* was including me in their list of the twenty-five most influential evangelicals, some powerful evangelicals were putting me on different kinds of lists. Whether their critiques were intended to correct me and keep me in the fold, or simply to discredit me so my influence wouldn't spread, I can't be sure. But as much as I disliked controversy, I knew that I couldn't be intimidated to return to their fold of modern, Western, hyperconfident, no-second-thoughts, industrial-strength religion.

I was nudged further in my intellectual and spiritual journey through a conversation with African theologian Dr. Mabiala Kenzo, a delightful and brilliant Congolese theologian of Twa descent.[2] He said that my term *postmodern* was one side of a coin that had two sides, and both sides were essential parts of one emerging global conversation. He helped me realize that *postmodernity* was a key term in a conversation among the excessively confident. This concept helped us in the West to understand and undermine our own colonial culture's confidence-mania and uncertainty-phobia. To attack or undermine what people like me saw as the twin sources of that overconfidence— foundationalism and destructive framing stories (as we saw in the previous chapter)—we in the West focused on the field of epistemology, which explores how we have rational confidence that what we call knowledge or truth is really, truly true.[3]

Kenzo then helped me see that *postcolonial* was the other side of the coin, a key term in a parallel conversation among those who had been dominated and colonized by the excessively confident. The formerly colonized, whether Native Americans, African-Americans, or Twa like Kenzo himself, were trying to rebuild a new kind of confidence among people whose confidence had been shattered and ground into the dirt through arrogant Western colonialism. They needed a restored confidence to face the ugly aftermath of centuries of domination and exploitation. They didn't focus on philosophical questions of truth and epistemology, but rather on social questions of justice, which are ultimately questions about the moral uses of power.

The only way ahead, I became convinced, was for the former colonizers and the formerly colonized to face both sides of the coin together, never wanting truth without justice or justice without truth.

This dynamic interplay of truth and justice was captured by South African archbishop Desmond Tutu, echoing a similar statement by the first Kenyan president, Jomo Kenyatta: "When the missionaries came to Africa they had the Bible and we had the land. They said, 'Let us pray.' We closed our eyes. When we opened them we had the Bible and they had the land." I have been told that during the apartheid years, Archbishop Tutu, when speaking to white Christian leaders, would then hold up the Bible and say, "Now, my brothers, based on this Bible you have given us, I call you to give us back our land!"[4]

At that moment, truth and justice would come together: if the truth is that God doesn't play favorites, if the truth is that God is not a racist, if the truth is that land theft and slave labor are wrong even (especially!) when done by people who call themselves Christians, if the truth is that all human beings are created in the image of God and deserve to be treated with equal dignity, even sanctity—then we must face the injustices of our past and seek justice for everybody everywhere. That is the only way that the world of tomorrow will be a better place, and it is the only way to live by the truth.

Somehow, this integration of postmodern and postcolonial concerns—for both justice and truth, for both a proper confidence and a proper use of power—made it possible for me to turn from a set of intramural religious arguments (which had preoccupied me for several years) to the more global exploration articulated in my two preoccupying questions: *What are the biggest problems in the world today?* and *What do the life and teachings of Jesus have to say about these global problems?*

IDENTIFYING THE TOP GLOBAL PROBLEMS

The first task in my research was to review the literature addressing global problems—which, to my surprise, occupied comparatively few inches of shelf space in a library, next to wide shelves sagging with tell-all celebrity biographies, self-help books, and apocalyptic fiction. One might wish there were more books on averting the destruction of the earth than books amusing us while it proceeds. Perhaps that paucity of attention is itself a key dimension of the crises.

Copenhagen Consensus

Thankfully, there have been a few serious attempts to identify and rank our top global problems. For example, the Copenhagen Consensus, led by Danish economist Bjorn Lomborg, brought together a panel of the world's leading economists, along with other experts in various fields, to identify the problems that cause the most suffering and danger in the world, and to prioritize potential solutions based on cost-benefit analysis.[5]

They came up with a list of the top ten global problems:

1. Hunger and malnutrition
2. Climate change[6]
3. Conflicts
4. Financial instability
5. Water and sanitation
6. Subsidies and trade barriers
7. Population/migration
8. Communicable diseases
9. Education
10. Governance and corruption[7]

Millennium Development Goals

While the Copenhagen Consensus has continued its work, the 191 member nations of the United Nations identified a list of eight key problems they pledged to address by 2015.[8] Articulated as the

Millennium Development Goals (MDGs), they offer a slightly different take on the world's top problems:

1. Eradicate extreme poverty and hunger.
2. Achieve universal primary education.
3. Promote gender equality and empower women.
4. Reduce child mortality.
5. Improve maternal health.
6. Combat HIV/AIDS, malaria, and other diseases.
7. Ensure environmental sustainability.
8. Develop a global partnership for development.[9]

J. F. Rischard

Another important list of global problems has been assembled by the World Bank's vice president for Europe, J. F. Rischard.[10] As one might expect in light of his position, he shows special sensitivity to economic and regulatory matters, offering a list of twenty urgent global problems under three general headings.

He identifies six *ecological problems* under the heading "sharing our planet": global warming, biodiversity and ecosystem losses, fisheries depletion, deforestation, water deficits, and maritime safety and pollution.

He names six *humanitarian problems* that require global commitment and cooperation: stepping up the fight against poverty, peacekeeping (including conflict prevention and combating terrorism), providing education for all, eliminating global infectious diseases, reducing the digital divide, and preventing or mitigating natural disasters.

He names eight *regulatory problems* that require political and economic innovations: reinventing taxation; creating rules for biotechnology; updating global financial architecture; stopping the spread of illegal drugs; improving rules for trade, investment, and competition; creating protections for intellectual property rights; developing rules for e-commerce; improving regulations for international labor and migration.[11]

PEACE Plan and Fifteen Challenges

Another important voice has arisen in recent years to join the Copenhagen Consensus, the architects of the MDGs, and Rischard. In the wake of his record-breaking best seller *The Purpose-Driven Life*,[12] evangelical pastor Rick Warren chose to leverage his growing fame and success to topple what he called five global giants. (The numbers in parentheses show how Warren's five items correspond with the eight Millennium Development Goals above.)

1. Spiritual emptiness, which he would address by *planting churches* that would proclaim the Christian gospel. (8)
2. Selfish, lazy, ineffective, or corrupt leadership, which he would address by *equipping servant leaders*. (8)
3. Poverty, which he would address by *assisting the poor* through various forms of humanitarian aid. (1)
4. Disease, which he would address by *caring for the sick*. (4, 5, 6)
5. Ignorance, which he would address by *educating the next generation*. (2, 3, 7)[13]

Under the banner of a five-point PEACE plan (an acrostic derived from the italicized words above), Warren called local churches to participate in "a second reformation." The first Reformation, led by Martin Luther, Warren explains, "was about belief. This one will be about deeds. It is about what the church should be doing in the world."[14]

Meanwhile, the United Nations University, the primary research arm of the United Nations, produced yet another list, in my opinion, one of the best.[15] Their fifteen global challenges are put in terms of questions the community of nations must answer:

How can . . .

1. sustainable development be achieved for all?
2. everyone have sufficient clean water without conflict?
3. population growth and resources be brought into balance?

·everything must change

4. genuine democracy emerge from authoritarian regimes?
5. policymaking be made more sensitive to global long-term perspectives?
6. the global convergence of information and communications technologies work for everyone?
7. ethical market economies be encouraged to help reduce the gap between rich and poor?
8. the threat of new and reemerging diseases and immune micro-organisms be reduced?
9. we improve our capacity to decide as the nature of work and institutions change?
10. shared values and new security strategies reduce ethnic conflicts, terrorism, and the use of weapons of mass destruction?
11. the changing status of women help improve the human condition?
12. transnational organized crime networks be stopped from becoming more powerful and sophisticated global enterprises?
13. growing energy demands be met safely and efficiently?
14. scientific and technological breakthroughs be accelerated to improve the human condition?
15. ethical considerations become more routinely incorporated into global decisions?

A New Way of Thinking About These Problems

As I reflected on these and other lists of global problems—twenty, fifteen, ten, eight, or five—I wanted to try to integrate them somehow, to show how so many of the identified problems were causes of one another, or effects of one another, or a mixture of both. I wanted to take Rischard's advice and try to think in radically new ways about these problems, especially in light of the oft-quoted words of Albert Einstein: "No problem can be solved from the same level of consciousness that created it."

It was clear to me, as it is to almost any somewhat knowledge-able person, that conventional ways of thinking aren't working. Billions of dollars of government aid in Africa have saved lives, but the forces that threaten to take more lives seem to go unchallenged. Government welfare programs may have provided a needed safety net, but they also had a wide range of negative unintended consequences—includ-ing offering disincentives for some people to rise from poverty. Con-ventional approaches based on conventional thinking were yielding the unacceptable results we currently have, and it didn't make sense to expect otherwise in the future.

As I reviewed these lists in relation to my two questions, I con-cluded that we can no longer deal with global problems as discrete, unrelated issues. We can't simply make a global to-do list and start with number one and work our way to the end.

That's why I was especially encouraged to discover the work of another group of scholars: Bob Goudzwaard, Mark Vander Vennen, and David Van Heemst. Like others, they created a list of key areas of global concern—in their case, a shorter list of three: global poverty, environmental destruction, and increasing violence.[16] This group (which I will call the New Vision Group, drawing from the subtitle of their groundbreaking book *Hope in Troubled Times: A New Vision for Confronting Global Crises*)[17] went on to see these three global problems as symptoms of a deeper disease, a disease of ideology.[18] Until we address our deeper ideological sickness, they concluded, we will face "solution deadlock" when we tackle global crises.

At that point, I was simply trying to understand the crises—not imagine how to solve them—but I felt I was making slow but sure progress in my understanding. There was a lot of overlap between the lists, and unmistakable patterns of interrelationship began to emerge. So, month after month I kept reading, studying, and talking with knowledgeable friends with all of these problems simmering on the back burner of my mind. I filled a couple of yellow legal pads with scribblings, comparing and integrating the lists, grouping and regrouping the items, sketching out all kinds of diagrams and flow charts to capture the cause-and-effect interrelationships between problems. With each exercise, I felt I was becoming more familiar with the problems and their complex interrelations, but I still lacked a way of bringing the complexity together. I felt stuck in complexity, and I couldn't get out of it.

GROUP DIALOGUE QUESTIONS

1. Have you read any of this author's other books? If so, how did you respond to them? Have you encountered any controversy about his previous books? How do you respond to the controversy?
2. Respond to the quotes by Jomo Kenyatta and Desmond Tutu: "When the missionaries came to Africa they had the Bible and we had the land. They said, 'Let us pray.' We closed our eyes. When we opened them we had the Bible and they had the land."
3. Why do you think there are so few popular books on global crises? Why would a topic of this importance not attract more attention?
4. Which list of global crises most impressed you? Have you encountered any of these lists before? Where?
5. Reflect on the quote from Albert Einstein: "No problem can be solved from the same level of consciousness that created it." Can you relate his insight to any experience in your own life?
6. Have you ever felt "stuck in complexity" like the author was? Share an experience when complexity overwhelmed you, and then share how you responded to that complexity.
7. How does the material in this chapter affect you in terms of your own personal faith and your spiritual journey?

Three Interlocking Systems

It took a conversation with Dr. Leonard Sweet some months later to get me "unstuck" from my own "solution deadlock." Without fail, when I'm around this brilliant and contagiously thoughtful scholar and author, I think new thoughts in new ways. I forget exactly what the context was, what a group of us was talking about, or what Len said before or after, but one offhand comment from Len seized my attention like an alarm buzzer: "It's like we've created some sort of suicide machine."

My intuition immediately shouted: *That's it! That image captures the way the world's most serious problems are linked in a vicious, self-reinforcing cycle.* The global problems I had been studying weren't like an uncoordinated herd of stampeding buffalo or a flotilla of stinging jellyfish; they were like a single system, a single mechanism of awe-inspiring engineering and roaring power.

Later, I discovered that several other people had coined similar language.[1] For example, Jared Diamond, in *Guns, Germs, and Steel,* spoke of how some ancient cultures "committed ecological suicide by destroying their own resource base."[2] David Korten, in *The Great Turning,* spoke of "suicidal corporate global economy."[3] Brazilian theologian Leonardo Boff wrote on the first page of his 1995 masterpiece, *Cry of the Earth, Cry of the Poor,* "A death machine is mowing down life in its most varied forms." Later he spoke of the societal "killing machine" and "the predatory and lethal machinery of our model of society and development."[4]

Suicide machine is, of course, a metaphor. Metaphors help us see invisible or unfamiliar things by comparing them to visible and familiar things. They help us grasp intangible things by rendering them as tangible things. They help us leap from the known and familiar to the unknown and unfamiliar.[5] For all the help they give us, they do not give us exhaustive knowledge of the thing they seek to explicate. The fact is, we don't fully know the people closest to us, nor do we know ourselves fully. Even after years of being a spouse or parent, we are often mystified or just plain wrong about one another, and our own motivations are often even more opaque to us than they are to others. So we should remember that the most helpful metaphor can give us a false confidence, and we should use metaphors with appropriate caution.

Even further, we must acknowledge that metaphors can be terribly dangerous. For example, when tribal conflict was brewing in Rwanda leading up to the genocide in 1994, one tribe (the Hutu) used two powerful metaphors to dehumanize the other (the Tutsi). By calling them *cockroaches* or *tall trees*, it became easier to squash them and cut them down, so that genocide seemed more like pest control or landscape improvement than the grotesque and inhuman mass murder that it was.[6]

Keeping in mind the powers, limitations, and dangers of metaphors, I hope that *suicide machine* can serve as a helpful metaphor (among others) for the systems that drive our civilization toward un-health and un-peace. It can help us visualize the way several facets of contemporary life connect, gear in gear, to destroy good and living things, devalue what is precious, overvalue what is worthless, foul up the results of millions of years of evolution, and so desecrate and frustrate what I believe is a sacred and ongoing work of the Creator, in us, among us, and through us.

Machines are the quintessential modern metaphor, meaning they reflect the habit of the mind in modern Western societies to describe things by comparing them to machines or mechanisms. As modern Western people, when we find objective, impersonal, universal laws—the kind that run machines—we tend to feel we have found the deepest truth about things, from physics (thanks to Sir Isaac Newton with his laws on mechanisms of physics) to biology (thanks to Gregor Mendel with his genetic mechanisms or Charles Darwin in biology with his evolutionary mechanisms) . . . from psychology (thanks to B. F. Skinner with his mechanisms of operant conditioning or Sigmund Freud with his psychosexual aggressive mechanisms) to religion (thanks to gospel "formulas" such as "the four spiritual laws," which are actually four spiritual mechanisms).[7]

A machine is a complex creation of human beings that harnesses energy to achieve a desire. (A tool, by contrast, is a simple creation of human beings that directs energy to achieve a desire.) We have a desire to travel, so we create traveling machines called automobiles and flying machines called airplanes. We have a desire to measure time and weight, so we create measuring machines called clocks and scales. We desire to communicate with people who are distant from us, so we create communication machines—telephones, televisions, and computer and Internet systems. Then, when we combine many machines together, we create complex systems—transportation systems, manufacturing systems, computer systems, telecommunication systems, economic systems, medical systems, and so on. And when we combine many systems together, we create the unified supermachine we call "society" or "civilization."

When the social, political, and economic machinery of a society gets out of control, or through some flaw of design or operation begins to destroy its creators and intended beneficiaries, then it has become a suicide machine.

THREE SUBSYSTEMS IN SOCIETY

With the suicide machine metaphor on the front burner of my thinking, I went back to all my yellow legal pads full of diagrams, flow charts, lists, and other scribblings. I began to conceive of our societal machine as a supersystem comprised of three primary interlocking subsystems, and I named them for the good and legitimate desires they are intended to fulfill: desires for *prosperity, security,* and *equity.*

Prosperity System

The prosperity system seeks to fulfill our desire for happiness—our desire not just to survive, but to thrive. We associate happiness with enjoyable sensations, so through the prosperity system we create ways to fulfill that desire—for good tastes, for pleasant and interesting sights and sounds, for enjoyable tactile, intellectual, and emotional experiences—and for relief from their opposites (such as disease, injury, or boredom).

To fulfill this hunger for happiness, the prosperity system feeds civilization with the products and services that people want to obtain—or "consume" if you will. The prosperity system comprises a host of subsystems that cooperate to keep the prosperity coming—agriculture systems, manufacturing, energy, transportation, education, entertainment, communication systems, and so on.

Of course, when some individuals or groups of people have a bigger share of desired products and services than others, jealousies arise. Sometimes those jealousies erupt into violent attempts to steal some of that prosperity, or at least to interrupt another's monopoly of the means of achieving it. The danger of interference from others in the pursuit of happiness means that all who desire prosperity will also desire security—protection from the danger of interference.

Security System

To protect a successful prosperity system from interference, a society develops a security system, also comprising a wide array of subsystems: weapons systems, intelligence systems, border control systems, policing and surveillance systems. Then, of course, it must recruit, train, and support personnel and infrastructure to manage these security subsystems.

Security systems are important, but they are often very expensive in terms of both money and personnel, all the more so when enemies and criminals keep developing new means of subverting yesterday's defenses. So, along with the desire to pursue greater happiness through the prosperity system, and then to guard all means of achieving that happiness through an expanding security system, a society must develop ways to equitably spread the rising cost of systems maintenance and development. Thus, the third component of the societal machine comes into play.

Equity System

The equity system seeks not only to fairly spread the expense of the security system, but also to support the expansion of the prosperity system in equitable ways. For example, by breaking up monopolies, the equity system assures that some members of society don't gain unfair advantage over others. Or by equitably spreading the expense of building roads, the equity system helps the prosperity system transport more products and services to more people who want to enjoy them in more places, and it makes possible the happiness that comes from travel itself.

The equity system fulfills the desire for fairness in four primary ways. First, it *develops and enforces laws* to protect people's freedom to pursue prosperity and security—including protecting one person or group's freedom from inequitable encroachment by others.[8] Second, it *levies taxes* to distribute the shared expenses of developing and maintaining all three systems. Third, it *establishes or protects the press and court systems* so they can investigate and report the truth about inequities. When laws, taxes, the press, and courts fail to address human suffering and inequity, impromptu organizations spring up to supplement the equity system—nongovernmental organizations, charities, and the like—organized to *alleviate suffering* through a range of interventions and projects.

Equity, as I'm using the term, doesn't mean equality. This distinction is important. *Equity* means fairness and justice, the outcome of wise and virtuous judgment, without prejudice, favoritism, or corruption, but with a human sense of mercy and compassion.[9] *Equality*, which means mathematical sameness, can actually be an expression of inequity: for example, most of us would agree that it would be inequitable for a sick or disabled person who can't work to be treated exactly the same as a healthy, able-bodied person who refuses to work. Or we might say that men and women should be paid and treated equally, but then we may agree that a pregnant woman or nursing mother should be given more leniency in regard to time off; the inequality would in this case be considered equitable. We'll return to the relationship between inequality and inequity in part 7.

THE SOCIETAL MACHINE

The three systems that make up the societal machine can't function independently. For example, without the equity system, the prosperity system becomes riddled with corruption, violence, and other inefficiencies that ultimately undermine prosperity. Without the equity system, the security system won't have policies to enforce and limits to observe, and then it may in their absence act against some or all of the people it is supposed to serve. And without taxes raised by the equity system, the security system won't have sufficient funds to operate—or it may demand more funds than it actually needs.

So, each system interacts with the others and needs them. Functioning together, they make up the social machinery upon which we have all come to depend. So we can begin to picture the machine like this.

The Societal Machine

But even though this diagram takes us many steps forward in our journey of seeking to understand global crises, we still have a long way to go. The societal machine not only *has* parts, but it also *is a part* of a bigger system. When we fail to take that bigger system into account, we help the machinery go suicidal.

GROUP DIALOGUE QUESTIONS

1. How do you respond to the comparison of civilization to a machine? In what ways does this metaphor work or not work for you?
2. The author suggests that our civilization is driven by the desire for three things: prosperity, equity, and security. How do you see these desires at work in your own life? How do you see them at work in today's newspaper?
3. Make a list of specific institutions in society that you have encountered in the last twenty-four hours— schools, police, churches, museums, TV stations, stores, and so on. How does each one fit into the three systems described in this chapter?
4. The author ends the chapter by suggesting that the human societal system must be seen as part of a larger system. What might that system be? Why would failure to see the larger system be potentially suicidal?
5. How does it feel to consider yourself as part of a social machine? What experiences most make you feel this way? What experiences make you feel differently—that you're free from being part of a machine?
6. How does spirituality function for people who see life largely in terms of machinery and mechanisms?

That Could Never Happen to Us

A lot of us are very happy to go through life knowing as little as possible about economics, politics, and ecology. As long as we can pay our credit card bill, avoid going to jail, and enjoy a cold drink, we'd rather not deal with the complexities of the societal machinery around us. But if we start becoming concerned about emerging global crises and the effects they may have on our own future and the lives of our children and grandchildren, then maybe we'll want to learn a little bit more about how the world works. That's what this chapter is about.

The societal machine we introduced in the preceding chapter doesn't float in a vacuum, suspended in space, hanging in an abstract dimension of ethereal concepts. No, it exists within the physical, visible ecosystem of planet earth.[1] You can't think of the societal machine apart from earth's soil and rain, photosynthesis and carbon cycle, glaciers and wind, sewage and sunshine.

With this new insight in mind, we can expand our diagram in several more stages, first by situating the machine in its environment[2] (see figure 8.1 on the following page).

Next we can clarify how the societal machine interacts dynamically with the ecosystem, constantly giving, constantly receiving. (see figure 8.2 on the following page).

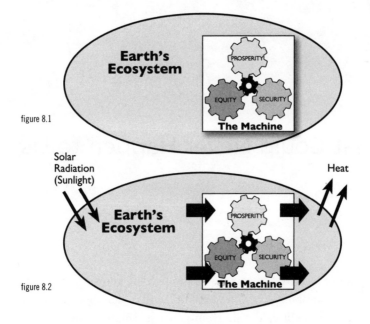

figure 8.1

figure 8.2

The machine takes in two resources, represented by the two incoming block arrows in our diagram: matter (which economists call raw materials—things like rubber, wheat, aluminum, and cotton, which the machine turns into products such as sandwiches, salads, beer, cars, computers, soccer balls, chairs, automobiles, x-ray machines, bandages, and so on) and energy (which we require to turn raw materials into products, and which we derive from oil and coal, hydroelectric dams, nuclear power plants, wind generators, solar panels, and the like).

Nearly all of the energy available to the machine is ultimately solar energy (represented by the two line arrows in our diagram), which is the only significant resource entering the ecosystem.[3]

Just as a living creature consumes matter and energy in the form of food and produces waste products, the societal machine (which, remember, is a metaphor for living creatures called human beings, acting in groups) takes in matter and energy and produces waste products—trash, wastewater, heat, emissions from cars and factories. These waste products are represented by the two arrows (one for matter like garbage and sewage, the other for energy like heat or radiation) going from the machine back into the ecosystem.

As the next enhancement of our diagram illustrates, some resources within the ecosystem are especially important to us. We need to monitor these critical resources with special care because of our dependence on them. We can represent the availability of these resources by inserting a bar graph into our diagram (see figure 8.3).

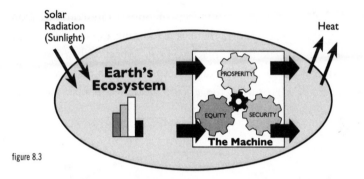

figure 8.3

Let's say the four bars represent current stocks of topsoil, oil, swordfish, and timber. Some of these stores or supplies are non-renewable; once we've used them, they're gone forever. Others reproduce themselves to replace what is taken, providing a potentially sustainable supply. So, while we can plant more trees and farm more fish, for example, we can't create more oil or topsoil—at least not very quickly. Even renewable resources have limits, since they can be depleted faster than they can renew themselves, as illustrated in the diagram on the following page.

If we draw down our supply of swordfish (the third bar in the graph) too quickly, the species may go extinct and we would lose that resource entirely, forever. Meanwhile, we may draw down our available forests (the fourth bar) but then replenish them to higher-than-ever levels. So, over time, the supply of any specific resource will vary, depending on how fast we're using it up or, where possible, renewing the supply (see figure 8.4).

Even though our machine diagram is almost complete (for our

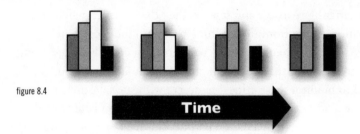
figure 8.4

purposes, that is—reality is millions of times more complex than any diagram or metaphor), there is a looming question we must consider: how big should the machine be in respect to the ecosystem? This is one of the most important questions we can ask as we begin to understand what makes the suicide machine suicidal. Consider two versions of our diagram below:

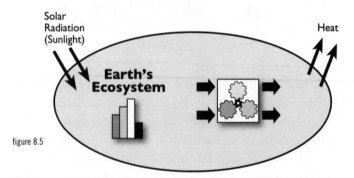
figure 8.5

Here the machine is relatively small in comparison to the whole ecosystem and the stores of resources. You could think of it as a very small goldfish in a very big fishbowl. It has plenty of room to grow, plenty of oxygen to breathe, plenty of food to eat, and its wastes can be absorbed back into its environment.

But imagine that the goldfish continues to grow and eventually reaches a point where the water in the bowl can't absorb oxygen fast enough for the fish to breathe, where the available food is consumed faster than it can be replenished, and where its wastes can no longer be absorbed and so accumulate to toxic levels. That would be analogous to the situation in the next diagram (see figure 8.6).

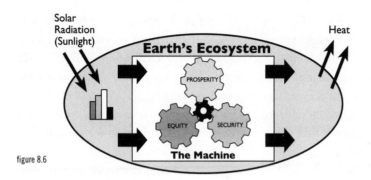

figure 8.6

Eventually, you'd have to agree, the societal machine could grow to a size where it demanded more resources than the environment could provide and produce more wastes than the environment could absorb. At that point, the machine would go suicidal.

This is why so many forward-thinking people are concerned about global warming and our addiction to the carbon-based fuels that contribute to it. It's why the issue of nuclear waste is so alarming. It's why some of us talk so much about peak oil or the loss of fertile topsoil (which can take centuries per inch to produce) or the loss of rainforests or the overharvesting of fisheries. It's also the core of terror in the word *terrorism*—because by far the worst terrorist scenario is the detonation and counterdetonation of nuclear weapons that would not only kill multiplied thousands immediately, but also unleash radioactivity and other debris into the environment that would have far-reaching and long-lasting effects on the one and only environment in which we live.

We have realized that our societal goldfish can get too big or too dirty for the goldfish bowl in which we live. We can arrogantly deny our limits as creatures and (in our own eyes) become like gods— independent, beyond constraint, with nothing to fear, clueless about our stupidity until we have been banished forever from our fertile, well-balanced garden into a bleak world of thorns and sweat and gloom.

That, of course, could never happen to us.

The previous statement is a nearly perfect lie. Just as the denial of an addict *(I can quit anytime! I don't have a problem!)* makes possible his ongoing self-destruction, this form of societal denial is capable of turning the engine of our civilization into a suicide machine. It is a lie so seductive—and so pervasive—that most readers would do well to either (a) stop reading and take a walk so they can think about it for a while, (b) call a friend or two with whom to process this chapter over a cup of coffee, or (c) immediately reread the chapter until they feel the wonder of the ecosystem in which we live and the danger of it being destroyed by a suicide machine of our own making.

I wish that this lie were the only lie, the only way our societal machinery can go suicidal. But it's not. As I continued my research and reflection on our global problems, I realized this was only one of four potentially suicidal dysfunctions of our societal machinery.

GROUP DIALOGUE QUESTIONS

1. How helpful did you find the diagrams in this chapter? Try drawing them from memory to explain "how the world works" to one another.
2. The author speaks of "wonder and danger" in the next to last paragraph. When and where do you most feel this wonder? This danger?
3. This chapter began by suggesting that many people want to know as little as possible about how the world works. It ends with people saying, "This could never happen to us." Why do you think many people respond to life in these ways? What are the consequences of these attitudes? What can be done to change this?
4. Do you see any spiritual dimensions to better understanding how the world works?

The Stories We Tell Ourselves

To more accurately understand the dysfunctions of our societal machinery, we must add one more component to our diagram, a component that answers questions like these: Since machines don't operate themselves, what controls the three systems of the societal machine? What helps the machine restore balance after instability, what determines the speed at which it operates, and what determines the ends for which it works? If the global societal machine is not operated by a single person but by all of humanity acting together, how are the varied desires of millions of people harnessed into a unified corporate will? How do millions of discrete minds, hearts, and wills form some sort of coherent corporate mind, heart, or will that directs the machine?

You can find an analogy to answer these questions next time you look in the mirror. Maybe you've never considered yourself this way, but you are a complex society of sixty trillion cells. In fact, there are about ten thousand times the number of cells in your body as there are people on earth. These cells are organized into ten organ systems: skeletal, muscular, circulatory, nervous, respiratory, digestive, excretory, reproductive, endocrine, and immune. All of these systems are integrated and unified into one person—you—in a completely unique way, through what we could call the framing story of your life. Your story may unify your cells and systems to become an Olympic gymnast and father of three children, while someone else uses her cells and systems to become a drug dealer or astronaut or kindergarten teacher. The unique framing story of you describes how you have unified your ten systems so far, and that story then frames how you will do so in the future. For example, if you constantly tell yourself, "I have always had bad luck, and I always get taken advantage of by other people," that story about your past will frame your future. If you tell yourself, "I have overcome every obstacle that ever presented itself to me, and nobody's attempts to take advantage of me have ever caused me to quit," you'll be framing quite a different future.

Similarly, just as your ten biological systems and trillions of cells are unified, integrated, motivated, and guided by the framing story you tell yourself as a person, our societies are unified, integrated, motivated, and driven by the framing stories we tell ourselves as groups. These stories align the desires of billions of individuals through the three societal systems we have introduced, providing a framework within which we live and act and desire and dream.[1] Any particular society or civilization at any given time lives by a dominant framing story (the dark gear in the center of "The Machine" below), and that story will no doubt evolve and adapt over time, for better or for worse, borrowing from or reacting to the stories of its neighbors.[2] Whenever we belong to a group—from a family to a church to a fan club to a political party to a nation—we are under the influence of that group's framing story, learning where we come from, what's going on, where

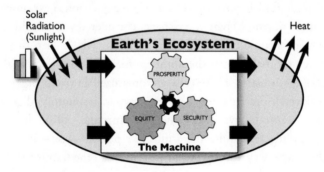

everything must change

we are situated in the story's plotline, where we are going, how we should act, and what we are here for.

If our framing story is wise, strong, realistic, and constructive, it can send us on a hopeful trajectory. But if our framing story is dysfunctional, weak, false, unrealistic, or destructive, it can send us on a downward arc, a dangerous, high-speed joyride toward un-peace, un-health, un-prosperity, and even un-life.[3]

THE EFFECTS OF A FRAMING STORY

If our framing story tells us that we humans are godlike beings with godlike privileges—intelligent and virtuous creatures outside a limited environment of time and space, without potentially fatal flaws—we will have no reason to acknowledge or live within limits, whether moral or ecological. Similarly, if it tells us that the purpose of life is for individuals or nations to accumulate an abundance of possessions and to experience the maximum amount of pleasure during the maximum number of minutes of our short lives, then we will have little reason to manage our consumption. If our framing story tells us that we are in life-and-death competition with each other, that only the fittest will survive, that each species and group is in a violent struggle to outcompete and gain independence and safety from or dominance over all others, then we will have little reason to seek reconciliation and collaboration and nonviolent resolutions to our conflicts. If it tells us that we are simply masses of atoms in a complex and ultimately meaningless fermentation and decay process, that there is no ultimate purpose to existence, no higher value to the story, then we will have little reason to seek transcendence.

But if our framing story tells us that we are free and responsible creatures in a creation made by a good, wise, and loving God, and that our Creator wants us to pursue virtue, collaboration, peace, and mutual care for one another and all living creatures, and that our lives can have profound meaning if we align ourselves with God's wisdom, character, and dreams for us . . . then our society will take a radically different direction, and our world will become a very different place.

Our Framing Story Is Failing

In this light, our growing list of global crises, together with our inability to address them effectively, gives us strong evidence that our world's dominant framing story is failing. We might say that it is too weak. It doesn't provide strong enough inspiration and motivation to transcend the greed, class conflict, sexual irresponsibility, ethnic hatred, religious bigotry, or nationalistic militarism that threaten us. We could also say that our framing story is too strong—but strong in a misguided way, in that it actually catalyzes and energizes those same self-destructive forces. In coming chapters we will sharpen our description and diagnosis of our dominant framing story, but for now we can safely conclude, in the words of one of my mentors, that our societal systems are perfectly designed to yield the results we are now getting. Any attempts to change the results without changing the system, starting with its framing story, will fail. Consider how our current dominant story is failing us.

The Prosperity Dysfunction

Our story does not guide us to respect environmental limits, but instead inspires our pursuit of as much resource use and waste production (also known as *economic growth*) as possible, as fast as possible. As a result, we burn through nonrenewable resources without concern for their eventual disappearance, draw down renewable resources faster than they can be replenished, and produce more waste products than our environment can absorb, manifesting a host of negative symptoms, some realized, others largely invisible to us as yet. Rapid and extravagant resource use (with corresponding waste production) is so profitable for some people that they can avoid or remain in denial about most of these negative symptoms for a very long time. In fact, their "success" makes it highly improbable that they will ever be willing to acknowledge the unsustainability of their way of life. This is the prosperity dysfunction.

The Equity Dysfunction

Our framing story does not lead us to work for the common good. Instead, it legitimizes the growing gap between rich and poor in a variety of ways. For example, the story may imply that God has blessed and favored the rich and powerful, or that the poor and vulnerable are lazy and irresponsible and therefore are getting what they deserve. All the while the bellies of the poor ache from hunger and their children die of treatable diseases.

The poor respond in various ways. Some poor people decide to join the story of the rich by immigration—legal or illegal. Other poor people resent the rich for not helping them and may blame the rich for their own poverty. They graft their growing resentment into their unique versions of the framing story, justifying their strategies for crime, war, terrorism, and hatred. Meanwhile, the rich see how the rage of the poor grows as the gap between themselves and the poor grows. The rich express their growing fear through guard dogs, high walls, and razor wire, through expanding defense budgets, and through preemptive war doctrine. The more the poor infringe upon the comfort of the rich through immigration, crime, war, and terrorism, the more the rich protect themselves and shut the poor out, creating a vicious cycle of us/them alienation and polarization. Every social grouping—national, religious, ethnic, tribal, political, social, or educational—is drawn into a vortex of rich/poor conflict. Each group becomes a competing us/them faction that seeks advantage for "us," not a common good for all. This is the equity dysfunction.

The Security Dysfunction

Our framing story does not lead these competing factions to reconcile peacefully. Instead we find, nested in the larger framing story shared by both rich and poor, a huge bank of patriotic and religious stories that celebrate how "redemptive violence" has helped good people ("us") to defeat evil people ("them") throughout history.[4] Thus when push comes to shove, good people and evil people alike trust violence as the way to peace, and our framing story squelches the search for creative, peaceful alternatives. When more and more nations (or religious or ethnic militia) arm themselves with more and more lethal weapons—not to mention when some groups acquire biological, chemical, or nuclear weapons—everyone feels less secure, and every regional conflict contains the seeds of terrifying escalation, resulting in an increasingly anxious global society. Gradually, the world becomes locked in a vicious cycle of tension between an anxious global empire of the rich and an angry global terrorist revolution of the poor. This is the security dysfunction.

Again, a look in the mirror can make this all very clear. Your sixty trillion cells and ten biological systems can be thrust into a life of service to humanity or a life of crimes against humanity depending on the framing story you live by. The various subplots of your life—we can call them episodes or narratives—all take shape within this larger framing story: the narrative of your marriage, your career, and hobbies, for example, live in dynamic relation with the framing story to which they contribute and by which they are to some degree driven.

DESTRUCTIVE NARRATIVES

Consider addiction as a framing story: the addict's addiction becomes the framing story in which many subplots emerge—divorce, declining health, car accidents, crime, unemployment, and so on. Similarly, in a society infected with an unhealthy framing story, various destructive narratives or subplots will proliferate. These destructive subplots, instead of feeding our communities with a kind of spiritual or social nutrition so we can live productive, healthy, sustainable, and coherent lives, can function more like heroin or crack. They produce a buzz, a high, an illusion of well-being and power, but the high is a false hope, tragic in the end because it distracts us from our actual situation. As we become hooked on these destructive narratives and the larger framing story they constitute, our society becomes sicker and sicker, stuck in self-reinforcing, addictive cycles that drive us toward insanity and potentially toward suicide in certain grimly predictable ways. For example:

Violent Narratives

Victim and *revenge narratives* keep old memories of past offenses alive; victimization becomes an excuse for current problems and a stimulus for future retaliation. This offense-revenge cycle can preoccupy a society for centuries, even millennia: each offense is memorialized, perhaps to the point of sacredness, as a part of a society's identity. The cycle demands retaliatory actions which in turn provide equal and opposite offenses for their enemy's national psyche, creating a tragic death-dance of hot and cold war. These narratives work closely with *warrior and revolution narratives,* justifying new violence and injustice to oppose existing violence and injustice. Some nations may upgrade their warrior narratives for *domination* or *imperial narratives,* which tell them that they deserve to be in control of other nations and that they aren't actually secure unless they're in control.

Withdrawal or Isolation Narratives

Other nations may tire of these overtly violent narratives and instead may choose *withdrawal* or *isolation narratives.* They are similarly addictive, but instead of an offense-revenge cycle, they work with a fear-protection cycle. Leaders keep their people in a state of constant fear of outside attack or internal uprising, aided and abetted by the news media and sometimes by religious leaders as well. As long as leaders provide protection, they are assured of remaining in power, and the people feel, if not security, the next best therapy for chronic anxiety: obsessive-compulsive vigilance. The feeling of being in danger itself becomes addictive: without a real or imagined threat, the society loses its framing story and must find or create a new potential enemy.

Theocapitalist Narratives

Other societies work on what we will call *theocapitalist narratives,* which mythologize markets and their products with a divine power to bring happiness. The economy's "invisible hand" moves mysteriously to solve all problems and meet all needs. These consumerist narratives must stir desire for material wealth beyond the level of need or even comfort by making the constant stimulation and satisfaction of desire an end in itself. This desire appears productive (especially in comparison to the previous framing stories) but easily becomes no less addictive than the other narratives—whether its addiction focuses on oil, amusement, sex, food, technology, work, leisure, or an abstraction such as growth.

This list does not pretend to be complete, but it illustrates the power of destructive narratives that find sanctuary within an unhealthy framing story. Human social life on the planet today can be seen as a swirl of cultures working, losing, adopting, and adapting these destructive narratives, all caught in the spin of our planet's master framing story, which is forming as we speak, slowly developing like a perfect storm.[5]

An Alternative Framing Story

If our societies are driven by a dysfunctional framing story, and if the global crises we face are symptoms or consequences of that dysfunction, how can we solve our crises while we're still in the grip of the story that helped cause them? Won't all our actions—including our attempts to solve global crises—be likely to push the human project closer and closer to breakdown, or worse still, complete suicide, since the solutions themselves are subplots within the same overarching framing story?[6] Without altering our framing story, we will never successfully solve our crises.

And right here—at the level of our framing story—we have tapped into the current that runs between our two original questions: what are our top global crises, and what does the message of Jesus say to them? I am convinced that Jesus confronted the framing story that drove the society of his day and offered a radical alternative, seeking to turn their trajectory from a downward arc of self-destruction to an ascending spiral of transformation and hope. One of the primary challenges for believers in Jesus today is to understand that confrontation and imagine how we might follow his example and continue his work.

So, looking back, we've tried to understand our global crises. We've consolidated various lists into a model of human society as a machine with three subsystems or mechanisms—prosperity, equity, and security. We have situated this societal machine within the ecosystem of Earth, and we have understood it to be driven by a dominant framing story in which many narratives or subplots nest and interact. And we have raised the possibility that Jesus' message might be seen as an alternative framing story that, if believed, could save the system from suicide. To test this possibility, we will need to consider the possibility that "Jesus" as we have understood him has himself been domesticated and made part of the dominant framing story. For Jesus to save the system, we must first, in a sense, save Jesus—by reframing him outside the confines of our dominant and largely unquestioned assumptions.

GROUP DIALOGUE QUESTIONS

1. Describe how it feels to think of yourself in the terms described at the beginning of this chapter—as a society of sixty trillion cells working in ten systems.
2. What framing stories are at work in your life right now? What stories are you telling yourself about yourself? How could these stories frame your future?
3. What framing stories have been important in your family's life? In your nation's life?
4. Review the destructive narratives that are outlined in this chapter. Where do you see them at work in our world today?
5. How do you react to the author's idea of saving Jesus?

Part 3

REFRAMING JESUS

How Much More Ironic

Jesus, I believe, saw that his contemporaries were stuck in their own suicidal system, driven by their own defective framing story. He proposed a radical alternative—a profoundly new framing story that he called *good news*. *News*, of course, means a *story*— a story of something that has happened or is happening that you should know about. *Good* news, then, would mean a story that you should know about because it brings hope, healing, joy, and opportunity. Jesus was saying, in essence, "There are a lot of bad stories in our world. But I have a good story that frames the bad ones, that puts them in a new light, that says they aren't the last word. I have a good story that inspires healing and transformative action in our world."

TWO VIEWS OF JESUS' GOOD NEWS

Before we can consider the relevance of Jesus' message to our day, though, we need to see it in its native historic, social, political, and religious situation. Doing so will surprise many of us, because we bring to the life and message of Jesus an unhelpful set of assumptions.

I can better explain by comparing two views of Jesus' good news. Of course, there aren't really just two views; there are hundreds—at least as many as there are denominations of Christianity, and maybe even as many as there are individual Christians, since each of us has a view of Jesus both like and unlike the views of others. But these two views—perhaps starkly or even crudely described—will serve to show two ends of a broadening spectrum.

The Human Situation: What is the story we find ourselves in?

Conventional View: God created the world as perfect, but because our primal ancestors, Adam and Eve, did not maintain the absolute perfection demanded by God, God has irrevocably determined that the entire universe and all it contains will be destroyed, and the souls of all human beings—except for those specifically exempted— will be forever punished for their imperfection in hell.[1]

Emerging View: God created the world as good, but human beings—as individuals, and as groups—have rebelled against God and filled the world with evil and injustice. God wants to save humanity and heal it from its sickness, but humanity is hopelessly lost and confused, like sheep without a shepherd, wandering further and further into lostness and danger. Left to themselves, human beings will spiral downward in sickness and evil.

Basic Questions: What questions did Jesus come to answer?

Conventional View: Since everyone is doomed to hell, Jesus seeks to answer one or both of these questions: How can individuals be saved from eternal punishment in hell and instead go to heaven after they die? How can God help individuals be happy and success-ful until then?

Emerging View: Since the human race is in such desperate trouble, Jesus seeks to answer this question: What must be done about the mess we're in? The *mess* refers both to the general human condition and to its specific outworking among his contemporaries living under domination by the Roman Empire and who were confused and conflicted as to what they should do to be liberated.

Jesus' Message: How did Jesus respond to the crisis?

Conventional View: Jesus says, in essence, "If you want to be among those specifically qualified to escape being forever punished for your sins in hell, you must repent of your individual sins and believe that my Father punished me on the cross so he won't have to punish you in hell. Only if you believe this will you go to heaven when the earth is destroyed and everyone else is banished to hell."[2] This is the good news.

Emerging View: Jesus says, in essence, "I have been sent by God with this good news—that God loves humanity, even in its lostness and sin. God graciously invites everyone and anyone to turn from his or her current path and follow a new way. Trust me and become my disciple, and you will be transformed, and you will participate in the transformation of the world, which is possible, beginning right now."[3] This is the good news.

Purpose of Jesus: Why is Jesus important?

Conventional View: Jesus came to solve the problem of "original sin," meaning that he helps qualified individuals not to be sent to hell for their sin or imperfection. In a sense, Jesus saves these people from God, or more specifically, from the righteous wrath of God, which sinful human beings deserve because they have not perfectly fulfilled God's just expectations, expressed in God's moral laws. This escape from punishment is not something they earn or achieve, but rather a free gift they receive as an expression of God's grace and love. Those who receive it enjoy a personal relationship with God and seek to serve and obey God, which produces a happier life on Earth and more rewards in heaven.

Emerging View: Jesus came to become the Savior of the world, meaning he came to save the earth and all it contains from its ongoing destruction because of human evil. Through his life and teaching, through his suffering, death, and resurrection, he inserted into human history a seed of grace, truth, and hope that can never be defeated.

This seed will, against all opposition and odds, prevail over the evil and injustice of humanity and lead to the world's ongoing transformation into the world God dreams of. All who find in Jesus God's hope and truth discover the privilege of participating in his ongoing work of personal and global transformation and liberation from evil and injustice. As part of his transforming community, they experience liberation from the fear of death and condemnation. This is not something they earn or achieve, but rather a free gift they receive as an expression of God's grace and love.

The conventional view is very familiar to many of us; it is frequently defined as "orthodoxy" and any departure from it as "heresy." It contains much of value; however, more and more of us agree that for all its value, it does not adequately situate Jesus in his original context, but rather frames him in the context of religious debates within Western Christianity, especially debates in the sixteenth century.[4]

True, even this conventional view of Jesus can be modified with an almost infinite number of variations—Protestant or Catholic, Calvinist or Armenian, Pentecostal or traditional—but the basic shape of the story is similar despite differences in details: Earth is doomed, and souls are eternally damned unless they are specifically and individually saved, and the purpose of Jesus was to provide a way for at least a few individuals to escape the eternal conscious torment of everlasting damnation. Supporters of the conventional view can justify it with many quotations from the Bible, and in so doing they bring much of value to light. But many other passages of the Bible are marginalized in the conventional view, and it has proven to entail many unintended negative consequences.

THE CONVENTIONAL VIEW'S UNINTENDED NEGATIVE CONSEQUENCES

Simply put, the conventional view of Jesus poses little or no significant challenge to the dominant framing story that currently directs our societal machinery in its suicidal trajectory. It not only fails to confront and correct the current dysfunctions of our societal machinery, but energetically aids and abets its suicidal tendencies in at least six unintended but nevertheless harmful ways.

First, while the emerging view sees Jesus as a medicinal cure to a lethal infection that plagues humanity (diagnosing and treating the individual and societal sickness called *sin*), the conventional view sees Jesus primarily as the legal solution to a capital infraction against God (legally resolving the capital offense of imperfection and the eternal punishment it demands).[5] By framing Jesus in this way, the conventional view relegates Jesus to practical irrelevance in relation to human social problems in history; his message is about the soul, its guilt before God, and its afterlife, not about our world and its crises.

Second, while the emerging view sees God's primary focus as the transformation and salvation of humanity within history, the conventional view offers relatively little hope for history, but rather anticipates its complete destruction and replacement. This historical hopelessness easily becomes "an opiate of the masses," pacifying them with dreams of a better afterlife "by and by" rather than motivating and mobilizing them to transform our world here and now.

Third, from the emerging viewpoint, God's concern is more holistic or integral, seeing individual and society, soul and body, life and afterlife, humanity and the rest of creation as being inseparably related. The conventional view, however, is more dualistic, with human souls and other "spiritual" things in one category and human bodies and other "secular" things in another. This dualism conveniently keeps faith a private and personal "spiritual" matter so believers see themselves as "just passing through" this world, steering them away from "worldly" social engagement beyond their personal, family, and church-related concerns.

Fourth, in the emerging view, God cares about all people, and special blessings that come to one person or one group are to be shared for the common good. The specially blessed understand themselves to be blessed for the benefit of everyone. But in the conventional view, God offers blessings to an elect group and little or nothing (except condemnation) to everyone else. Each religious community that follows this view runs the risk of becoming yet one more elite, us-versus-them group seeking its religious self-interest, relatively oblivious to the common good.

Fifth, in the emerging view God seeks to save us and our world from the suicidal machinery of a society driven by a destructive and false framing story. But in many versions of the conventional view, God must destroy the world and all it contains because of our sin, so it is *from God*—and specifically God's wrath and eternal damnation—that we must be saved. Since God's essential attitude toward the world is one of wrath, we are discouraged from seeing God as our ally in our world's transformation.

Finally, by postponing the essence of salvation to the afterlife, and by assuming that God plans to destroy the earth, the conventional view leads us to assume that the world will get worse and worse, and that this deterioration is in fact God's will or plan. This assumption would tend to create a self-fulfilling prophecy. Not only that, but in some versions of the conventional view, the worse the world gets, the better we should feel since salvation—meaning postmortem salvation after the world is destroyed—is approaching. In too many cases, the conventional view can lead people to celebrate humanity's "progress" in self-destruction rather than seeking to turn it around. To put it bluntly, in terms of humanity and this earth, the conventional view too easily creates—unintentionally, of course—a kind of religious death-wish.

Again, I see much truth and value in the conventional view, and I understand why many defend it: convinced that it is indeed what the Bible teaches, they believe the conventional view is "as good as it gets." Many good and sincere defenders of the conventional view will seek to enhance it by keeping it as the main "contract" of belief, and then add elements of the emerging view as "fine print." Others who embrace the emerging view as their main contract will similarly try to keep elements of the conventional view as fine print. At the very least, those who defend the conventional view either in their main contract or fine print will need to consider how they will respond to the six suicidal tendencies we've just considered.

Personally, I am convinced that Jesus' good news was and is better news than we have been led to believe by the conventional view. In spite of the stress and anxiety associated with calls for radical rethinking and, where necessary, radical reformation, I believe we need to face the real possibility that the conventional view has in many ways been domesticated, watered down, and co-opted by the dominant framing story of our modern Western culture and, as a result, has become "a gospel *about* Jesus" but not "the gospel *of* Jesus."

More starkly, I believe our conventional view has accidentally put Jesus in the very framing story Jesus originally sought to subvert. In terms of our two original questions, then, Jesus in the conventional view has little or nothing to say regarding the world's global crises. The real issue is our individual souls and their eternal postmortem destiny. We are so familiar with this version of Jesus and the gospel that it is truly difficult to imagine any other alternative. It's as if we've only seen trained lions in circuses behind iron bars, snarling at whips snapped by performing trainers, jumping through hoops and leaping through rings of fire; we can't imagine what a lion living wild and free on the Serengeti Plain would be like. We've got to release Jesus into the wild of his native habitat to let a fresh view emerge.

JESUS RESITUATED

The Roman Empire was Jesus' original habitat and the dominant social reality in which he lived. Its framing story demanded ultimate submission. The empire could demand this submission because it could boast amazing successes: a system of roads and ports to facilitate commerce, urban planning that featured unprecedented engineering advances like aqueducts and amphitheatres, an economic system that provided a common currency, and a cultural system that spread Roman values through the Greek language.

Driven by the kinds of narratives we considered in the previous chapter, the Roman Empire promised peace, security, and equity through domination. The *pax Romana* recipe was elegantly simple, as it is for all empires. Concentrate the power of violence in one source—the emperor (literally, the king of kings, the supreme king to whom all regional kings defer and submit). Decisively crush any and all opposition to the emperor. Then, unified under the emperor's supreme will, the empire will defeat its enemies and punish its criminals so that all will experience prosperity, equity, and peace.

All, that is, except slaves and servants, whose free and low-cost labor were essential to the empire's prosperity and who therefore had no rights, or next to no rights.

And then there were the small farmers. As we've seen, when taxes would rise to enhance the empire's prosperity, security, and equity systems, small farmers often couldn't keep up. Fortunately, there were benevolent wealthy landowners nearby who were more than willing to pay taxes to the empire in exchange for the title to the land. Beyond this kindness, the wealthy landowners were even willing to let the small farmers stay on the land and keep farming it for their wealthy benefactors. The former small farmers, now tenant farmers, could even keep a portion of the crops for themselves—maybe even enough to stay alive.

And of course, like tenant farmers, women would generally enjoy considerably less of the empire's prosperity than its first-class male citizens. After all, a woman's primary job was to bear as many sons as possible to be soldiers to protect the empire, and as many citizens as possible to enrich it through their work and taxes. This duty was considerable because of high infant mortality, high death rates of women in childbirth, and high losses of grown male children through warfare. The average girl in the Roman Empire had to marry by the age of fourteen and begin bearing children immediately. Simply to maintain the population, the empire depended on her to raise five children to adulthood—on average.[6]

So the empire benefited everyone—except for slaves, servants, tenant farmers, and women—and perhaps we should add those who lived at the borders of the empire.

Those at the empire's margins faced several recurring problems. First, some of the empire's neighbors lived in constant fear of being conquered and annexed into the empire, so they would heavily arm and fortify themselves, requiring border dwellers to do the same. This need for constant vigilance and militarization did not constitute a peaceful life. Meanwhile, other neighboring nations or tribes would grow jealous of the prosperity enjoyed within the borders of the empire, so they were prone to launch raids that would certainly involve plunder and would frequently include rape and other acts of revenge for past offenses. Again, this threat made for a less than peaceful and prosperous life. And when neighbors would encounter times of extreme hardship (famine, drought, or attack by another neighbor), large numbers of them would wish to immigrate to enjoy the relative prosperity and security of the empire.

But the empire didn't want its own people to suffer by sharing slices of the pie with a flood of unwanted immigrants, so borders had to be carefully protected. As a result, border dwellers could expect constant militarization and frequent skirmishes, if not all-out war; the security of those at the center required constant insecurity for those at the margins. Better to fight the enemy on the distant soil of the borderlands than to let the security of the homeland be disturbed.

So unless you were a slave, servant, tenant farmer, woman, or border dweller, you had a great life of prosperity, security, and equity in the empire. Until, of course, full-scale wars broke out. Then it wasn't good to be a conscriptable male. But thankfully, the sons of the wealthy and those in power wouldn't be conscripted to go to the front lines. The common people and their sons would be given that honor.

Obviously, to protect the precious freedom of the empire's wealthy and powerful men, there would have to be taxes—taxes that fell disproportionately on the non-elite. But these were small prices to pay for the pleasure of being part of a great and peaceful empire—a pleasure enjoyed by all except slaves, servants, tenant farmers, women, border-dwellers, conscriptable males, and those who were not given tax breaks.

There was one other small price to pay so that powerful, wealthy men could enjoy the prosperity, security, and equity of the empire: freedom of speech, of thought, of religion. Of course, all three were officially celebrated and defended by the empire—except when they might undermine support for imperial policy. For example, if people were tempted to use their free speech to complain about excessive taxation in the empire, or if their religion came into conflict with the patriotic ethos of the empire—perhaps by doubting the supreme, divine authority given to the emperor—they'd better keep quiet about it, or they may experience the dark side of the *pax Romana*: the cross.

How ironic that the cross—the icon of the dominating Roman framing story—became the icon for the liberating framing story of Jesus. And how much more ironic if we who believe in Jesus don't get the irony.

GROUP DIALOGUE QUESTIONS

1. Summarize and respond to the two views of the gospel (or good news) presented in this chapter.
2. Why do you think the author presented them in this point-counterpoint way? How did you respond to this articulation of the two views?
3. Review and responde to the six unintended consequences of the conventional view.
4. How did you respond to the description of the Roman Empire? Why did the author use an ironic tone?
5. When you think of Jesus as someone living under the Roman Empire, how does it change your view of Jesus?
6. The author obviously is dissatisfied with the conventional view. Do you share that dissatisfaction? What questions do you have about the emerging view he presents as an alternative?

Switching Jigsaw Lids

The cross was Rome's brilliant way of eliminating uncooperative people. Imperial security forces would erect crosses conspicuously on hillsides near well-traveled roads near major cities of the empire. By impaling rebels like insects on pins for public view, security forces would demonstrate both the absolute and fearsome power of the empire and the complete and pathetic powerlessness of writhing, gasping, crying would-be insurrectionists. It would just take one quick glance at a cross, perhaps supporting a naked victim covered in sweat and blood, feces dripping down his leg, screaming and moaning and sobbing, and the lesson would be learned. Or perhaps a second quick glance a few days later, the Roman cross holding high the rebel's rotting remains as they were attended to by scavenging crows, a vulture or two, feral dogs, a cloud of flies, and maggots.

The quickest glance at a cross would cure almost anyone of the impulse to shake up the blissful status quo of the *pax Romana* that benefited everyone equally—except slaves, servants, tenant farmers, women, the people of border territories, soldiers, those not given tax breaks, and those unable to control their dreams of freedom and impulses for free speech.

One might also think that British muskets and canons would have cured American colonists of the dream of liberation prior to

1776. Or that the slave master's whip and the frontiersman's gun would have cured blacks and Native Peoples of their dream of liberation in nineteenth-century America. Or that South African tanks and razor wire would have cured black South Africans in the 1980s under apartheid, or that Israeli tanks, bombs, prisons, and walls would cure the Palestinians under Israeli domination today. But something in the human spirit isn't easily cured of being on the underside of dominating societal machinery, of being treated as less than fully human, of being less than free.

The Counternarratives of Jesus' Day

In Jesus' day, the Jews refused to be pacified by the *pax Romana*. They had a narrative of their own that they would not easily subordinate to the imperial narrative of Rome. Their religion was strictly monotheistic. The God of Abraham, Isaac, and Jacob was not open to accepting Caesar as a peer, nor did the Lord wish to be seated among the many gods of Greco-Roman culture. So the Jews of Jesus' day were not remotely interested in adding emperor worship or patriotic idolatry to their religious equation. This made them particularly difficult for the Romans to rule, and in fact, the Romans never really succeeded in domesticating them.

It is not surprising that, under these circumstances, many Jews fantasized about an armed revolt. After all, they had the story of David and Goliath—a reminder that a smaller people without advanced weapons could, with God's help, defeat a larger, better-armed opponent. So various counternarratives developed among them.

These counternarratives provided them two essential social resources: an explanation for their current subjugation and a plan of action. Subjugation came, in short, because of their own complacency—complacency in the past and present, complacency expressed in their lack of both courageous faith and scrupulous piety.

When it came to a plan of action, the Zealot party would call for repentance from complacency and immediate, bold, remedial action along these lines: *If we would just rise like David to face the*

Goliath of Rome, if we would take the first step by slitting some Roman throats and burning some Roman buildings, God would raise up a heroic liberator among us to lead us to victory![1]

Meanwhile, the Pharisee party, sympathetic to the Zealots, would focus more on the lack of scrupulous piety, scapegoating blame along these lines: *If we would repent and stop our complacent tolerance of the drunks, the prostitutes, the gluttons, and those who don't pay their tithes to the temple, if we would faithfully observe every detail of the Law, God would send a heroic liberator among us to lead us to victory! We could eject the Romans and finally live in prosperity, security, and equity as God's chosen people!*[2]

The Herodians and Sadducees were the political realists of their day, seeing the Zealots and Pharisees as hopelessly naive: nobody could beat the Romans militarily, and to try was suicide. So, following the old wisdom of "If you can't beat them, join them," or "If you can't beat them, at least try to make a profit off of them," they called for a path of accommodation and coexistence: learn to live in public within the Roman imperial narrative but hold their own Jewish narrative as a private personal value. If necessary, let the former modify the latter, but avoid the reverse. That's not collaboration; that's not compromise—it's being clever and realistic (or so a Jewish tax collector might say—to the chagrin of those Jews who couldn't so easily nestle up to the powers that be).[3]

A few, like the Essenes, rejected all of these approaches, calling instead for a withdrawal into the wilderness to try to avoid the whole simmering mess.[4]

At first glance, all of this might seem rather remote to us today, although there has been much talk in recent years about the United States as a new imperial power.[5] But upon further reflection, it's clear that these counternarratives have various counterparts in our world today, maybe including some of us, or maybe parts of each of us. For example, some groups call believers to withdraw into isolated subcultures like the Essenes—with their own TV stations, radio stations, literature, and schools. Others stir people to "take America back for Jesus," often using the rhetoric of warfare, recalling the

Zealots. Some identify various scapegoats—*liberals* and *gays* have been popular in this role—to blame for our world's problems. Others call on believers to support their president or party without criticism and to accept the current political arrangement as the will of God, echoing Herodians and Sadducees.

THE EMERGING VIEW OF JESUS

At this point, we can distinguish between various forms of empire-related framing stories. First, *imperial* or *dominant narratives* legitimize the powers that be. Second, *counternarratives* or *revolutionary narratives* explain the situation of those who experience the downside of an empire, stirring them to action. Third, *dual narratives* allow one to live in a compartmentalized way, living by the dominant imperial narrative in public and another domesticated narrative in private. Fourth, *withdrawal narratives* justify nonparticipation and isolation for subcultures that equally reject imperial, revolutionary, and dual narratives.

It would have been nice if there were a fifth option waiting in the wings in the days of the Roman Empire. But there wasn't.

There wasn't, that is, until Jesus came.

This emerging view of Jesus—framed against the backdrop of empire and its narratives and counternarratives—makes possible a valid (I would even say a better) way to understand him, his life, his message.[6]

From this viewpoint, when Jesus proclaimed his central message of the kingdom of God, he was proclaiming not an esoteric religious concept but an alternative to empire: "Don't let your lives be framed by the narratives and counternarratives of the Roman empire," he was saying, "but situate yourselves in another story . . . the good news that God is king, and we can live in relation to God and God's love rather than Caesar and Caesar's power."

Like most churchgoing people, I grew up with the conventional view of Jesus, not this emerging view. Frankly, he never completely made sense to me in that framework, but I was hesitant to admit it for fear that such an admission would be taken as heresy. You may have had a similar experience.

My friend Steve Chalke describes our situation like this: we have a jigsaw puzzle in a box, but someone put the wrong lid on the box.[7] We keep trying to use the picture from the wrong lid as a guide to putting the pieces together. With the wrong picture implanted in our imaginations, some of the colors on the pieces don't seem to belong, and some shapes don't fit. We may assume they were included by mistake and push them to the side, or maybe let them drop off the table edge altogether. And we keep searching for other colors and shapes that we see in the picture on the lid but which for some reason aren't included in our box of pieces. What do we do? We push more and more unfitting pieces aside. We take out some scissors and colored markers and "adjust" some of the pieces that remain. We do our best to conform the pieces in the box to the picture on the lid. We do the best we can.

Some people become so disillusioned and frustrated that they throw out the whole thing—pieces, box, and all. They give up puzzling altogether. Others decide that it's the box lid rather than the pieces that determines "orthodoxy," and they zealously defend the lid and bestow on all who dare to question it the labels "heretic" and "apostate."

Others become uncomfortable with the realization that their loyalty is more to the picture outside the box than to the pieces inside the box. They wonder what would happen if they reversed that loyalty and refused to accept a lid that doesn't do justice to all the pieces in the box. They refuse to cut corners or alter colors. Eventually they decide the problem isn't with the pieces—they actually fit together: the problem is with the picture on the lid.

If our low get-it factor resembles the dullness of the first hearers of Jesus' message, then it's no wonder that Jesus spoke so much about blindness and deafness or that so many of his signs and wonders addressed sight and hearing. The problem isn't simply with what's out there in reality, he would be saying; the deeper problem is with how we're not accurately seeing or hearing what's out there. The healing of physical blindness or deafness would signify our need to be healed of a more subtle kind of insensibility. Jesus wants us to see and hear the big picture he saw and heard, but our eyes and ears need healing before that can happen.[8]

If the transforming framing story we're imagining together here is indeed better and truer than the way of understanding Jesus many of us were given, if this picture on the lid better matches the actual contents of the box, it may help fulfill the unfulfilled potential of the Christian religion in its many forms. And perhaps it could help us face and then turn away from at least some of the more disappointing failures that have plagued the Christian religion in its first two millennia. Perhaps it could even overflow the bounds of the Christian religion and bring some benefit to other religions and ideologies as well.

And maybe, just maybe, it will prove capable of liberating us from today's societal machinery, driven by its dysfunctional framing story, which is gaining strength and momentum in our world now, even as I write, even as you read.

GROUP DIALOGUE QUESTIONS

1. Describe the meaning of crosses in the Roman Empire. Was this a new insight to you? How does it compare to the associations most people have with the cross today?
2. Review the metaphor of the puzzle lid. How do you relate to this metaphor? Does it fit with any of your religious experiences?
3. How do you feel about the "emerging view" of Jesus and his message now that it has been more fully described? What questions still remain?
4. Suggest some ways that the emerging view could, in the author's words, "help us face and then turn away from at least some of the more disappointing failures that have plagued the Christian religion in its first two millennia."

everything must change

No Junk DNA

A year or so ago I was boarding a plane, and I sat in an aisle seat next to a serious-looking young man in the center seat. As I stowed my carry-on, I asked if he was heading away or heading home. "Away. Work," was his reply. "What kind of work?" I asked, trying to be polite, but getting the feeling that he didn't really want to talk. He answered, "I'm one of the world's experts on the genetics of the fruit fly, drosophila. I'm going to give a lecture to the world's other leading drosophila geneticists." He assumed this would shut me up, I suspect, but being in an unusually garrulous mood, I said, "That sounds fascinating."

My taciturn neighbor, it turned out, seldom met anyone interested in his area of expertise. Elbow to elbow with an interested student, he became an enthusiastic teacher. By the time we reached cruising altitude, he was explaining how long the DNA in a single human cell would be if it were extracted and stretched out in one long filament. As we landed, he was refuting the common misconception that much of the material contained in a gene is "junk DNA." Nothing is wasted, and there is no junk, he explained. "Maybe we don't yet understand the function of some parts of the gene, but the more we learn, the more we see how each part has a role to play. We only call those parts *junk* when we assume we know what they're supposed to do, and they don't do it. But our assumptions are wrong. The problem isn't the gene: it's the thinking of geneticists."

We said good-bye at baggage claim, and I was pulling out of the rental car facility when I began thinking about how relevant his comments about genetics were to the conventional way we read the Bible, and especially the four Gospels. The Bible's purpose, we assume, is to explain how to go to heaven, to legitimize certain religious institutions, to define in detail universal timeless truths, to provide a detailed timeline for the end of the world, and so on. But based on that assumption, there appears to be a lot of junk revelation in there, a lot of extraneous material about history, agriculture, economics, art, ethics, and other "earthly" things, extra stuff that doesn't really matter in relation to getting souls to heaven. So, what might we discover if we become willing to question that assumption? Then we could test an alternative hypothesis: that the Bible instead is the story of the partnership between God and humanity to save and transform all of human society and avert global self-destruction. Perhaps if we read the Bible afresh from this perspective, a lot of the supposed filler will suddenly come alive with new importance and meaning. Perhaps what seemed to be extraneous material will turn out to be profoundly relevant to our two basic questions about our world's crises and the relevance of Jesus' message to them.

Our task in the next three chapters will be to test this hypothesis. First, in this chapter we'll consider a dozen specific features of the Gospels, and then in the subsequent chapters we'll examine key passages from the beginning, middle, and end of Jesus' life and ministry.[1]

Twelve Features of Jesus' Ministry That Are Not "Junk"

Consider first how in the canonical Gospels, Jesus is constantly in conflict with the Sadducees and Herodians on one side and the Pharisees (and their allies, the Zealots) on the other. Each party tests him to see if he plays into their imperial or counterimperial narratives.

The imperial narrative of the Sadducees and Herodians accepts the presence of the Roman Empire and calls for docile cooperation, while the counternarrative of the Pharisees and Zealots rejects the Roman Empire's presence and calls for resistance and revolution. In this light, it is striking to see Jesus choose a counterimperial Zealot named Simon as one of his disciples, and equally striking to see Jesus choose Matthew, who is identified as an imperial tax collector. Jesus thus brings together people formerly affiliated with both imperial and counterimperial narratives, inviting them into his own framing story, which provides an alternative to both.

Next, consider the persistent role of "tax collectors" and "sinners" in the Gospels. Their role is significant because, again, tax collectors were collaborators with the imperial narrative (raising taxes for Caesar and his empire, thus supporting the oppressive regime) who were rejected by the Pharisees. Along with collaborating tax collectors, sinners were scapegoated by the Pharisees as the cause of Jewish troubles. By his habit of socializing (through table fellowship) with these people marginalized by the champions of the counterimperial narrative, Jesus would be highlighting that his approach was indeed a "third way," undomesticated and incapable of being categorized in terms of the standard political polarization of his day.

Similarly, consider how a question about paying taxes to Caesar becomes a test of narrative affiliation (Luke 20:20ff.), and consider how many of the other test questions posed to Jesus become transparent attempts to put Jesus in either the imperial box or the counterimperial one so he can be disposed of (Luke 20:1ff., John 8:4ff.). But again, his narrative is different, so it won't fit in either box.

Next, consider how Jesus constantly rebukes hypocrites—masked people who try to live by a dual narrative. They wear an imperial mask in public, living by its narrative, but then they unveil another counterimperial face in private (or vice versa). Jesus calls people to live with integrity, wholeheartedly inhabiting one integrated, holistic framing story rather than playing at two. "No one can serve two masters"—a repeated theme of Jesus—also speaks to the impossibility of living faithfully by a dual narrative (Luke 16:13; Matthew 6:24).

Also, consider the anonymous "rich young ruler" who interviews Jesus (see Mark 10:17–31, for example). On the one hand, as a rich man he is profiting under the imperial system, and as a ruler he has been given a co-opting position of authority within it early in his career. On the other hand, he is sincere and devout, a wholehearted keeper of Jewish law. His life is a study in dual narratives. When he expresses interest in "eternal life," he is not simply asking how he can go to heaven after he dies, as is commonly assumed. Although the question of how to go to heaven has been deeply important in Christian history, it was not a preoccupying question in Jesus' day. The phrase "eternal life" (*zoein aionian* in Greek) would be better translated "life of the ages," meaning a life that transcends "life in the present age." It is, in other words, "life in the kingdom of God." In fact, Jesus substitutes *kingdom of God* for the term later in the story (vv. 24–25).[2] Jesus' response, "Sell all you have and give it to the poor . . . and come, follow me," is not simply about a problem with materialism in the privacy of "his heart" that might keep him out of heaven, as is so often preached. Instead, it's an electrifying call to defect from the imperial narrative and join Jesus in serving those who suffer under it.

Parables about Stewards. Consider how many of Jesus' parables about stewards come alive within this framework. Stewards aren't simply nice professional fund managers, as is commonly assumed. Instead, stewards are intermediaries standing between the wealthy landowners who profit under the Roman Empire and the poor tenant farmers who suffer under it. As we saw conceptually explained in chapter 9, when poor farmers can't afford the imperial taxes demanded by Rome, their wealthy countrymen step in and pay the taxes for them, and then in return, the wealthy demand title to the poor farmers' land. The poor are thus reduced to tenant farmer status, even as the landholdings of the rich swell. Each year, when tenant farmers must pay rent in the form of a percentage of their farm's produce, stewards are the ones who collect this rent and manage the tenant farmers on behalf of the wealthy elite. They represent people who aren't directly oppressing others, but profit indirectly from an oppressive system. Stewards are thus at the epicenter of tension between competing narratives in the imperial framing story. For Jesus to use them so frequently in his parables is a master stroke of political irony, sparkling with tension and innuendo.

Parable of the Unjust Steward. Specifically, consider the so-called parable of the unjust steward in Luke 16:1–16. Seen in terms of the imperial narrative, the story is transformed from an ethically difficult text to a politically dynamic one. The steward in the story "switches sides." He stops working for the wealthy landowner and starts working for the oppressed poor. So he isn't actually *unjust*—that would be the judgment of people within the imperial narrative who see the landowner's position as legitimate. From Jesus' perspective, outside that imperial narrative and within God's liberating framing story, the steward is *wise* rather than unjust—wise enough to defect (as the rich young ruler should have done) from the service of the wealthy elite to give a break to the poor who are being crushed by the societal machinery driven by the imperial narrative. Jesus is saying that switching sides—choosing to serve the needs of the poor instead of working the system that favors the rich—is a way of "laying up treasure in heaven," of working for a higher spiritual economy rather than the "unclean" imperial economy. Switching sides is not unjust; it's smart. It's a good investment, far better than short-term profiteering from an economic system based on the imperial narrative.

"Jesus the Christ." Consider the revolutionary term *Christ*—so common in the New Testament that many think it is Jesus' last name. It is actually a Greek translation of *messiah*, meaning "the liberating king promised by God." For those who suffer under the oppression of an empire, this is not a sophisticated or esoteric theological term at all: it is a profoundly political one, suggesting one who would liberate from an oppressive empire. Jesus' words in Luke 9:23—"If anyone would come after me, he must deny himself and take up his cross daily and follow me"—mean far more than a call to private, personal devotion: since crosses were used to publicly execute those who plotted insurrection against Caesar, Jesus is saying,

"Risk everything, including your life, to stand up to Caesar and join me in my revolution—not by fighting and killing, but by being willing to die with me."

"Son of Man." Similarly, the fascinating and complex term *Son of Man* (used by Jesus eighty-one times in the Gospels—see Mark 8:31, for example, where the term is used in parallel to the term *Christ*) evokes a dream of liberation from the book of Daniel. Daniel was written in the context of empire (ostensibly in the Babylonian and Medo-Persian empires, but more likely, some scholars would say, in the later Greek and Syrian empires). The book of Daniel churns with the life-and-death challenge of living unbowed within a hostile imperial narrative, and it elicits dreams of liberation from all empires. Daniel recounts a vision in which one "like a son of man" approaches "the Ancient of Days" (God) and is given "authority, glory, and sovereign power; all peoples, nations, and people of every language worshiped him. His dominion is an everlasting dominion that will not pass away, and his kingdom is one that will never be destroyed" (7:13–14). Later, significantly, this kingdom is identified as being "handed over to the saints," and is described as the kingdom of God in contrast to the Assyrian, Babylonian, Greek, and Roman kingdoms or empires (v. 27).[3] Each use of "Son of Man" nearly glows when this rich context is brought to it.[4]

"Lord." Consider how the title *Lord* is equally dynamic in this context. Sometimes the Greek term *kurios* simply means "sir," but it is also the term used for the emperor. He is the ultimate "sir," the ultimate authority, the king of all kings, and the lord of all lords. The earliest confession of the earliest followers of Jesus—Jesus is Lord—was not in this light primarily a theological confession of Jesus' divinity, as many today assume; it was a very earthly declaration that Jesus, not Caesar, was the ultimate authority.[5] It was a statement of defection from ultimate allegiance to the emperor, the empire, and the imperial narrative and a corresponding affirmation of faith in Jesus as the leader of the kingdom that really matters, the kingdom of God.[6]

In this light, exorcisms become "signs and wonders"—prophetic actions that first depict the "possession" of Israel by the demonic forces of empire, and then predict their expulsion by the kingdom of God. Of particular interest is the expulsion of a demon identified as Legion (a clear reference to the Roman military) and then sent into a "troop" (another military reference) of pigs (which had no business being in Jewish territory—another reference to the occupying Gentile Romans), as recorded in Mark 5:1–20. The pigs "charge" (yet another use of military language) into the sea (not the lake, perhaps suggesting that the Romans go back to where they came from—across the Mediterranean, and also highly evocative of the liberation of the Israelites from Egypt).[7]

The term *kingdom of God*, which is at the heart and center of Jesus' message in word and deed, becomes positively incandescent in this kind of framing. As a member of a little colonized nation with a framing story that refuses to be tamed by the Roman imperial narrative, Jesus bursts on the scene with this scandalous message: *The time has come! Rethink everything! A radically new kind of empire is available—the empire of God has arrived! Believe this good news, and defect from all human imperial narratives, counternarratives, dual narratives, and withdrawal narratives. Open your minds and hearts like children to see things freshly in this new way, follow me and my words, and enter this new way of living.* At every point, the essence of his kingdom teaching subverts the "common sense" of the Roman Empire and all its predecessors and successors:

Don't get revenge when wronged, but seek reconciliation.
Don't repay violence with violence, but seek creative and
    transforming nonviolent alternatives.
Don't focus on external conformity to moral codes, but on
    internal transformation in love.
Don't love insiders and hate or fear outsiders, but welcome
    outsiders into a new "us," a new "we," a new humanity
    that celebrates diversity in the context of love for all,
    justice for all, and mutual respect for all.
Don't have anxiety about money or security or pleasure at

the center of your life, but trust yourself to the care of
God.

Don't live for wealth, but for the living God who loves all
people, including your enemies.

Don't hate your enemies or competitors, but love them and
do to them not *as they have done* to you—and not
before they do to you—but *as you wish they would do* for
you.

These features of the Gospels, along with many others, come
alive as never before in this framing of the biblical story into which
Jesus is born and in which he grows, lives, works, and teaches. They
are no longer "junk DNA" or extra puzzle pieces but rather essential to understanding Jesus, his message, and his mission. If we take
them seriously, I believe we will find resources to confront the destructive narratives of our day and envision the possibility that Jesus is
still right: the kingdom of God is still, at this moment, at hand.

GROUP DIALOGUE QUESTIONS

1. Summarize the idea of "junk DNA" in relation to the
   Bible.
2. Which of the author's twelve examples was most
   interesting or enlightening for you? Which of them was
   the least convincing?
3. Reread the summary of Jesus' teaching near the end of
   the chapter. Does it strike you as a radical reversal of the
   "common sense" of the Roman Empire?
4. How would you define or explain, in your own words,
   what Jesus meant by "the kingdom of God"?
5. How does this chapter impact your own spiritual life
   and your personal view of Jesus?

Jamming the Accelerator, Slamming the Brakes

In the next two chapters, we'll continue our reframing of Jesus by considering four pivotal episodes—one from the beginning of Jesus' life, one from the beginning of his public ministry at age thirty, one from the middle of his ministry, and one from just hours before his crucifixion. Considering these anew helped release me from the puzzle lid that held hostage my understanding of Jesus, and a better picture began to take shape.

SONGS OF MARY AND ZECHARIAH

First, in Luke's narrative of Jesus' birth, we find two fascinating songs or poetic prayers: one uttered by Mary about the child growing in her own womb, and one by Zechariah, her cousin's husband, on the birth of his son, who would grow up to be John the Baptist.

Mary's song, commonly known as the Magnificat (Luke 1:46–55), begins like this:

My soul glorifies the Lord
and my spirit rejoices in God my Savior,
for he has been mindful
of the humble state of his servant.

From now on all generations will call me blessed,
for the Mighty One has done great things for me—
holy is his name. (vv. 46–49)

Her joy and surprise here suggest a great reversal—that she, a common peasant woman, someone at the bottom of the ladder of status in the imperial narrative, has been noticed by God—not in spite of her "humble state," but because of it.

This sense of reversal continues as Mary sees the proud being scattered, the powerful being put down, and the humble being raised high—the language of social upheaval and transformation:

His mercy extends to those who fear him,
from generation to generation.
He has performed mighty deeds with his arm;
he has scattered those who are proud in their inmost thoughts.
He has brought down rulers from their thrones
but has lifted up the humble.
He has filled the hungry with good things
but has sent the rich away empty. (vv. 50–53)

Who is creating this reversal? Political revolutionaries? No, God! God is not the one who legitimizes the wealthy and powerful in their elite status at the top of the ladder. God is the one who shakes the ladder and turns imperial narratives upside down so that powerful rulers will tumble and so that a poor, oppressed, occupied country like Israel can again have high hopes:

He has helped his servant Israel,
remembering to be merciful
to Abraham and his descendants forever,
even as he said to our fathers. (vv. 54–55)

According to the conventional puzzle lid I was given in my religious upbringing, Mary's Magnificat is all wrong. She should have said something like this:

My soul glorifies the Lord and my spirit rejoices in God my personal Savior, for he has been mindful of the correct saving faith of his servant. My spirit will go to heaven when my body dies, for the Mighty One has provided forgiveness, assurance, and eternal security for me—holy is his name. His mercy extends to those who have correct saving faith and orthodox articulations of belief, from generation to generation. He will overcome the damning effects of original sin with his mighty arm; he will damn to hell those who believe they can be saved through their own efforts or through any religion other than the new one he is about to form. He will condemn followers of other religions to hell but bring to heaven those with correct belief. He has filled correct believers with spiritual blessings but will send those who are not elect to hell forever. He has helped those with correct doctrinal understanding, remembering to be merciful to those who believe in the correct theories of atonement, just as our preferred theologians through history have articulated.

But Mary's song is not about the solution to the theological problem called *original sin*. Nor is it about how she and others can go to heaven after they die. Nor is it about how they can be happy and successful individuals through God, or even about how they can have deeper spiritual experiences of communion and contemplation—as valid as all of these things may be. At this moment of celebration and worship, Mary celebrates that God is going to upset the dominance hierarchies typical of empire so that the nation of Israel can experience the fulfillment of its original promise.

Zechariah's song (Luke 1:68–79) explores strikingly similar themes, no less directly and powerfully:

Praise be to the Lord, the God of Israel,
because he has come to his people and redeemed them.
He has raised up a horn
of salvation for us

in the house of his servant David
(as he said through his holy prophets of long ago),
salvation from our enemies
and from the hand of all who hate us—
to show mercy to our ancestors
and to remember his holy covenant,
the oath he swore to our father Abraham:
to rescue us from the hand of our enemies,
and to enable us to serve him without fear
in holiness and righteousness before him all our days.
(vv. 68–75)

The religious words "redeem" and "salvation" here clearly do not mean what the conventional puzzle lid suggests they should mean: salvation from hell or rescue from the ontological (a technical term you can skip if it's not familiar, roughly meaning "intrinsic to and rooted in our essential being") condition of being fallen and damned by God, or even redemption from feelings of moral shame and psychological distress. Zechariah celebrates the coming of Jesus as the coming of a strong king who will rescue—or liberate—the people of Israel from their enemies, the Romans, who hate and oppress them.

The salvation that Zechariah celebrates is not located in an otherworldly afterlife; it is what we might call political and social liberation so that the people of Israel can serve God *without fear*—of invasion, occupation, domination, oppression, or humiliation—*all our days*, meaning in this life.

At this point in his song, Zechariah addresses his newborn son, John, combining spiritual and political concerns:

And you, my child, will be called a prophet of the Most High;
for you will go on before the Lord to prepare the way for him,
to give his people the knowledge of salvation
through the forgiveness of their sins,
because of the tender mercy of our God,
by which the rising sun will come to us from heaven

to shine on those living in darkness
and in the shadow of death,
to guide our feet into the path of peace. (vv. 76–79)

Salvation—previously defined as rescue from enemies and those who hate us—is now related to forgiveness of sins. How are the two kinds of salvation related? If we recall the counternarrative of the Pharisees that focused on Israel's religious complacency, and the counternarrative of the Zealots that focused on liberation from oppression, we can see how forgiveness of sins is inseparable from finding the path of peace. Rebellious, sinful people don't deserve to be liberated, nor will they be open to God's leading into peace: repentant and forgiven people will. Little John will one day prepare the way for God's promised king. This "rising sun" will tenderly and mercifully help Israel to face and repent of her sins so as to receive forgiveness, leading the people in a path leading out from the darkness of oppression under Rome to the daylight and open spaces of freedom and *shalom*—well-being and peace.

NOT A TAME PROPHET

Similar political, economic, and spiritual themes interweave strongly in the opening episode of Jesus' public ministry in Luke's Gospel. Jesus goes to his hometown and attends the synagogue gathering on the Sabbath, as he customarily did, but this time something dramatic happens:

He went to Nazareth, where he had been brought up, and on the Sabbath day he went into the synagogue, as was his custom. He stood up to read, and the scroll of the prophet Isaiah was handed to him. (Luke 4:16–17)

Synagogues were what we might call lay-led congregations, so it was not unusual for a young man like Jesus to volunteer to read from the sacred writings and offer a comment on its meaning. What was unusual, though, was the passage he chose in Isaiah and the comment he offered:

"The Spirit of the Lord is on me,
because he has anointed me
to proclaim good news to the poor.
He has sent me to proclaim freedom for the prisoners
and recovery of sight for the blind,
to set the oppressed free,
to proclaim the year of the Lord's favor."

Then he rolled up the scroll, gave it back to the attendant and sat down. The eyes of everyone in the synagogue were fastened on him, and he began by saying to them, "Today this scripture is fulfilled in your hearing." (vv. 18–21)

The brevity of the summary is striking, but its content is even more striking.

Jesus claims to be anointed by the Spirit of the Lord to do what these words said: proclaim good news to the poor (we've already seen how the Roman Empire, through taxation, created a new class of poor tenant farmers), proclaim freedom for prisoners (likely implying those who are held against their will under Rome's imperial control), and, proclaim new sight for the blind (with blindness referring to his physical healings, or perhaps to the removal of blindness that would come through his insightful teaching, or both). He would also proclaim the year of the Lord's favor—referring to the Jubilee year, when all are to be released from debt and lands are returned to the families that had owned them in the past, relevant on many levels for people whose lands had been seized both by the Romans and by opportunistic fellow Jews.

In between these proclamations is a single phrase that may appear to be a redundancy, but actually is not. Not only will he proclaim freedom for prisoners or captives, but he will also actually *set the oppressed free*. Those are revolutionary words for oppressed people. Those are the words of a liberator.

Equally striking is his use of the word "today." This liberation is not postponed until after death or on the other side of an apocalypse that may include the literal destruction and recreation of the space-time universe. What was promised is now unfolding, in this history and geography. Its fulfillment begins today, and it begins here. No wonder the people react as they do: "All spoke well of him and were amazed at the gracious words that came from his lips" (v. 22).

But Jesus doesn't accept their praise. He pushes back, perhaps playfully at first (quoting a proverb about hometown prophets never being accepted), but then almost aggressively, as if he's daring them to reject him. The episode ends:

> "Truly I tell you," he continued, "prophets are not accepted in their hometowns. I assure you that there were many widows in Israel in Elijah's time, when the sky was shut for three and a half years and there was a severe famine throughout the land. Yet Elijah was not sent to any of them, but to a widow in Zarephath in the region of Sidon. And there were many in Israel with leprosy in the time of Elisha the prophet, yet not one of them was cleansed—only Naaman the Syrian." (vv. 24–27)

By evoking the memory of two Gentiles being blessed, Jesus in a sense explodes the expectations he had just raised. Yes, he claims to be the long-awaited liberator, overturning the imperial narratives of the Romans and their collaborators by freeing the oppressed— but no, he will not do so in the exclusive, parochial, or nationalistic mode demanded by their counternarratives. His scope of liberation will be, as with the prophets of old, far broader than simply the members of his own religion and nation. Even outsiders, even Gentiles will be included in the scope of Jesus' good news.

Yes, he claims the title of prophet, but he will not perform like a tame prophet who works safely within established conventions. If you want him, you'll have to accept more than you bargained for. He comes with his own narrative, and it won't be negotiated or compromised. The people who had been praising him a moment earlier now turn ugly:

> All the people in the synagogue were furious when they heard this. They got up, drove him out of the town, and took him to the brow of the hill on which the town was built, in order to throw him off the cliff. But he walked right through the crowd and went on his way. (vv. 28–30)

This is not the smooth launch of a typical campaign to be voted in as the next messiah. It's more like Jesus is jamming his foot on the accelerator of expectations and then slamming on the brakes. It's not a smooth ride, but a driver like this definitely gets your attention.

GROUP DIALOGUE QUESTIONS

1. Respond to the author's rewriting of Mary's prayer to fit with the conventional understanding of Jesus and the gospel. How did this rewriting affect you?
2. Which of the passages especially seized your attention— Mary's prayer, Zechariah's prayer, or Jesus' first sermon?
3. How would you define the word *salvation* in light of this chapter?
4. How would you summarize Jesus' mission in light of this chapter?
5. Why do you think the crowd turned against Jesus in the final story? Do you think Jesus intentionally elicited this reaction? If so, why?
6. Imagine you were at this final scene. You come home and recount the story to a family member who didn't attend the synagogue that day. How would you tell the story?

Or So It Appeared

As we continue "test-driving" this emerging understanding of Jesus—locating him in relation to the narratives and counter-narratives of empire—we come to two more episodes: one from the middle of Jesus' public ministry and one from its climax.

PETER'S DECLARATION AT CAESAREA PHILIPPI

It was a tense time in an unlikely place. The traveling rabbi and emerging prophet Jesus had taken his band of disciples to a city called Caesarea Philippi. The city's name was itself evocative: it was an outpost city of the emperor whose regime occupied and dominated Jesus' people and homeland. To reach the city, Jesus' entourage had to walk twenty-five miles north from the Sea of Galilee, which was the context for much of Jesus' early ministry. It wasn't the kind of trip you would make unless you actually wanted to be there; we have only one record of Jesus ever traveling any farther north than this excursion (an episode we'll consider in depth later, in chapter 19).

The city was built near the base of an escarpment, where an important spring emerged from a cliff face. The spring had been a center for worship of the Canaanite god Baal; but the place was renamed Panias (or Banias), when the Greek god Pan replaced Baal as the focal point of worship. Elaborate niches (still visible today) were carved into the cliff face so that statues of Pan and associated Greek deities could be housed there. Panias also had a reputation like Gettysburg or perhaps Waterloo or Little Bighorn in the history of the region: it was known as the site of an important battle where Syrians took control of the whole region. This regime change signaled the rise of the Seleucids to power, which meant worse days for the Jews, as the Seleucids sought to impose Greek religion on the Jews.

Eventually the Romans replaced the Seleucid regime, and when the regional Roman ruler Herod the Great died, his son Herod Philip was given control of the region around Panias. He changed the name to Caesarea Philippi—the first name honoring Caesar Augustus, the Roman emperor, and the latter name honoring himself and distinguishing the city from another city named Caesarea (Maritima—on the coast).

The Jewish people resented being ruled by a man enmeshed with pagan practices, who added to them by having his image inscribed on a local coin, a transgression falling under the category of "graven image" in their minds. Taken together, the religious associations (Baal, Pan) and political associations (Caesar, Philip) would have been fused, because for people in that time, politics and religion were not separated into distinct categories as they are for many of us today. Take, for example, how the Greco-Roman gods helped legitimize the Roman political machine. For Jesus to lead his disciples to this city, then, would be an intentional move evoking many layers of meaning—perhaps akin to a leader today bringing his followers to Auschwitz, Hiroshima, Soweto, or the Gaza Strip.

So this Jewish prophet and his band of closest friends come to the foreign city named for the occupying emperor and a puppet regional ruler, the site of a battle that led to some of Israel's worst days, and a location known as a center for the worship of false gods. Very possibly in the shadow of the cliff face with its idols set into their finely carved niches, Jesus asks, "Who do people say the Son of Man is?" (Matthew 16:13).

I imagine an awkward silence follows—it is a rather strange and self-conscious question, after all, especially in a place like this—but then the answers flow. "Some people say you're John the Baptist [resurrected]; others say Elijah; and still others, Jeremiah or one of the prophets" (v. 14).

Then Jesus sharpens the question: "What about you? Who do you say I am?" (v. 15). Another silence, and then Peter, a leader among them, speaks: "You are the Christ, the Son of the living God" (v. 16).

Peter must know exactly what he means by these words. He must know that he is making a profound and dangerous political statement.[1] As we saw in chapter 12, *Christ* is the Greek translation for the Hebrew term *messiah*, which means *liberating king*. To say *liberating king* anywhere in the Roman Empire is dangerous, even more so in a city bearing Caesar's name: "You are King Jesus who will liberate us from King Caesar. You are the liberator promised by God long ago, the one for whom we have long waited. You are the one who will turn the bad news of our occupation and domination by a foreign empire into good news of liberation."

Similarly, *Son of the living God* takes on special radiance in this setting. Caesars called themselves "sons of the gods," but Peter's confession asserts that their false, idolatrous claim is now trumped by Jesus' true identity as one with authority from the true and living God. The Greek and Roman gods may be used to legitimize the dominating rule of the Caesars, but the true and living God is the one who legitimizes the liberating authority of Jesus.

Jesus responds by saying that God has blessed Peter with this revelation and speaks in dazzling terms of Peter's future role in God's mission, confirming that Peter's answer is absolutely correct. "The gates of hell" will not prevail against their joint project, Jesus says, using a phrase that could aptly be paraphrased "the authority structures and control centers of evil." The phrase would be explosively evocative at this control center of Roman authority enmeshed with Greco-Roman religion, with echoes of Canaanite Baal worship before it.[2]

But shortly after they accelerate their hope and expectations to this ecstatic speed, Jesus once again slams on the brakes. He begins explaining that he will now travel south to Jerusalem where he will be captured, imprisoned, tortured, and killed by the religious and political establishment of their nation. Peter appears not to hear the happy ending, only the horrible middle. So he responds, exactly as we would have, with complete incredulity and denial: "Never, Lord! This shall never happen to you!" (v. 22).

Do you feel Peter's shock? If Peter had been right, as Jesus has just affirmed—that Jesus is the liberating king, the revolutionary leader anointed and authorized by the living God to overthrow the Roman occupation—then the one thing Jesus *cannot* do is be captured, imprisoned, tortured, and killed. No, he must capture, imprison, humiliate, and defeat their oppressors. He must crush their enemies and be victorious. So Peter corrects Jesus: "Stop talking like this! This could never happen!"

At that moment, in one of the most dramatic cases of conceptual whiplash ever recorded in literature anywhere, Jesus turns to Peter and says, "Get behind me, Satan!" It's a shattering moment: the one who so recently was deemed the blessed recipient of divine enlightenment is now called a mouthpiece of the dark side. One of the leaders of this fledgling movement that Jesus promises will defeat the gates of hell is now working on the side of hell.[3] What's going on here?

For Peter, a whole set of settled assumptions suddenly exploded and fell to the ground in pathetic, deflated fragments. Previous knowledge and settled certainty were instantly deconstructed and reduced to shards and questions, misconceptions and confusion. In short, Peter's framing story—his counternarrative to the imperial narrative—was exposed to be the opposite of what he had always assumed: evil, not good . . . Satanic, not holy. Whatever Jesus was up to, it wasn't part of the dominant imperial narrative of the Romans and their collaborators, nor was it part of the counternarrative of good Jews like the Pharisees and Zealots, nor was it a dualist narrative that tried to negotiate between the two, and of course it wasn't part of the Essenes' fatalistic narrative of withdrawal. It was something radically different, radically new.

everything must change

JESUS STANDS BEFORE PILATE

The newness and differentness of Jesus' narrative grow all the more clear as we come to another climactic event that leads to the crucifixion and death that Jesus has just predicted and Peter could not accept. John's Gospel contains this episode. In Matthew, Mark, and Luke, without question, the evocative language of the kingdom of God is at the heart of Jesus' message. But the Gospel of John seems rather demure about the language of the kingdom, mentioning it directly only three times, two of them in the same passage (3:3, 5; 18:16).[4]

Indirectly, though, a careful reading makes clear that John is not changing the message; no, he is simply translating the term *kingdom* into parallel terms: life, abundant life, life of the ages.[5] But even in the Gospel of John, at this climactic moment in the story, kingdom language is unavoidable.

Jesus stands before Pilate, the local representative of Caesar, two rungs down on the chain of command that runs from Caesar in Rome, to the king of Syria, and then to Pilate, who oversees Judea on the empire's behalf. As a good politician who works within the imperial narrative, Caesar's puppet only has one question on his mind: is Jesus claiming to be a king with a kingdom?

> Pilate then went back inside the palace, summoned Jesus and asked him, "Are you the king of the Jews?"
>
> "Is that your own idea," Jesus asked, "or did others talk to you about me?"
>
> "Am I a Jew?" Pilate replied. "Your own people and chief priests handed you over to me. What is it you have done?"
>
> Jesus said, "My kingdom is not of this world. If it were, my servants would fight to prevent my arrest by the Jewish leaders. But now my kingdom is from another place."
>
> "You are a king, then!" said Pilate.

Jesus answered, "You are right in saying I am a king. In fact, for this reason I was born, and for this I came into the world, to testify to the truth. Everyone on the side of truth listens to me."

"What is truth?" Pilate asked. (John 18:33–38)

Yes, Jesus is a king. But his kingdom is "not of this world." What does this mean? Does it mean Jesus is promoting a "spiritual" kingdom, something people feel warming their hearts, or something they will experience after they die? Hardly. Jesus has just used a similar "not of the world" construction in the previous chapter, as part of a rich and lengthy prayer. There Jesus makes it clear that he doesn't want his disciples to be removed "out of the world." Instead, he sends them "into the world," but as they are "in" the world, they are not to be "of" the world, just as he is not "of" the world (John 17:13–19).

"My kingdom is not of this world," then, means the very opposite of "My kingdom is not in this world." Instead, it means my kingdom is very much in this world, but it doesn't work the way earthly kingdoms or empires do. The word *this* becomes especially significant in relation to Pilate's location in the Roman chain of command: *this* world of Pilate, of Roman swords and spears and threats of crucifixion, of imperial domination and hierarchy and violence—*this* world is not the origin or character of Jesus' kingdom.

Then Jesus specifies: earthly kingdoms fight, but his kingdom, being "from another place," has another nature and another strategy. Instead of winning by violence and domination, his kingdom simply tells the truth and sees who listens: "for this reason I was born, and for this I came into the world, to testify to the truth" (John 18:37).[6]

Pilate's reply—"What is truth?" (v. 38)—makes perfect sense to me as someone who has lived most of my life just outside of Washington, DC. To those in power, truth is plastic. It's twistable like Silly Putty, spinnable like a fast pitch. In comparison to unarmed truth, they feel, well-armed power is solid steel. "What is your kingdom's cute little truth," Pilate might be saying, "in comparison to the brute power of the empire I represent?"

A few hours later, when Jesus was hanging from the cross, the answer looked pretty clear. Pilate and his kingdom won. Or so it appeared.

GROUP DIALOGUE QUESTIONS

1. How does the background information about Caesarea Philippi enrich your understanding of this episode in Jesus' life?
2. Imagine you are Peter. How do you feel as the first story unfolds? How do you identify with Peter in this story?
3. Imagine you are Pilate. How do you feel as the second story unfolds? How do you identify with Pilate in this story?
4. How do these two stories affect your understanding of Jesus?
5. Based on these stories, what adjectives would you use to describe Jesus?
6. Imagine Jesus speaking to a powerful person in the world today—you pick the person. Create an imaginary dialogue they might have.
7. Imagine yourself standing at the cross as Jesus' body is taken down. It appears that Pilate's regime has won. What would that mean to you?
8. Has there ever been a time in your experience when it seemed like God's kingdom lost and other forces won?

Part 4

REINTRODUCING
JESUS

Peace Through Domination

Perhaps now, having resituated Jesus in his native context, we are ready to be reintroduced to him so we can explore how his message might relate to our world and its crises today. But doing so is always risky, and we would be wise to face the full force of the risk.

Fundamentalist religious movements typically try to do just the sort of thing I'm proposing, and they generally do so in the worst possible way: they take words spoken five hundred or fourteen hundred or two thousand or fourteen hundred years ago and apply them, sharia-style, as if they were intended to serve as today's annotated legal code, today's constitution, today's how-to manual. They underestimate how the original words and teachings were situated—how deeply their sacred texts were rooted in gritty contemporary problems and human social contexts; instead, they see their sacred texts as timeless, placeless utterances coming from an arid, Platonic plane of universal abstractions.

And these fundamentalist movements also underestimate how equally situated their own interpretations and applications are. They don't recognize how movements and countermovements swirl around sacred texts like currents in a river, or how those shifting currents influence their interpretations and applications at every turn. Instead, they assume that since their methods are "scholarly," their conclusions are "objective" and therefore certain and timelessly true. Too few of them realize how the very scholarly terms they use constantly gain and shed negative and positive connotations. Nor are they aware of the power dynamics hidden in their methods and vocabularies. This naïveté is so pervasive and so accepted that one can hardly blame people for being taken in by it. Yet with suicide bombings in the news day after day, we can see where this naïveté can lead.

With so much fundamentalist talk being used as a shortcut to claiming that God is on the quoter's side, *Newsweek*'s managing editor, John Meachum, offers some needed caution in his review of Garry Wills's *What Jesus Meant*:

> The popular Christian question "What would Jesus do?" is not an especially useful one, Wills notes, for Jesus did many things we would not, and should not, do. Should Christian believers today, Wills asks, "like Jesus, forbid a man from attending his own father's funeral . . . or tell others to hate their parents? . . . Are they justified in telling others, 'I come not imposing peace, I impose not peace but the sword' . . . ? Or 'I am come to throw fire on the earth' . . . ?" Such moments in the Gospels, Wills writes, "were acts meant to show that he is not just like us, that he has higher rights and powers . . . [as] a divine mystery walking among men."[1]

Wills himself put it like this: "To read the Gospels in the spirit with which they were written, it is not enough to ask what Jesus did or said. We must ask what Jesus meant by his strange words and deeds."[2] In other words, if we focus on what Jesus *said* without determining what he *meant* in his original context, we run the risk of misquoting Jesus even when quoting his words.

I often experience this problem when I speak to groups about our responsibility to care for the poor, for example. Whenever the subject of poverty comes up in some circles (say, in reference to Mark 10:21), someone is bound to respond by quoting Matthew

26:11, "The poor will always be with you." (This just happened to me again yesterday—twice, in fact.) They're suggesting that Jesus' words tell us it's fruitless to help the poor, so we should just concentrate on meeting people's "spiritual" needs (and keep our money to ourselves, thank you).

Many religious conversations, using this handy technique, devolve into a kind of theological football game, where after kneeling on the line of scrimmage, someone yells, "Hut! Hut!" and offensive and defensive scriptures clash until someone blows a whistle. Then, like cranky kids playing on a backyard lot, players start crying, "Foul!" and "You fouled me first!" Then they line up and do it again. It's all elegantly simple and largely fruitless, apart from providing an outlet for pent-up aggression not unlike professional wrestling.

Quoting Jesus' words from Matthew 26:11 to defend a complacency toward the poor becomes manifestly ridiculous when one looks at the passage of the Old Testament Jesus is himself quoting: Deuteronomy 15. After saying, "There will always be poor people in the land," the text says, "Therefore I command you to be openhanded toward . . . the poor and needy in your land" (v. 11). And earlier in the chapter (v. 4), we read, "However, there should be no poor among you," because the land can produce an abundance for all if that abundance is fairly distributed through a just legal system—or to use our terms in this book, a just equity system. It's risky business to superficially quote Jesus!

So we must carefully seek to determine not just what Jesus said, but what he meant, and how he would have been heard by his original hearers. Only then can we venture to explore what his original meaning would mean for us today, and even then, we must do so with great humility and awareness of our amazing human capacity to be wrong.[3] This process is far more complex than simply marshaling quotes, and it is also more fruitful. It requires more than an ability to lift quotations out of context and fire them at an opponent like a missile. It requires the ability to get a sense for the shape, feel, and direction of Jesus' life and words, in the swirl and spin of his times, and find patterns of resonance with our own. It is from start to finish a matter of interpretation, which, like reading itself, is as much art as science.

The New Vision Group compares this artistic interpretive process with discerning the grain of a species of wood:

> But what can ancient stories teach us today? Clearly, we cannot somehow simply "apply" them to today's situation—nor should we try. Nevertheless, these peace-building stories—indeed, all of Scripture—contain a clear direction, a grain as unmistakable as the wood grain of oak or cherry.[4]

We need this kind of interpretive sensitivity to discern and articulate the alternative narrative or framing story of Jesus, remembering that "narrative" and "framing story" are exactly the kinds of highfalutin scholarly terms Jesus would never have used. Interestingly though, as we've seen, he did use a related term to identify his message: *good news*.

THE GOOD NEWS OF JESUS

It's important to remind ourselves that *good news* was neither a scholarly nor religious term in Jesus' day. It was a political one, a term of public life, as contemporary scholars like N. T. Wright and John Dominic Crossan make clear.[5] Crossan presents an inscription (one of many like it) written a few years before Jesus' birth, in which the Asian League of Cities—a subsidiary structure of the Roman Empire—decided to change all calendars so that Caesar Augustus' birthday would be the first day of the year:

> Since the providence that has divinely ordered our existence has applied her energy and zeal and has brought to life the most perfect good in Augustus, whom she filled with virtues for the benefit of mankind, bestowing him upon us and our descendants as a savior—he who put an end to war and will order peace, Caesar, who by his epiphany exceeded the

hopes of those who prophesied good tidings (*euaggelia*), not only outdoing benefactors of the past, but also allowing no hope of greater benefactions in the future; and since the birthday of the god first brought to the world the good tidings (*euaggelia*) residing in him. . . . For that reason, with good fortune and safety, the Greeks of Asia have decided that the New Year in all the cities should begin on 23 September, the birthday of Augustus . . . and that the letter of the proconsul and the decree of Asia should be inscribed on a pillar of white marble, which is to be placed in the sacred precinct of Rome and Augustus.[6]

Crossan directs our attention to the prominence of language that is familiar to us because of its association with Jesus, but which obviously works in dynamic tension with this earlier association: "Augustus is a 'savior' whose 'epiphany' brought 'peace' to 'mankind.' He is the greatest benefactor of past, present, and future, so that 'the birthday of the god' is the ultimate 'good tidings' for the world. . . . The imperial inscription's plural term *euaggelia* comes from the same root as our Christian singular term *euaggelion*, gospel, or good news."[7]

Using the term *good news*, then, the Roman Empire spread its own colonial or imperial framing story, news of an emperor-king who brought peace so profound that we should adjust our calendars to mark the newness of the age. Along with Luke's Christmas angels (2:10), Mark tells us that Jesus employs this "good news" language to describe his work:

After John was put in prison, Jesus went into Galilee, proclaiming the good news of God. "The time has come," he said. "The kingdom of God is near. Repent and believe the good news!" (1:14–15)

The empire's "good news" is a framing story of peace through domination, peace through redemptive violence, peace through centralized power and control, peace through elimination of enemies. It involves the gods legitimizing those in power so that resistance to their sacred regime becomes not only treason but also heresy. The imperial narrative that drives them to dominance often drives them on to self-destruction.[8] Jesus' alternative framing story, as we've seen, involves God's bringing down those in power (Luke 1:52–53) so that the poor can be legitimized (Luke 4:18), and so that the religious collaboration with the empire can be exposed as hypocrisy. The empire uses crosses to punish rebels and instill fear and submission in the oppressed: Jesus will use a cross to expose the cruelty and injustice of those in power and instill hope and confidence in the oppressed.

HEARING JESUS WITH FIRST-CENTURY EARS

Bishop N. T. Wright helps us hear Jesus' words afresh, with what he calls "first century ears." The words of Jesus' alternative narrative, he suggests, have been co-opted by later theological systems (the puzzle lids we referred to earlier), so readers today need "to unlearn our meanings" and discover how Jesus' words would have sounded to their original hearers:

> Consider, for example, the Jewish aristocrat and historian Josephus, who was born a few years after Jesus' crucifixion and who was sent in AD 66 as a young army commander to sort out some rebel movements in Galilee. His task, as he describes it in his autobiography, was to persuade the hot-headed Galileans to stop their mad rush into revolt against Rome and to trust him and the other Jerusalem aristocrats to work out a better *modus vivendi*. So when he confronted the rebel leader, he says that he told him to give up his own agenda and to trust him, Josephus, instead . . . he told the brigand leader to "repent and believe in me," *metanoesein kai pistos emoi genesesthai*.
>
> This does not, of course, mean that Josephus was challenging the brigand leader . . . to give up sinning and have a religious conversion experience. . . . [Similarly, Jesus] was

telling his hearers to give up their agendas and to trust him for his way of being Israel, his way of bringing the kingdom, his kingdom-agenda.[9]

The phrase "kingdom of God" on Jesus' lips, then, means almost the opposite of what an American like me might assume, living in the richest, most powerful nation on earth. To a citizen of Western civilization like me, kingdom language suggests order, stability, government, policy, domination, control, maybe even vengeance on rebels and threats of banishment for the uncooperative. But on Jesus' lips, those words describe Caesar's kingdom: God's kingdom turns all of those associations upside down. Order becomes opportunity, stability melts into movement and change, status-quo government gives way to a revolution of community and neighborliness, policy bows to love, domination descends to service and sacrifice, control morphs into influence and inspiration, and vengeance and threats are transformed into forgiveness and blessing.

In his message of the kingdom of God, then, Jesus proposes a radical new framing story, and he wants people to trust him enough to give his way to peace a chance. How does he do so? In public, he teaches people (often using parables, which stimulate them to think rather than mandating what to think) and heals them (which is often described as *freeing* or *liberating* them from disease and demons)— rather than propagandizing them (telling them what to think while simultaneously keeping them from thinking for themselves) and controlling them (oppressing them under sick and demonic systems of oppression). In private, he eats meals with people—all the wrong sorts of people—to demonstrate that the kingdom of God transforms by grace and acceptance rather than by fear and threats of exclusion.[10] In the midst of Rome's empire, wherever Jesus goes, he creates a family meal where all are welcome.

Some will be quick to note that Jesus also used strong language of exclusion—being thrust into "outer darkness," for example, where there is "weeping and gnashing of teeth." But in an irony that is so powerful it can hardly be overstated, Jesus applies that language to the typically exclusive (religious scholars, Pharisees, etc.), and asserts that the typically excluded (prostitutes, sinners, even Gentiles) will be included before them (Matthew 23:13; Luke 13:28–30; Luke 4:24–27). Clearly, Jesus is deconstructing the dominant system of exclusion—not fortifying it.

No wonder Jesus mixes metaphors so freely: *kingdom* can be useful in confronting the kingdom of Herod and the empire of Caesar, but it also needs to be deconstructed and augmented by other more intimate and less violent metaphors. So Jesus habitually refers to God as *Father* rather than *King*. As the famous prodigal son parable profoundly communicates, the rebel and the upright are equally God's children, as (we could extrapolate) are the Jew and Gentile, the free and slave, the religious scholar and the prostitute, and female and male. The Father's deep desire is to bring all the children home into his feast (Luke 15:11–32).[11]

Seventeenth-century French bishop and mystic Francois Fenelon seemed to grasp this when he said, "All wars are civil wars, because all men are brothers. Each one owes infinitely more to the human race than to the particular country in which he was born."[12] Wars play out a framing story of *us versus them* that seeks to take precedence over the deeper and higher framing story of God's global family table, where *us* and *them* are equally invited, equally wanted, in the biggest "us" of all.

No less striking than his family imagery, though less often appreciated, is Jesus' sensitivity to ecology—evident in his many parables about farming and fishing and weather. He knows the natural world intimately and makes hillside and seashore his preferred classrooms. One imagines him being interrupted by an incoming flock of crows, who then appear in his next parable, or one imagines children gathering flowers while their parents listen to Jesus speak, and then those flowers appear in the next part of his sermon.

We may immediately think of Saint Francis, known for his deep love for all God's creatures.[13] Arnold Toynbee (quoted by Leonardo Boff) observed that "in order to keep the biosphere habitable for two thousand more years, we and our descendants" must choose between the way of Francis and the way of his money-hungry father, Pietro Bernardone, who was passionately committed to the earliest forms of today's dominant framing story. "The example given by St. Francis [whom he calls 'the greatest of all the men who have ever lived in the West'] is what we Westerners ought to imitate with all our heart, for he is the only Westerner in this glorious company who can save the earth."[14]

Francis himself would urge us to go beyond his own example to consider the story in which he was rooted and by which he lived: Jesus' message of the kingdom of God.

GROUP DIALOGUE QUESTIONS

1. How do you react to the author's discussion about how sacred texts are abused by fundamentalists? Have you experienced religious people abusing a sacred text? How do you think this kind of abuse can be overcome?
2. How did you respond to the author's analysis of Jesus' oft-quoted words about the poor always being with us?
3. Have you ever "played theological football" the way the author describes? How do you think this kind of "game" can be avoided?
4. The author includes quotes from the Asian League of Cities and the ancient historian Josephus. What insight did you gain from these quotes into the life and message of Jesus?
5. The author refers to Saint Francis. What do you know about Saint Francis? Perhaps someone in your group can do some research on Francis and report to the group.

Occupying Regime, Equity Gap, Excrement Factory

J esus' metaphor *kingdom of God* encapsulates his alternative framing story, but for reasons I detailed in *The Secret Message of Jesus*, I believe the metaphor is problematic today.[1] If Jesus were speaking today, I'm sure he would find equally relevant and subversive metaphors to help us envision a new framing story for our world, and so transform our suicide machine into a creative and humane society—a *beloved community*, to use Dr. King's beautiful phrase.[2]

In this chapter, I will briefly sketch three examples of the kind of metaphors Jesus might use today if he were confronting our security, equity, and prosperity systems, and then explore a fourth by which he might challenge our essential imperial framing story.

DIVINE PEACE INSURGENCY

To address the global security crisis, Jesus might speak of the *divine peace insurgency*. When a nation is conquered and occupied by another nation, insurgent movements seek to expel the occupiers. The insurgents see themselves not as criminals or rebels fighting a legitimate authority, but rather as a resistance movement fighting illegitimate occupiers. They are freedom fighters seeking liberation from tyranny; they are legitimate power seeking to expel an illegitimate one. If this world is indeed the creation of a good, holy, compassionate, wise, and just God, and if it has been conquered and occupied by this destructive, unholy, merciless, tyrannical, stupid, and devious system we are calling the suicide machine, then Jesus came to launch an insurgency to overthrow that occupying regime. Its goal is to resist the occupation, liberate the planet, and retrain and restore humanity to its original vocation and potential. This renewed humanity can return to its role as caretakers of creation and one another so the planet and all it contains can be restored to the healthy and fruitful harmony that God desires.

But this insurgency can never use the weapons of the occupying regime; otherwise, it simply becomes another manifestation of it. So it is a merciful insurgency, a wisdom insurgency, a hope insurgency, a generous insurgency, a courage insurgency, a compassion insurgency, a faith insurgency, a peace insurgency.

God's Unterror Movement

To confront the global equity crisis, Jesus might speak of *God's unterror movement.* The societal machine becomes suicidal when humanity trades God's original creative narrative for a selfish and destructive framing story of its own. Driven by this alien story, some seek profit that will make others poor. They seek security that will make others insecure. They seek equity for themselves but are insensitive to the plight of others. Their pleasure inflicts pain on others. Their gain means loss for others. They seek and use power and freedom in ways that will injure, dehumanize, reduce, or oppress others. The impoverished, oppressed, reduced, and aggrieved respond by seeking revenge, redress, and opportunity, often through crime, immigration (legal or illegal), and acts of terrorism—adding to the growing toxins of pain and destruction, distorting God's beautiful dream further and further into a terrifying nightmare.

The equity gap that separates rich from poor renders them enemies rather than neighbors, so everyone is caught up in the ultimate vicious cycle of terror and counterterror, violence and counterviolence, hate and counterhate. We can only escape by defecting from this whole vicious, suicidal system . . . walking away from the king in Rome, walking away from the armed rebels who dream of overthrowing him, and following a weaponless prophet in Galilee.

When groups of seemingly disparate people defect and band together in the way of Jesus, they form what we might call unterror cells. They secretly plot detonations of hope. They quietly conspire to set off explosions of spontaneous kindness. They plan gentle coup d'etats to replace regimes of domination and oppression with movements of empowerment and service. In a complete overthrow of violent terrorism, they fly airplanes of generosity into towers of need and plant improvised encouragement devices by roadsides and in neighborhoods everywhere, seeking God's kingdom and God's equity.

NEW GLOBAL LOVE ECONOMY

Jesus might confront the global prosperity crisis by announcing the *new global love economy*. The divine insurgency and unterror movement prepare the way for the construction of a new love economy to fulfill God's creative dream. Our current prosperity system, as we shall see, is amazingly powerful—growing more so every day—yet it is unsustainable long-term, an example of self-delusion and denial about our creaturely limits that may be one of the most striking characteristics of modern times. As part of this insane and suicidal economy, we act as though the resources we consume are infinite and the wastes we deposit are invisible. Just as our bodies consume food and produce excrement, in this economy we consume trees and produce smoke, consume clean air and produce smog, consume clean water and produce sewage and toxic waste, consume rock and produce radiation, consume oil and coal and produce gases that turn our planet into an overheating oven in which storms boil and oceans rise and deserts spread and forests whither. Our prosperity system thus becomes an excrement factory.

Socially, in this economy we consume time and produce fatigue, consume art and talent and produce entertainment and amusement, consume work and leisure and produce paychecks and heart attacks.

And ultimately we consume communities and produce extended families, consume extended families and produce nuclear families, consume nuclear families and produce individuals, consume individuals and produce consumers, and finally consume consumers themselves and produce disembodied fragments called "wants" and "needs" and "markets" and "segments" and "anxieties" and "drives" that the economy consumes and excretes and reconsumes in a kind of cannibalistic ferment or rot. In the process, we commonly produce successful megaconsumers of unimaginable wealth who are more or less bankrupt in compassion for their poor neighbors. And in a stroke of suicidal genius, we simultaneously produce poor people whose greatest dream is to be like those megaconsumers who don't care at all about them.

Politically, we produce and sell weapons in unimaginable numbers and then tax the profits to build defenses against those to whom we sold the weapons. We build an economy of war in hopes that it will produce for us a world of peace.

That's why if Jesus were here today, I imagine he would speak frequently of the new global love economy of God—not an industrial economy, and not an information economy, and not even an experience economy, but a wise relational economy that measures success in terms of gross national affection and global community, that seeks to amass the appreciating capital of wise judgment, profound forethought, and deepening virtue for the sake of rich relationships.

GOD'S SACRED ECOSYSTEM

Jesus might encapsulate his alternative framing story in the image of *God's sacred ecosystem.* The goal of the insurgency or un-terror network or divine love economy is to see God's primal creative dream for our world come true—the dream of a sacred ecosystem whose dynamic dance of give and take, procreation and death, production and recycling, thriving and struggle, and extinction and evolution together produce unimaginable beauty, novelty, and possibility. Like lovers whose mutual affection overflows and seeks to express itself in the triune miracle of intercourse, conception, and birth, the living God creates a universe to express and share a generous overflow of love, joy, and life. Within it, our planet is a blue jewel in which a unique and beautiful ecosystem constantly generates meaning, hope, and wonder. This is the story we find ourselves in.

Among the greatest gifts the loving Creator can bestow on us in this beautiful ecosystem are freedom, dignity, and creativity. But these very gifts make possible our abuse and rebellion, as we create evil, ugliness, and discord rather than goodness, beauty, and harmony. In this way, we reject our role as creative caretakers and colleagues in earth's sacred ecosystem and become its rapists, vandals, plunderers, and destroyers. We consider ourselves outside of it, above it, disconnected from it, and we consider it not God's sacred ecosystem and our responsibility, but rather our battlefield, a "resource" of "raw materials" to be processed by our societal machine into things we call "goods," but that are often not very good.

In this way, God's beautiful ecological dream can become an ugly nightmare of pain for Creator and creation alike. If God embraces that pain and its ugliness, and responds not with unquenchable fury and irreconcilable revenge but with justice and mercy, truth and grace, then humanity has the option of responding to God's kindness, regretting its foolish abuse and rejection of its original gifts, and returning to embrace God's beautiful dream. This mutual embrace— God embracing our pain and ugliness, and humanity embracing God's mercy and beauty—creates the possibility of a new beginning where we stop working against God. Instead of pursuing our own selfish dreams—whether they are individual, ethnic, religious, political, economic, or national—we seek for God's dream for creation to come true, and we are restored to our place in God's sacred ecosystem.

THE REAL CULTURE WAR

Author and activist David Korten understands this strategy of Jesus and its relevance to our contemporary situation. He describes the struggle between what he calls *empire* and *earth community* as the real "culture war" going on in our world, and says, "The outcome will depend in large measure on the prevailing stories that shape our understanding. . . . Perhaps the most difficult and yet essential aspect of this work is to change our stories."[3]

In his perspective, the political left and right both play for the empire, but he expresses a special concern about the recent ascendancy of the New Right: "Thus, the true believers of the New Right gained power not by their numbers, which are relatively small, but by their ability to control the stories that answer three basic questions: How do we prosper? How do we maintain order and keep ourselves secure? How do we find a sense of meaning and purpose in life? We might call these our prosperity, security, and meaning stories."[4]

While Korten finds the answers of the New Right unhelpful, he finds inspiration for a new vision of earth community in Jesus, who, he says, "dedicated his life to changing the prevailing stories."[5] I hope you are beginning to see what Korten sees.

GROUP DIALOGUE QUESTIONS

1. The author doesn't believe Jesus would speak in terms of "kingdom" if he were communicating today. Do you agree or disagree? What can be problematic about the language of kings and kingdoms today?
2. Respond to each of the four alternative metaphors the author proposes. What are the strengths and weaknesses of each one?
   Divine Peace Insurgency
   God's Unterror Movement
   New Global Love Economy
   God's Sacred Ecosystem
3. Can you think of some other ways of speaking of the kingdom of God for people today?
4. How do you think Jesus would respond to the three basic questions proposed by Korten?

How Different It Would Be

Properly understood, *the sacred ecosystem of God* can be like a seed from which a transforming framing story can send down roots and send up shoots in our world today. That story, at the center of our societal machine, can lead to the transformation of our prosperity, equity, and security systems.

What I mean will become clear as we reflect on a climactic passage in Jesus' Sermon on the Mount, found in Matthew 5–7, a passage that comes alive when it is seen as a radical subversion of the imperial narrative:

> Do not store up for yourselves treasures on earth, where moth and rust destroy, and where thieves break in and steal. But store up for yourselves treasures in heaven, where moth and rust do not destroy, and where thieves do not break in and steal. For where your treasure is, there your heart will be also. (Matthew 6:19–21)

At the heart of the imperial narrative is insecurity, deep anxiety: *the wealth we have amassed may be stolen; the goods we have hoarded may be devalued by rust or rot.* This anxiety is what drives the Romans to constantly expand their empire: enough is never enough.

Jesus says that giving—and we know, elsewhere, that he specifically means giving to the poor (see Mark 10:21)—is a more secure investment than accumulating and hoarding. So he proposes a framing story of prosperity, equity, and security through generosity rather than anxious hoarding. He applauds solidarity with the poor rather than with the hoarders and protectors and empire builders.

The ongoing emphasis on generosity appears to be interrupted by the next paragraph:

The eye is the lamp of the body. If your eyes are healthy, your whole body will be full of light. But if your eyes are unhealthy, your whole body will be full of darkness. If then the light within you is darkness, how great is that darkness! (Matthew 6:22–23)

If the words "healthy" and "unhealthy" (in Greek, *aplous* literally means "single" and *poneros* literally means "evil") are understood in this context to mean "generous" and "stingy," the whole section flows more smoothly. An anxious, stingy, hoarding outlook—or framing story of greed, we could say—creates personal and societal darkness, but a framing story of generosity and abundance creates light and health, exactly the kind of light Jesus described earlier in the sermon (5:14–16).

Now Jesus turns to expose the dual narrative so common in his day among tax collectors and stewards, among the rich and the religious elite who in their hearts think of themselves as Jews but who wear the hypocrite's mask by living their public lives in collusion with the Roman regime. Beneath their political and spiritual hypocrisy, Jesus sees this same narrative of greed at work: "No one can serve two masters. Either you will hate the one and love the other, or you will be devoted to the one and despise the other. You cannot serve both God and Money" (6:24).

This love of money, this stingy, hoarding, ungenerous narrative, will eventually drive you to hate God, Jesus says. So, having exposed the narrative of anxiety and greed that drives the Roman Empire and all who collaborate with it, Jesus now moves to describe his alternative framing story:

> Therefore I tell you, do not worry about your life, what you will eat or drink; or about your body, what you will wear. Is not life more important than food, and the body more important than clothes? Look at the birds of the air; they do not sow or reap or store away in barns, and yet your heavenly Father feeds them. Are you not much more valuable than they? Can any one of you by worrying add a single hour to your life? (vv. 25–27)

To convey his alternative framing story, Jesus refers to the birds. They live in a story centered in a caring and faithful God—"your heavenly Father"—who feeds them day by day. Then Jesus uses one of his favorite figures of speech: the "how much more" construction. These little sparrows are so valuable to God that God feeds them. How much more valuable are you to God than sparrows? If you are even more precious to God than sparrows, can you see how fruitless it is to live by the anxious narratives of greed and anxiety? Why not defect from the Roman narrative and live instead the narrative of the sparrows?

Jesus continues the pattern with a parallel example:

> And why do you worry about clothes? See how the flowers of the field grow. They do not labor or spin. Yet I tell you that not even Solomon in all his splendor was dressed like one of these. If that is how God clothes the grass of the field, which is here today and tomorrow is thrown into the fire, will he not much more clothe you, O you of little faith? (vv. 28–30)

Using another ecological image, of a field full of summer grasses and wildflowers, Jesus suggests that there is a natural abundance, a natural provision that flows from God. Wealth—even the extravagant wealth of Solomon—can't improve upon that natural abundance, that natural provision from God.

Jesus makes it clear that he's thinking of the Roman occupiers and their framing story when he concludes:

> So do not worry, saying, "What shall we eat?" or "What shall we drink?" or "What shall we wear?" For the pagans run after all these things, and your heavenly Father knows that you need them. But seek first his kingdom and his righteousness, and all these things will be given to you as well. Therefore do not worry about tomorrow, for tomorrow will worry about itself. Each day has enough trouble of its own. (vv. 31–34)

When we hear "pagans," we typically think of the irreligious in contrast to the religious, but the Greek word *ethne* (the original word translated "pagans") simply means Gentiles, or non-Jews, who in Jesus' day are none other than members of the Roman Empire. Their drive to "run after all these things" is a sign that they are driven to conquest and empire by a framing story other than the one that flows from faith in a God who cares for birds and flowers.

These words are no less powerful when applied to our civilization today. Interestingly, one of the characteristics of the Enlightenment was to distance humanity from creation, or in Leonardo Boff's terms, to place ourselves *over* and *above* and *against* it rather than *with* it and *alongside* it and *for* it.[1] Great pains were taken in recent centuries to describe how different and distant human beings were from animals, even when evolutionary theory suggested that we were part of one family tree.[2] This distancing of humans from creation was no less strong in religious communities, and no doubt there were some good reasons for it. But there were some poor reasons for it too.

The industrial world was driven by its own imperial, colonial framing stories, we need to remember, and these narratives thrust Europeans into the world to conquer, plunder, profit, and control. Non-Europeans were "savages," not neighbors and fellow human beings in God's world. God's creation was no longer "brother sun and sister moon," but instead, a store of raw materials buyable at a price to be exploited by industrialists. In the theological wing of colonialism, God no longer cared about sparrows and wildflowers; God cared for people's souls (and perhaps only for some special "elect" people's souls), each of which would be extracted like a Hostess Twinkie from its cellophane wrapper either at death or at the end of the world.

The human soul was given intrinsic value because it was eternal and immaterial. For Jesus, though, who was in no way this kind of dualist, the value of humans was rooted in their identity as God's creatures, alongside flocks of chattering sparrows and fields of brilliant wildflowers. Greater value, yes, but that greater value was only meaningful assuming the lesser value was more than zero.[3] To say that a human being is a million times more valuable than a sparrow is only meaningful if a sparrow has some real value; after all, a million times zero is zero.

This division between humanity and creation ultimately makes little sense, but it is deeply rooted in modern Western society.[4] The biblical framing story Jesus inhabited, of course, was not so human-centric or utilitarian. In his narrative, God actually cares for each creature, without its value needing to be justified by being useful to human beings. Each has intrinsic value in relation to its Creator. Even if there were no human beings on the planet (as there weren't for billions of years in scientific time, or for five and a half days in the Genesis narrative), God would still judge creation good, precious, of real value. In fact, economist Herman Daly suggests that we should reverse our human egoism and consider our value in relation to our service to others of God's creatures: "We grant ourselves intrinsic value. . . . But we do not count our instrumental value to other species, which is too often negative but could be positive if we cared about it."[5]

So Jesus counters the imperial framing story that isolates humanity from creation by placing us back with our fellow creatures in a story of creation, secure and beautiful under the care of God, not driven by anxiety to remove ourselves from that natural system of care. In God's global economy of love we find all the prosperity, equity, and security we need.

For Jesus, God's natural ecosystem is not only one of care, but also of limits. So when Jesus is tempted (Luke 4:1–13), he refuses to turn stones into bread (which would subvert God's natural system of provision), refuses to take a religious shortcut to authority and kingship (which would subvert God's natural system of gaining honor through humble service), and refuses to indulge in spectacle to prove himself (which would subvert God's natural system of being proven through trials and experience).

The framing story of the Romans, like the narratives common in our world today, creates its own systems of prosperity, equity, and security, but it runs them on an anxious, stingy framing story of scarcity, driven by fear and greed, all of this disconnected from creation. And thus divorced from its creaturely context, it respects no creaturely limits, but justifies all means in light of arbitrary and self-serving ends it sets for itself. Throughout his ministry, Jesus calls people to defect from that dysfunctional framing story and live by a new one: a story in which God provides through creation's natural systems, a story in which we acknowledge our creaturely dignity and limits within those systems, a story in which we celebrate our kinship with birds and flowers, with season and soil. The word *repent* means, in this context, a profound defection from one framing story and a profound investment of trust in another.

From Jesus' perspective, we don't live in a hermetically sealed man-made environment called a society or nation or empire or religion or culture or economy, where we are at the top of the food chain, where we are the global CEO and board of directors. No, we live as beloved creatures in God's magnificent creation, among other creatures that also experience God's care, together called to live wisely within creaturely limits, enjoying the bounty in which we live and move.

Sadly, because we are so fully indoctrinated by the imperial framing narrative of our day, few of us can begin to imagine how different it would be to live in the framing story of Jesus.

GROUP DIALOGUE QUESTIONS

1. The tension between generosity and greed runs strong in this chapter. Talk about your own experience of this tension. What kind of hold does greed have on you? What are some of your experiences with generosity?
2. The author quotes Leonardo Boff, who describes the contrast between placing oneself over and above creation and placing oneself with, alongside, and for it. Try to explain that contrast in your own words. In what ways do you see people placing themselves over and above creation today? In what ways do you see people placing themselves with, alongside, and for it?
3. Jesus speaks of learning from the birds and flowers. Are there ways in which aspects of creation teach you?
4. Try to describe what it would be like to decrease our distance from creation and to see ourselves as part of God's sacred ecosystem, as this chapter recommends.

Which Jesus?

Nobody helps me become more aware of my own blind complicity with false imperial framing stories than author Wendell Berry. Listen to his reflections on ways in which institutional churches play by the very greed-based framing story they are supposed to oppose:

> . . . the churches, which claim to honor God as the "maker of heaven and earth," have lately shown little inclination to honor the earth or to protect it from those who would dishonor it. . . . The *organized* church comes immediately under a compulsion to think of itself, and identify itself to the world, not as an institution synonymous with its truth and its membership, but as a hodgepodge of funds, properties, projects, and offices, all urgently requiring economic support. . . . If it comes to a choice between the extermination of the fowls of the air and the lilies of the field and the extermination of the building fund, the organized church will elect—indeed, has already elected—to save the building fund. . . . [T]he fowls of the air and the lilies of the field can be preserved only by true religion, by the practice of a proper love and respect for them as the creatures of God.

No wonder so many sermons are devoted exclusively to "spiritual" subjects. If one is living by the tithes of history's most destructive economy, then the disembodiment of the soul becomes the chief of worldly conveniences.[1]

This "disembodiment of the soul" produces a kind of perverse *ecstasy* (which means, literally, to stand outside ourselves)—not unlike a drug-induced euphoria or a hypnotically induced trance. When we stand outside our bodies and the creation in which they participate, we feel liberated from creaturely restraint, liberated from all duty as embodied, environmented creatures. No longer seeing ourselves as intricately interactive participants in God's natural ecosystems, we desperately relocate ourselves into our artificial constructs above, outside, and against them, an arrangement that is inherently convenient and profitable to the suicide machine. This ecstasy, however, like any narcotic, ultimately leads first to *derangement* (being removed from our natural range or place in the world) and then to *decomposition* (*composition* meaning placing things together, with one another, and *de-composition* meaning divorcing what had been previously joined)—which is synonymous with death. Our ecstasy machine, then, is also a derangement machine, a decomposition machine, a suicide machine.

What Berry calls "true religion"—a proper love and respect for all God's creatures—names the sacred ecosystem of God, which is the kingdom of God, which is the only sane alternative to the destructive economies and narratives that drive our world today, as it was in the days of Jesus. That "true religion" jolts us to awaken us from our depraved ecstasy and its attendant dislocation, derangement, and decomposition, to be relocated, resituated, recomposed, and so find a better and more wholesome joy in a story of creation, among the birds of the air and wildflowers of the field, as children of the Creator, not simply citizens of Caesar's empire.

Please, please don't make what I'm saying ridiculous by calling it a "flower child" theology or relating it to some kind of idealistic, romantic nonsense.[2] Please ask yourself: What if Jesus isn't being cute and romantic in the Sermon on the Mount? What if he is completely serious and means to be taken seriously? What if he is proposing the ultimate deconstruction—the deconstruction of all human structures, whether scientific preanalytic visions, governments, economies, ideologies, civilizations, and the framing stories that drive them—so that we can be recomposed in our true identity, resituated in God's primal framing story of creation? What if he is trying to excavate through layer upon layer of carpeting, plywood, ceramic tile, blacktop, gravel, trash, broken glass, and cement, so our bare feet can once again feel the cool, moist, soft soil from which we were, and are, all created?[3]

WHICH JESUS ARE WE TALKING ABOUT?

I was speaking about these matters recently to a packed room of young adults in Buenos Aires, Argentina. In the discussion time that followed, one man raised a rather simple question: "Which Jesus are you talking about?"

Immediately I knew what he meant. The "Jesus" I have pitted against the suicide machine in these pages is a Jesus drawn from the canonical Gospels. But there are a number of other Jesuses in play in today's world, various distorted and domesticated images of Jesus trimmed to fit comfortably and conveniently within the existing societal machinery. One such Jesus, in particular, denies and contradicts almost everything said and done by the Jesus of the four Gospel accounts.

I'm not thinking of the fictitious Jesus of *The DaVinci Code,* nor of any of the manifold Jesuses evoked by the various Gnostic Gospels. I'm thinking of a certain portrait we could call the "Second Coming Jesus," a Jesus evoked by a certain eschatology or theory of the future.

A friend of mine, referring to how groups form and behave, says, "Architecture always wins," meaning that people's behavior is always shaped by the spaces in which they gather. Theologically, I think we could say, "Eschatology always wins."

Far from being an esoteric and speculative distraction, our beliefs about the end toward which things are moving profoundly and practically shape our present behavior. This is especially true in regard to violence and war, and is one of the reasons many of us have been increasingly critical in recent years of popular American eschatology in general, and conventional views of hell in particular. Simply put, if we believe that God will ultimately enforce his will by forceful domination, and will eternally torture all who resist that domination, then torture and domination become not only permissible but in some way godly. The implications for, say, military policy (not to mention church politics) are not hard to imagine.

The phrase "the Second Coming of Christ" never actually appears in the Bible. Whether or not the doctrine to which the phrase refers deserves rethinking, a popular abuse of it certainly needs to be named and rejected. If we believe that Jesus came in peace the first time, but that wasn't his "real" and decisive coming—it was just a kind of warm-up for the real thing—then we leave the door open to envisioning a second coming that will be characterized by violence, killing, domination, and eternal torture. This vision reflects a deconversion, a return to trust in the power of Pilate, not the unarmed truth that stood before Pilate, refusing to fight. This eschatological understanding of a violent second coming leads us to believe (as we've said before) that in the end, even God finds it impossible to fix the world apart from violence and coercion; no one should be surprised when those shaped by this theology behave accordingly.

If we remain charmed by this kind of eschatology, we will be forced to see the nonviolence of the Jesus of the Gospels as a kind of strategic fake-out, like a feigned retreat in war, to be followed up by a crushing blow of so-called redemptive violence in the end. The gentle Jesus of the first coming becomes a kind of trick Jesus, a fake-me-out Messiah, to be replaced by the true jihadist Jesus of a violent second coming.

This is why I believe that many of our current eschatologies, intoxicated by dubious interpretations of John's Apocalypse, are not only ignorant and wrong, but dangerous and immoral. By way of ignorance, they are oblivious to the conventions of Jewish Apocalyptic literature in particular, and literature of the oppressed in general. As a result, they wrongly—one might even say ridiculously—interpret obviously metaphorical language as literal. For example, they misread Revelation 19:15, where Jesus, in a blood-stained robe, "strikes down the nations" using a sword; they fail to notice that the sword *comes out of his mouth*—a rather unmistakable case of symbolism to a reasonable adult reader, I would think, unless he imagines Jesus actually thrashing his head around, slinging a sword between his teeth like a giant cigar of mass destruction.[4]

In light of the literary conventions of both literature of the oppressed in general and Jewish apocalyptic in particular, and assuming that Jesus' coming as told in the Gospels was not a fake-me-out coming, but actually was the climactic revelation of God as the New Testament seems to affirm (Philippians 2:5–11; Colossians 1:15–20; Hebrews 1:1–4), Jesus' "striking down the nations" with a sword "coming out of his mouth" has a very different meaning. Jesus' word—the unarmed truth of the gospel of the kingdom—is the force that overcomes the "kingdom of this world," the dominant system, the suicide machine. It conquers not with physical weapons but with a message of justice (Revelation 19:11), and the blood on Jesus' robe is not the blood of his enemies, but his own blood (12:11, cf. 5:6).

Read in this way, we don't have a violent "Second Coming" Jesus who finishes what the gentle "First Coming" Jesus failed to do, but we have a poetic description of the way the gentle First Coming Jesus powerfully overcomes through his nonviolent "weakness" (cf. 1 Corinthians 1:18–25), a prince of peace whose word of reconciliation is truly mightier than Caesar's sword.

THE JESUS OF LOVE AND GRACE

At the end of March 1968, Martin Luther King Jr. preached in Washington, DC, at the National Cathedral. He displayed this better and saner reading of the Apocalypse. John, he said, "caught a vision of a new Jerusalem descending out of heaven from God."

Then John "heard a voice saying, 'Behold, I make all things new; former things are passed away.' God grant that we will be participants in this newness and this magnificent development. If we will but do it, we will bring about a new day of justice and brotherhood and peace. And that day the morning stars will sing together and the sons of God will shout for joy."[5] Four days later Dr. King was assassinated, a martyr for peace in a world still working by violence.

"If we will but do it" seem like embarrassingly simple words—perhaps even naive. But they resonate with the similarly naive words of one of Dr. King's heroes, Mohandas Gandhi, who said, "The difference between what we do and what we are capable of doing would suffice to solve most of the world's problems."[6]

Their apparent naïveté brings us back to the question, *which Jesus?* The Jesus of one reading of the Apocalypse brings us to a grim resignation: the world will get worse and worse, and finally this jihadist Jesus will return to use force, domination, violence, and even torture—the ultimate imperial tools—to vanquish evil and bring peace. But exactly what kind of victory and peace are we left with when domination, violence, and torture have won the day? This version of Jesus brings us to a kind of fatalism that sees the future predetermined and our actions incapable of altering the divinely preset outcome. And it sees domination, violence, and torture as the eternal legacy of God's creative project.

The Jesus of the emerging reading we have considered in the preceding chapters tells us the opposite: that good will prevail by peace, love, truth, faithfulness, and courageous endurance of suffering, and that domination, violence, and torture are among the things that will be overcome. In this view, no good deed will be forgotten or wasted, so we should start doing the next good thing now, faithfully continue, and never give up until the dream comes true. Even if doing so will cost us our life, we must press on, because death is not the end, and even death itself cannot stop the advance of the peace and love of God.

For this Jesus, love and grace—not violence and domination—finally win. In the second half of this book, we'll need to relate this emerging view of Jesus and his message to what's going on in our world, not so we can attempt a fundamentalist imposition of Christian sharia-law, but so we can begin to imagine how much *what he meant* in his day can mean for the world and its crises in our day.

GROUP DIALOGUE QUESTIONS

1. How did you respond to the Wendell Berry quote?
2. Explain the statements "architecture always wins" and "eschatology always wins."
3. The author describes a popular view of the "Second Coming" Jesus that makes the "First Coming" Jesus a "strategic fake-out." Do you see the tension between these two views of Jesus, and if so, how do you reconcile that tension?
4. Read Revelation 19, and explain whether or not you think the author's analysis is accurate.
5. Describe some of the various views of Jesus that you have seen or heard—in churches, in religious broadcasting, among friends and relatives.

Part 5

THE
SECURITY
SYSTEM

Joining the Peace Insurgency

Jesus' good news alerts us to our derangement and dislocation from our true place in God's world and God's story. It presents to us a new framing story that Jesus called "the good news of the kingdom of God," and that, I've proposed, we might also call the transforming story of God's divine peace insurgency, God's unterror movement, God's new global love economy, or God's sacred ecosystem.

If we resituate ourselves in this new story, if we find identity, meaning, and purpose in this good news, we find ourselves beginning again, born again, facing a new start. As recomposed, resituated, *de*-deranged people, we can begin rebuilding our societal system, not as a suicide machine, but as a beloved community, the kind of garden city envisioned in John's Apocalypse (Revelation 21:1–4).

So let's imagine what it would be like to reevaluate, renew, and rebuild the three primary systems of our society in this new framing story. We'll begin with perhaps its most frightening element, the security system, and then proceed to its most powerful element, the prosperity system, and then conclude with its most underdeveloped element, the equity system.

RELIGION: ARMED AND DANGEROUS

Almost daily our headlines give us evidence of the ways in which religion baptizes and legitimizes violence as the means to security. Suicide bombers in the Middle East cry, "God is great!" as they blow their bodies—and those of innocent neighbors—to pieces. Religious leaders in the United States encourage presidents to "blow [enemies] away in the name of the Lord."[1] Churchgoers in the United States often seem to be the first to support and the last to abandon wars of questionable morality.

In light of this dark religious tendency, I'm surprised more people haven't chosen the path of Sam Harris, America's leading atheist. Even though I don't share his final conclusion, I must admit that the impulse behind his *The End of Faith*[2] and his *Letter to a Christian Nation*[3] resonates with me: we need to acknowledge and reject the ways in which religion aids and abets the violent turn in human nature and society.

In the aftermath of September 11, 2001, Harris decided not to aim the fury of his terrible swift pen at "terrorists" or "terrorism," but at the religion that drives them. And, he would add, at the religion that drives excessively violent counterterrorist responses—collectively, the monotheisms of Islam, Christianity, and Judaism.[4] All religion, he believes, even moderate religion, is culpable because it provides cover for the irrational and violent extremists at the fringes of the religious community who threaten our global survival. We have become, he says, "increasingly deranged by our own religious certainty. We have a society in which 44 percent of the people claim to be either certain or confident that Jesus is going to come back out of the clouds and judge the living and the dead sometime in the next 50 years. It just seems transparently obvious that this is a belief that will do nothing to create a durable civilization. And I think it's time someone spoke about it."[5]

Harris's frustration is, I think, nearly identical to the impulse behind Enlightenment rationalism and skepticism that arose in the wake of the Thirty Years' War in Europe (1618–1648). When religions perpetually incite war, violence, and mutually assured destruction, to me it is less a wonder that people want to reject or marginalize religion than it is that anyone sticks with it. And even when religions aren't directly violent, they still may promote fatalistic eschatologies of abandonment like the one Harris mentioned: the future is determined by God and predicted in a book, and it's going to get worse and worse, so why try to work against the destruction that is predestined? As one famous evangelist put it, if the *Titanic* is destined to sink, why rearrange the deck chairs on it? Far better to man the lifeboats![6]

Harris is especially hard on the early books of the Bible:

> There's no document that I know of that is more despicable in its morality than the first few books of the Hebrew Bible. Books like Exodus and Deuteronomy and Leviticus, these are diabolical books. The killing never stops. The reasons to kill your neighbor for theological crimes are explicit and preposterous. You have to kill people for worshiping foreign gods, for working on the Sabbath, for wizardry, for adultery. You kill your children for talking back to you. It's there and it's not a matter of metaphors. It is exactly what God expects us to do to rein in the free thought of our neighbors.[7]

Over two hundred years earlier, colonial American patriot Thomas Paine was no less outraged in his 1795 *Age of Reason*:

> Whenever we read . . . the cruel and tortuous executions, the unrelenting vindictiveness with which more than half the Bible is filled, it would be more consistent that we call it the word of a demon than the word of God. It is a history of wickedness that has served to corrupt and brutalize humankind. And, for my own part, I sincerely detest it, as I detest everything that is cruel.[8]

But Harris doesn't easily let Christians off the hook by using a meek and mild Jesus as an exemption from biblical violence. Yes, "in half his moods" Jesus speaks about peace and compassion, Harris says, but "there's another Jesus in there. There's a Jesus who's just paradoxical and difficult to interpret, a Jesus who tells people to hate their parents . . . coming back amid a host of angels, destined to deal out justice to the sinners of the world. That is the Jesus that fully half of the American electorate is most enamored of at this moment."[9]

These questions, Harris rightly realizes, are not arcane theological matters; they have to do with the survival of humanity. In the Cold War years, it was too easy to imagine mushroom clouds rising as the dueling secular ideologies of capitalism and communism unleashed mutually assured nuclear destruction. In the twenty-first century, it is equally easy to imagine holy jihad fueled and funded by Islamist factions locked in a death match with holy crusade fueled and funded by powerful Christian and Jewish factions, factions who are empowered by the silence and passivity of their moderate and progressive counterparts.

Harris can't be blamed for seeing a "moody" Jesus, peaceful one minute and vindictive the next, because the religion that bears his name has shown precisely this bipolarity through history: for every courageous and peaceful saint willing to live and die in the spirit of Saint Francis, there have been any number of bishops and theologians willing to justify the killing and torture of heretics, to bless unjustifiable wars, and to incite mistrust and prejudice toward unbelievers. For every Martin Luther King and Desmond Tutu proclaiming the Jesus who rode on a donkey and spoke of peace, there have been plenty who proclaim a different Jesus, well armed and dangerous.

A RADICAL REASSESSMENT OF JESUS

But as this book demonstrates, we are in the early stages of a radical reassessment of Jesus.[10] More and more of us realize how religious communities can be complicit with imperial narratives and edit their version of Jesus to fit their narrative. More and more of us understand Jesus' life and message as being centered on the articulation and demonstration of a radically different framing story—one that

everything must change

critiques and exposes the imperial narrative as dangerous to itself and others. More and more of us are discovering a fresh vision of a Jesus who seems less moody, irrational, and bipolar, and more consistent, focused, courageous, subversive, and brilliant.

Obviously, in this emerging reading phrases like "turn the other cheek" (Matthew 5:39), "love your enemies" (Matthew 5:44), and "all who draw the sword will die by the sword" (Matthew 26:52) are deeply significant. But in this alternative reading, many other stories of Jesus take on a powerful new luminosity as well, charged with mystery and wonder and dynamism in stark contrast to imperial narratives and counternarratives.

A prime example would be Matthew's story of the Canaanite woman (15:21–28), which has been read provocatively by Grant LeMarquand.[11] Matthew's version of the story is especially interesting because Matthew is known as the most Jewish of the four Gospel writers. Surprisingly, Matthew identifies the woman as a Canaanite, unlike Mark, who calls her a "Greek, born in Syrian Phoenicia" (7:26). Matthew's use of *Canaanite* is surprising, first, because the term appears nowhere else in the New Testament, and second, because Canaanites were, strictly speaking, nonexistent at the time. To call someone in Jesus' day a Canaanite would be an anachronism, like calling a contemporary Norwegian a Viking, or a contemporary Scot a Celt.

The term *Canaanite* evoked Israel's violent conquest of Canaan, a story found in those biblical books (Exodus and Deuteronomy) that so disturbed Harris, Paine before him, and thousands of others before and since.

Matthew's use of the term is intentional, LeMarquand argues, because in this story Jesus deconstructs the violent conquest narrative and suggests that the kingdom of God takes a radically different approach to "the other." Matthew has already included non-Jews in his story in striking ways—the naming of Gentiles (and Canaanites) Tamar and Rahab in the birth narratives (1:3, 5), the visit of the Gentile Magi (2:1–12), and the healing of a Roman centurion's servant (8:5–13). And Matthew will include Gentiles in an even more striking way at his story's end (28:18–20), affirming that Gentiles must be freely included in the circle of disciples. But here, in between, during Jesus' unique excursion into Gentile territory (shortly before his visit to Caesarea Philippi, which we considered in chapter 14), Jesus encounters this woman identified by Matthew as a Canaanite.

Their encounter is disturbing because Jesus certainly appears to be a racist. He responds to her request for mercy and healing for her daughter first by ignoring her, then by saying, "I was sent only to the lost sheep of Israel" (Matthew 15:24), and then by using language that to our ears sounds indefensibly dehumanizing and racist— "dogs"—to refer to her people (v. 26). Some readers, trying to "save" Jesus from the appearance of racism, along with the appearance of changing his mind, would say that Jesus was simply engaging in wordplay with the woman—that he knew all along that he was going to heal her daughter. However, playing with a distraught mother, and using dehumanizing language to do so, wouldn't "save" him or anyone in my opinion.

In Jesus' defense, we should note that he doesn't say, "I was sent only to the elite people of God, the chosen ones, holy Israel, not you hopeless dogs." No, Jesus identifies his fellow Israelites as "lost sheep"—hardly a great affirmation or compliment. In this light, I suspect that Jesus is saying something like this: "Lady, I'm sorry about your daughter. But I have enough problems with my own Jewish people. Herod, a Jewish ruler, just killed the prophet John, my close colleague. The Pharisees are misleading the people, and we just had a very harsh confrontation. In fact, they're plotting my assassination as we speak. So my own people have lost their way, and I've been sent to them; that's why I can't help you."

Her clever and persistent reply, however, seems to convert Jesus so that he gains new insight into the God-given scope of his mission. It may be that this clever woman knows the original call to Abraham: God will bless Abraham and make his descendants a great nation so they will bring blessing to all nations. Her statement about dogs eating scraps that fall from the table would then mean, "Yes, I understand that your calling is to your people. But since your people are supposed to bring blessing to the rest of us, wouldn't it be good to let this scrap of blessing fall to my daughter?"

Whatever she knows or doesn't know, in this encounter, instead of a Jew violently and mercilessly conquering a Canaanite in harmony with the old stories of Exodus and Joshua, the Canaanite wins and conquers the Jew so that he responds to her request for mercy. By the way, the other incident in which Jesus appears to change his mind also occurs in a conversation with a woman, and a mother—in fact, his own (see John 2:1–11). Perhaps just as in that encounter Jesus learns it is now time to "go public" and start doing miracles, in this encounter Jesus realizes it is now time to "go multicultural" and start caring for Gentiles.

Jesus now utterly reverses his earlier statement. "I was sent only to the lost sheep of Israel" recedes into the past, and he now moves dramatically forward to care not only for one Gentile girl, but for literally thousands of Gentiles. In the following episode, he dramatically heals multitudes—and they are quite obviously Gentiles (at least, they are for Matthew), because he specifies they "praised the God of Israel." And then, even more dramatically, he feeds them in a way that perfectly parallels his earlier feeding of five thousand Jews (Matthew 14:13–21).

But there is one critical difference. When Jesus feeds five thousand Jews, there are twelve baskets left over—the number clearly signifying the twelve tribes of Israel. But when he feeds four thousand Gentiles, how many baskets are left over? Seven. What could that number signify? For the probable answer, LeMarquand suggests, we need to turn to what is perhaps the most "detestable" (to use Thomas Paine's term) and "despicable" (to use Sam Harris's term) passage in the Hebrew Scriptures, in terms of justifying religious violence.

It's about 1400 BC. Moses gives the word of the Lord to Joshua, his successor in leadership, instructing him what to do when he leads his people into Canaanite territory:

> When the LORD your God brings you into the land you are entering to possess and drives out before you many nations—

the Hittites, Girgashites, Amorites, Canaanites, Perizzites, Hivites, and Jebusites, seven nations larger and stronger than you—and when the LORD your God has delivered them over to you and you have defeated them, then you must destroy them totally. Make no treaty with them, and show them no mercy. Do not intermarry with them. Do not give your daughters to their sons or take their daughters for your sons, for they will turn your sons away from following me to serve other gods. (Deuteronomy 7:1–5)

So, LeMarquand suggests, Jesus here takes the old "destroy the Canaanites" narrative and dramatically turns it around. The reversals are striking. Jesus does not follow Deuteronomy's "no mercy to Canaanites" policy, but rather shows mercy to this Canaanite woman and her daughter. Seven nations are to be destroyed "totally": seven loaves remain, a testimony to the fact that now Canaanites are not to be destroyed, but fed. Canaanite daughters are dangerous, in that they will lead Israelite sons astray: Jesus, an Israelite son, sees a Canaanite daughter not as a danger, but as a person in need, and heals her.[12]

If Jesus' first feeding miracle and its twelve-basket surplus suggest a reconstitution of the twelve tribes being led through the wilderness with a new kind of manna, then this second feeding miracle suggests a new kind of conquest—not with swords and spears, but with bread and fish; not to destroy, but to serve and heal. Jesus seizes the old narrative, shakes it, turns it inside out, and offers a new story that reframes a future radically different from the past.

Of course, his cross is an even more dramatic narrative reversal. As we've seen, Rome uses crosses to expose and pronounce a death sentence on rebels; Jesus uses the cross to expose Roman violence and religious complicity with it, while pronouncing a sentence of forgiveness on his crucifiers. His cross doesn't represent a "shock and awe" display of power as Roman crucifixions were intended to do, but rather represents a "reverence and awe" display of God's willingness to accept rejection and mistreatment, and then respond with forgiveness, reconciliation, and resurrection. In this kingdom, peace is not made and kept through the shedding of the blood of enemies, but the king himself sacrifices his blood to make a new kind of peace, offering amnesty to repentant rebels and open borders to needy immigrants.

If, as Dominic Crossan says, the Roman motto is peace through victory, or peace through the destruction of enemies, or peace through domination[13] . . . then for Jesus the motto is peace through nonviolent justice, peace through the forgiveness of enemies, peace through reconciliation, peace through embrace and grace.[14] If in the violent narratives of Rome the victorious are blessed—which means that the most heavily armed, the most willing to kill, and the most aggressive and dominant are blessed—then in the framing story of the kingdom of God, blessed are the meek, blessed are those who hunger and thirst for justice, blessed are the peacemakers, and blessed are those who are willing to suffer for doing good. In this light, these aren't simply greeting-card sentiments, but rather ways of starkly contrasting Jesus' framing story with the narratives and counternarratives of his day.

To be a follower of Jesus in this light is a far different affair than many of us were taught: it means to join Jesus' peace insurgency, to see through every regime that promises peace through violence, peace through domination, peace through genocide, peace through exclusion and intimidation. Following Jesus instead means forming communities that seek peace through justice, generosity, and mutual concern, and a willingness to suffer persecution but a refusal to inflict it on others. To follow Jesus is to become an atheist in regard to all bloodthirsty, tribal warrior gods, and to become a believer in the living God of grace and peace who, in Christ, sheds God's own blood in a manifestation of amnesty and reconciliation.

To repent, to believe, to follow . . . together, these mean nothing less than defecting from Caesar's campaign of violence to join Jesus' divine peace insurgency.

GROUP DIALOGUE QUESTIONS

1. Reflect on the way the author uses the words *derangement* and *dislocation* early in the chapter. How do those words describe human cultures today?

2. Why do you think atheism becomes attractive to some people? In what ways can you imagine God being happy about a person turning from some forms of religion to atheism?

3. How do you respond to the charge that the Bible is a violent book and that God seems to sanction violence in the Bible?

4. How do you respond to the reading given in this chapter of the story of Jesus and the Syrophonecian woman from Matthew 15?

5. The author suggests that through his encounter with this woman, Jesus enters a new phase of ministry. Has God ever used an encounter with an unlikely person to lead you into a new phase or chapter of life?

6. If someone asked you, "What is the divine peace insurgency?" how would you answer?

Whose Side Are We On?

In spite of the "Christianization" of Western culture, it is clear that few of us live consistently and purposefully within Jesus' framing story. It is clear that his peace insurgency has little if any influence on global or national security policy even in countries that claim a Christian heritage, including democracies like the United States that have a strong majority of voters (and politicians) professing belief in Jesus. Instead, we find ourselves within a framing story of redemptive violence, a narrative preaching to us, overtly or covertly, that peace may be achieved only through the elimination or domination of our enemies.

It is no wonder that in a narrative like this, human societies are willing to incur almost any expense for increased security, even if our expenditures don't seem to be paying off.[1] In 2004, for example, global military expenses exceeded $1 trillion, but serious international terrorist attacks rose from 175 to 655. During the Cold War period, from about 1948 to 1990, the nations of the world militarized as never before in the history of humanity. The two superpowers of the era, the United States and the Soviet Union, had amassed about seventy thousand nuclear warheads whose combined power was one million times greater than the bomb that destroyed Hiroshima. The Brookings Institution estimates that the United

States alone, since 1940, spent a mind-boggling $5.48 trillion on developing nuclear weapons and systems to deliver them.[2]

In 1969, midway through the Cold War era, one US nuclear submarine could destroy 160 Soviet cities simultaneously. The Soviets and Americans could achieve Mutually Assured Destruction—the infamous MAD ceiling had been reached. At that point, surely the military buildup would slow down. Why build more weapons when you had the power to completely destroy not only your enemy, but the entire planet?

THE HIGH COST OF STRATEGIC SUFFICIENCY

Contrary to all logic, the arms race did not slow down, but accelerated. In fact, US government leaders removed the Mutually Assured Destruction ceiling entirely: there would be no limit to the number of weapons the United States would develop. Former national security adviser and secretary of state Henry Kissinger describes this stunning decision with a kind of surreal coolness: "The joint Chiefs of Staff cooperated because they understood that the doctrine of assured destruction would inevitably lead to political decisions halting or neglecting the improvement of our strategic forces, and in time reducing them. We therefore developed in 1969 new criteria of strategic sufficiency."[3]

Soon, guided by this new, ironically named doctrine of "strategic sufficiency," America had the ability to destroy ten planet Earths with our nuclear weapons—our own world plus nine more like it. One might wonder if this level of militarization would be considered sufficient?[4] Yes, in the years since the end of the Cold War, many of these warheads have indeed been dismantled, but thousands still exist—still capable of destroying many planet Earths.[5] In fact, the United States spends $100 million *per day* to keep its weapons poised and ready for use in a preemptive strike.

During his first term as secretary of defense (1975–1977), Donald Rumsfeld expressed his openness to this chilling choice: "We do not exclude the possibility that for the defense of our interests we will be the first to use nuclear weapons."[6] Apparently, when President George W. Bush made his preemptive war doctrine overt and public in 2003, we shouldn't have been surprised: it had already been the covert American doctrine of both political parties for decades. Bill Clinton echoed Rumsfeld in a September 27, 1993, speech to the United Nations, affirming that America has the right to "unilateral use of military power" to ensure "uninhibited access to key markets, energy supplies, and strategic resources."[7]

Ten years after the Cold War ended, well before the 9/11 terrorist attacks, the US government's annual investment in defense had risen to 20 percent of its fiscal budget, more than a half-trillion dollars, and over half of the US national debt was military related ($2.9 of $5.6 trillion). Since 9/11, expenditures have exploded.

By 2003, the US military budget was larger than the next *fifteen* nations combined, spending $2 billion per day on the military; by 2006, the US military budget had swelled by 49 percent over its 2000 levels, *not including* expense for the wars in Afghanistan and Iraq. The US military budget was then larger than the next *twenty-five* nations combined. In other words, the strongest twenty-five countries in the world would have to switch from being US allies (as most of them are) to US enemies in order for the United States to be confronted by a greater force.

On top of all of these financial costs of a massive military, William Fulbright (Arkansas senator and chair of the Senate Foreign Relations Committee during the Cold War) has identified other costs, including the "brain drain" of many of our best engineers, scientists, and thinkers being drawn away from potentially productive and profitable research (such as developing alternative energy sources to reduce our dependency on oil, and in particular, Mideast oil) to spend their lives developing weapons, which he calls "sheer non-productive assets":

> Violence has become the nation's leading industry. It is not an enthusiasm for war but simple economic self-interest that has drawn millions of workers, their labor unions, and their elected representatives into the military-industrial complex. To those who build them, weapons mean prosperity, not war. For the industrialist they mean profits; for the worker,

new jobs and the prospect of higher wages; and for the politician, a new installation or defense order with which to ingratiate himself with his constituents. . . . Weapons are not reproductive; they are sheer non-productive assets. They do not contribute to the welfare of the country in any positive way. On the contrary, they drain resources—human as well as material—that could be applied to making our consumer products competitive, or to restoring the infrastructure that has been so rapidly deteriorating.[8]

What could drive a nation with such crushing military dominance to keep pushing harder and harder, further and further into a kind of militarist mania? In 1948, George Kennon, one of the US government's leading foreign policy planners in the twentieth century, explained it in these chilling words: "We have about 50 percent of the world's wealth, but only 6.3 percent of its population. . . . Our real task in the coming period is to devise a pattern of relationships which will permit us to maintain this position of disparity."[9]

So in terms of the suicide machine's three mechanisms, we could say it rather baldly and boldly like this: *the purpose of the US security system is to maintain the inequity of US prosperity.* Or, put alternatively, to maintain and expand the American Empire.

THE AMERICAN EMPIRE

Empire can be defined in various ways. Duane Clinker offers three characteristics: An empire expands beyond normal boundaries, so its national interests extend to include military installations abroad, multinational corporations owned by the empire's citizens, and the interests of its allies.[10] An empire normally develops extraordinary military power. An empire exerts its influence in a variety of ways—through economics, culture, religion, education, and politics.[11]

David Korten offers four characteristics of an empire: Empires embrace the idea of material luxury and excess for the ruling classes. Empires are dedicated to absolute military supremacy. Empires emphasize the masculine values of violence and domination over the feminine values of nurture and cooperation.[12] Empires create a ceiling for human development and impede development beyond its current level.[13]

In light of these kinds of descriptions, the three priorities of the National Security Strategy of the United States have a rather eerie significance:

1. Perpetuate US military dominance globally so no nation can rival or threaten the United States.
2. Be prepared to engage in preemptive military strikes, whenever the US government considers another nation to be a threat to the US, its forces or installations abroad, or its friends or allies.[14]
3. Maintain immunity for US citizens from prosecution by the International Criminal Court.[15]

In other words, dominate, intimidate, and refuse to play by the rules you expect everybody else to play by—a classic manifesto of the imperial spirit.

Americans are largely unaware that they are surfing the crest of this global military spending tsunami in pursuit of imperial dominance. Most are still under the illusion that the United States is the leading nation in the world for generosity, showering other nations with unmatched aid. Even in terms of brute numbers, though, this is not the case: Japan gives more.

The 2006 budget showed that US military expenditures were twenty-one times larger than diplomacy and foreign aid *combined*, and that the United States was *dead last* among the most developed nations in foreign aid as a percentage of gross domestic product.[16] One wonders what would happen if good-hearted Americans realized that a mere 10 percent of the US military budget, if reinvested in foreign aid and development, could care for the basic needs of the entire world's poor. Or if they realized that one-half of 1 percent of the US military budget would cut hunger in Africa in half by 2015. Would there be marches in the streets calling for budgetary reform?

Many Americans may also believe that this rush toward imperial militarization reflects a needed response to 9/11. But actually, it reflects a rather long-standing foreign policy. For example, many will recall the "shock and awe" campaign that launched the second Iraq war in 2003. The term *shock and awe* (which suggests an almost reverent and worshipful attitude toward crushing military attack) was not new at all; its roots can be traced back to 1996 during the Clinton administration, when the Pentagon's National Defense University released a report called "Shock and Awe: Achieving Rapid Dominance." Notice the report's reverential use of capital letters:

> One recalls from old photographs and movie or television screens, the comatose and glazed expressions of survivors of the great bombardments of World War I and the attendant horrors and death of trench warfare. These images and expressions of shock transcend race, culture, and history. Indeed, TV coverage of Desert Storm vividly portrayed Iraqi soldiers registering these effects of battlefield Shock and Awe.
>
> In our excursion, we seek to determine whether and how Shock and Awe can become sufficiently intimidating and compelling factors to force or otherwise convince an adversary to accept our will in the Clausewitzian sense, such that the strategic aims and military objectives of the campaign will achieve a political end.[17]

The similarity between the words "shock and awe" and "terror" should cause every reader some pause: when these 1996 words were put into play as part of the "war on terror" in Iraq in 2003, the US Department of Defense made clear its intent to fight the terror of terrorism with the terror of "Shock and Awe."

Perhaps we could say, then, that the war *on* terror had identified itself as a war *of* terror—or a war of competing terrors: organized and wealthy US terror against random and improvised jihadist terror. Such a war seems suicidal for all parties concerned, and for those caught in the crossfire as well.

No less concerning in the report should be the reference to Clausewitz. The nineteenth-century Prussian military officer Carl von Clausewitz was revered by Marx, Engels, Lenin, and Trotsky as the founder of "total war doctrine."[18] It appears that to the list of Clausewitz's Socialist and Communist admirers we can now add US leaders from the US Defense University. For Clausewitz, violence was simply another form of speech, a way of communicating, a kind of exclamation point if you will, in the political romance: "War is simply a continuation of political intercourse, with the addition of other means. . . . Is not war just another expression of [diplomatic] thoughts, another form of speech or writing?"[19]

What Happens When We Accept Total War Doctrine?

What happens to a country when its leaders have erased long-standing lines between attack and defense, diplomacy and war, non-violence and violence, suggesting that all are legitimate and acceptable forms of diplomatic communication? What happens to the world when a country with the capacity to destroy the whole planet many times over accepts a Clausewitzian "total war doctrine"?[20]

One recalls Alfred Nobel who, in 1866, invented dynamite. He called it "security powder," in hopes that it would be a tool of violence so terrible that it would bring peace. "I hope to discover a weapon so terrible that it would make war eternally impossible," he said. Eighty years later, bombs fell on Hiroshima and Nagasaki.[21]

And one recalls the words of Dwight Eisenhower, a man who knew something about war: "It happens that defense is a field in which I have had varied experience over a lifetime, and if I have learned anything, it is that there is no way in which a country can satisfy the craving for absolute security—but it can easily bankrupt itself, morally and economically, in attempting to reach that illusory goal through arms alone."[22]

This is the condition of our security system today, especially here in the United States. In the eyes of the rest of the world, our "craving for absolute security" has already driven us to the brink of moral bankruptcy. How much further will our addictive craving for security through domination drive us? Will it drive us to bankrupt our economy? Or will it drive us to the ledge of civilizational suicide through global nuclear war? We should hope and pray for the former.[23]

Or else we should hope and pray for a radical transformation of our framing story so that we switch sides from Caesar's way to Jesus' way—before it is too late. If it weren't for my faith in God, I would conclude that it is already too late, that the moment for transformation has long passed.[24]

But despair is boring and uncreative, and to succumb to it is to empower it. So I turn from it and turn to Jesus, to believe his narrative and to join his peace insurgency, to stop figuring out how to get him on our side, and instead to try to cross over to his side.

GROUP DIALOGUE QUESTIONS

1. How do you respond to the information in this chapter about global military expenses? Which statistic most struck you, and why?
2. Respond to William Fulbright's comment that weapons are "non-productive assets."
3. The author suggests that the United States is functioning as an empire. What do you know about empires in the past? How do you feel about the idea of an American Empire?
4. President Eisenhower spoke of the possibility of a nation going bankrupt in its search for security. Do you see that as a threat for your nation? How could that danger be avoided?
5. The author confesses the pull of despair in reaction to

the material in this chapter. Do you feel despair? Why or why not?
6. How can you tell whether you are trying to get God on your side, or you are trying to get on God's side, as the last paragraph suggests?
7. Define the concept of "redemptive violence." Would you say that Jesus' teachings can be reconciled with redemptive violence?

Layers and Layers More

The more imperial and aggressive the United States has seemed, the more other nations have felt resistance and resentment growing against the United States. The more the United States senses this resistance and resentment, the more fearful it becomes and the more it arms itself. The result? A tragic trajectory, a vicious downward spiral of militarization, growing fear and resentment, increasing militarization, mushrooming fear and resentment, and so on. The cycle is irrational, suicidal, idiotic.

But scratch the surface of its idiocy, and you find layers and layers more. For example, consider John Ralston Saul's description of "the McNamara trap" during and after the Vietnam War era: "McNamara concluded that it would be rational to limit armament costs by producing larger runs of each weapon and selling them abroad. The US also happened to be running a three-billion-dollar general trade deficit. Foreign arms sales would be a way to balance the situation."[1]

Do you see what is being said in these three crisp sentences? *Military weapons are expensive*, McNamara thinks. *So why not reduce the costs by producing extra weapons and then selling them to other nations for a handsome profit? The US military can then create a cottage industry, a second source of income, as a weapons dealer. And doing so will even help the economy by balancing the trade deficit.*

What could be more rational than Americans selling weapons to other nations who will then use them against American soldiers and their allies?

THE SUICIDAL LOGIC OF THE WAR BUSINESS

The United States isn't alone in this "rationality." It is joined by the other four members of the UN Security Council (Russia, Great Britain, France, and China) in cornering the market on global arms exports in 2004, with an impressive 86.7 percent market share. (The term *security racket* may come to mind to describe this kind of Security Council.) If you add other European nations into the mix, the figure rises to over 93 percent.

But even if you take all of the rest of the world's weapons sales and put them together, they don't match US weapons exports. My country can boast that we produce 53.4 percent of the world's weapons.[2] Most Americans are either uninformed about these figures, apathetic, or perhaps they believe that McNamara was more rational than President Jimmy Carter, who in 1976 said, "We cannot have it both ways. We can't be both the world's leading champion of peace and the world's leading supplier of arms."[3]

It gets worse. In 2003, 80 percent of the top buyers of US weapons (twenty of the twenty-five top clients) were countries that our own State Department labeled undemocratic or countries known for their failure to uphold human rights, such as Egypt and Saudi Arabia. In 1999, the US weapons industry supplied arms to 92 percent of the conflicts in process anywhere on the planet, and in a stroke of elegant fairness, often supplied both sides in conflicts. Perhaps most shocking and awful of all: between 1998 and 2001, the United States, Great Britain, and France earned more income from selling weapons to developing countries than they gave those developing countries in aid.[4]

If you want to be a major player in the war business long term, I guess McNamara's strategy is darkly rational. But if you value your sons and daughters and don't relish the thought of sending them off to kill or die, or both; if you detest the waste, suffering, carnage, poverty, and social degradation that come from war; if you believe that human anger and violence cannot accomplish the justice of God; and if you have a modicum of confidence in the message of Jesus, you'd have to say that McNamara's rationality—which is the current bipartisan rationality of the US government—is nothing short of suicidal. Many of us are ashamed, deeply ashamed, to be associated with it.

The voice of Archbishop Desmond Tutu rings with a vastly different sanity:

> For many years, I've been involved in the peace business, doing what I can to help people overcome their differences. In doing so, I've also learned a lot about the business of war: the arms trade. It is an industry out of control. Every day, more than 1,000 innocent people, including children, are killed by conventional weapons, according to the UN.
>
> There have been international treaties to control the spread of nuclear, chemical and biological weapons for decades. Yet, despite the mounting death toll, there still is no treaty governing sales of small arms and other conventional weapons, from handguns to attack helicopters. . . .
>
> This is allowed to continue because of the complicity of governments, especially the governments of rich countries that turn a blind eye to the appalling human suffering associated with the proliferation of conventional weapons. It is estimated that every year small arms kill more people than the atomic bombs dropped on Hiroshima and Nagasaki put together. Many more people are injured, terrorized or driven from their homes by armed violence.
>
> The world has the chance to finally say "no" to the continuing scandal of the unregulated weapons trade. . . . No longer should the peace business be undermined by the arms business.[5]

THE FORCE OF WAR

Chris Hedges knows too much to fall for the suicidal logic of the arms business. His professional career as a war-zone journalist has thrust him into the middle of many of the wars of recent decades. In his book *War Is a Force That Gives Us Meaning*, he reviews the wars of the twentieth century, and especially its last decade. In Afghanistan, 2 million died in war. In Sudan, 1.5 million. In Rwanda, 800,000. In Angola, 500,000. In Bosnia and Burundi, 250,000 each. In Guatemala, 200,000. In Liberia, 150,000. In Algeria, 75,000. In Eritrea and Ethiopia, Colombia, Israel and Palestine, Chechnya, Sri Lanka, Turkey, Sierra Leone, Kosovo, the Persian Gulf, and elsewhere, many tens of thousands more. Looking over the whole century, 43 million military personnel were killed in war, and 62 million civilians.[6]

Hedges recalls historian Will Durant's assessment that "there have only been twenty-nine years in all of human history during which a war was not underway somewhere."[7]

This drive to war resembles nothing more than an addiction. David Korten says, "Feeding on its own illusions, Empire becomes a kind of collective addiction—a psychological dependence on domination, violence, and material excess."[8] The addict, craving an emotional high, keeps reaching for the very bottle or syringe or white powder that is killing him. What high could be so powerful, seductive, and addictive that it could explain our societal death wish? After witnessing many wars at point-blank range, Hedges uses words like "exhilirated," "proud," "powerful," and "god-like" to describe the unique high that war brings.[9]

A powerful high indeed, even more attractive when it provides what Hedges calls "a potent distraction" from the malaise, trivia, pettiness, desperation, divisiveness, impotence, ordinariness, and boredom we may feel in our daily lives during times of peace— described powerfully by Shakespeare:

> Let me have a war, say I: It exceeds peace as far as day
> Does night; it's spritely, waking, audible, full of vent.
> Peace is a very apoplexy, lethargy, mull'd, deaf, sleepy,
> Insensible; a getter of more bastard children than war is a
> Destroyer of men.[10]

A Weapon of Mass Distraction

War, then, can be a potent "weapon of mass distraction"—distracting us from the deaf, sleepy, lethargic flatness of peacetime complacency. Of course, just as addicts "hit bottom" when the consequences of their addiction cause their lives to collapse, the horrors and pains of war sometimes precipitate "bottoms" that bring societies down from the high of their euphoric, ecstatic warrior trance:

> Wars that lose their mythic stature for the public, such as Korea or Vietnam, are doomed to failure, for war is exposed for what it is—organized murder. . . . Each side reduces the other to objects—eventually in the form of corpses.[11]

Hedges confesses, "Nearly every reporter has seen his or her mission as sustaining civilian and army morale. . . . The press usually does not lead. Mythic war reporting sells papers and boosts ratings." He adds that the press is generally "as eager to be of service to the state during the war as most everyone else. Such docility on the part of the press," he explains, makes it easier "to do what governments do in wartime, indeed what governments do much of the time, and that is lie."[12]

Of course, even if the news media were seeking merely to report news instead of being "of service to the state" or "sustaining civilian and army morale," it is doubtful whether the majority would listen to them. As Hedges explains, the nation or the group at war "falls into a collective 'autism' . . . and does not listen to those outside the inner circle."[13]

In this kind of addictive denial, society lies to itself through its leaders and the echoing, ratings-driven press. It holds its hands over its ears to avoid hearing unpleasant and inconvenient truths, and so helps a war to last longer than necessary. Then it creates a quick amnesia after a war is over, making it all the more likely that it will relapse quickly after a brief period of peaceful sobriety.

> The nationalist myth often implodes with a startling ferocity. It does so after the lies and absurdities that surround it become too hard to sustain. They collapse under their own

weight. The contradictions and torturous refusal to acknowledge the obvious becomes more than a society is able to bear. The collapse is usually followed by a blanket refusal, caused by shame and discomfort, to examine or acknowledge the crimes carried out in the name of nationalist cause.[14]

Twelve-step programs teach that it takes a spiritual program to treat addiction. A student of war will similarly conclude that only a spiritual program can break our world, including the United States, from the addictive high of war—the emotions that put our war machinery into motion. What Jesus said about choosing between God and money (Matthew 6:24) may be equally true regarding security: perhaps no one can serve two security masters, but must ultimately choose between the arms of militarization and the outstretched arms of Christ, between living by the peace of the sword and living by the peace of the Lord.

There are two roads, both claiming to lead to shalom, and both can't be right.

GROUP DIALOGUE QUESTIONS

1. The author uses strong language to describe our culture's love affair with war: *irrational, suicidal, idiotic.* Do you think this strong language is appropriate or excessive?
2. What statistic in this chapter was most disturbing to you, and why?
3. How might someone argue against Desmond Tutu's statement in this chapter?
4. The author presents an either/or choice in the final sentences of this chapter. Do you feel that the choice is that simple? Why or why not?
5. This chapter is potentially one of the most controversial and most important in the book. Talk about what it would mean in your life if you became convinced that this chapter is speaking the truth.

Joining Warriors Anonymous

The last sentences of the previous chapter were not setting you up for a call to ideological pacifism. I agree with the New Vision group: we need to move to a new dialogue beyond the old just-war and pacifist positions.[1] So I would rather sidestep these polarizations entirely and instead call adherents of both positions to a joint consideration of the addictive nature of war, an addiction we may already have but may be in denial about.

Chris Hedges concludes his book with a final allusion to addiction. Just as fine wines and well-crafted beers offer much for aficionados to appreciate (as would, I imagine, a well-bred strain of cannabis or opium), war offers many fine and noble things to be celebrated and appreciated. But in both cases, fine things can become an occasion for self-destruction:

> We believe in the nobility and self-sacrifice demanded by war, especially when we are blinded by the narcotic of war. We discover in the communal struggle, the shared sense of meaning and purpose, a cause. War fills our spiritual void. I do not miss war, but I miss what it brought. . . . And this is a quality war shares with love, for we are, in love, also able to choose fealty and self-sacrifice over security. . . . For the

covenant of love is such that it recognizes both the fragility and the sanctity of the individual. It recognizes itself in the other. It alone can save us.[2]

Here, Hedges identifies exactly the point at which Jesus seeks to deconstruct the security system of the suicide machine. To break our addiction to the "narcotic of war," Jesus must do two things. First, he must replace the craving for security with another craving, and second, he must fill the potential boredom of peace with something more fulfilling than the addictive white powder of war.

A Craving for Justice

What craving does Jesus propose as an alternative to the dark craving of human beings for violence? Clearly, he agrees with Hedges that only love can save us. But if we turn to the Sermon on the Mount, in its opening poem known to many of us as the Beatitudes, we will find him exploring *how* love can save us—through a craving for justice.[3]

> Blessed are those who hunger and thirst for justice,
>   for they will be filled.
> Blessed are the merciful, for they will be shown mercy. . . .
> Blessed are the peacemakers, for they will be called
>   children of God.
> Blessed are those who are persecuted because of justice, for
>   theirs is the kingdom of heaven. (Matthew 5:6–7, 9–10)[4]

The kingdom of heaven (or God)—which is elsewhere identified as life "to the full" (John 10:10), which would include a life full of prosperity, security, equity, meaning, and shalom—comes to people who crave not victory or even freedom but justice, who seek not revenge but reconciliation, who strive not for domination but peace, and who are courageously eager to suffer pain for the cause of justice, not inflict it.

If Jesus were in a conversation with Chris Hedges and others like you and me who are concerned about the pervasive human pull toward war, I think he might say something like this:

> You are right to acknowledge the violent streak in human society. The fact is, human beings have evolved as fighters. But if you do not redirect this primal drive, you will destroy yourselves and your world. So, acknowledging that you are natural fighters, it is time to rethink what kind of fighting you must do. This is why I came; this is what my life and message were about. My message of the kingdom of God is intended to replace the drugs of nationalism, tribalism, partisanship, ethnocentrism, and religious elitism—and the war addiction they support. Instead of resorting to violence for national or other lesser interests, my kingdom invites you to defect from all war making and invest yourselves in peacemaking for God's global interests and the common good of all God's creations on the planet.
>
> You need to choose another type of fighting: instead of fighting against each other, you must fight with each other against injustice, for the good of each other. Instead of fighting for dominance or revenge, you must fight for peace and reconciliation. And make no mistake: this form of struggle requires no less courage than war. It requires the willingness, if need be, to stand up to the most powerful forces in the world, vulnerable and without weapons, and tell the truth, to be willing to drink the cup of suffering in the cause of justice. So replace your craving for security with a passionate hunger and thirst for justice, and you will be immune to the temptation to snort the tempting white powder of war, or shoot the mysterious yellow syringe of war, or swallow the sparkling, bubbling, golden champagne of war.

If this is how Jesus replaces one craving with a better hunger and thirst, with what does Jesus transform the potential flatness and triviality of peace? The answer is simple: with life, life in the kingdom of God, a life which he describes life "like streams of living water" flowing from one's inmost being (John 7:38). His sign and wonder of turning water into wine evokes this transformation of life from plain, mundane, tasteless, and flat to something dynamic, spirited, alive. Those who follow his way, this imagery suggests, will be so intoxicated with life that they will never want to squander it in war.

This new vibrancy moves people back from the brink of war—far, far back. Consider these passages from the Sermon on the Mount (Matthew 5:21–26, 43–48):

> You have heard that it was said to the people long ago: "You shall not murder, and anyone who murders will be subject to judgment." But I tell you that anyone who is angry with a brother or sister will be subject to judgment. Again, anyone who says to a brother or sister, "Raca," is answerable to the Sanhedrin. And anyone who says, "You fool!" will be in danger of the fire of hell. (vv. 21–22)

Jesus' disciples must work to dehabitualize and delegitimize even small expressions of aggression like name-calling. They must realize the dangers of language that dehumanizes the other—whether it is Hutus in Rwanda calling Tutsis "cockroaches" and "tall trees," or political and religious leaders using language like "infidel" or "terrorist" or "axis of evil," or a husband and wife trading insults in a loud, late-night argument.

Care on the level of dehumanizing language helps preempt escalations that lead to violence, murder, and war. One backs away from the narrow ledge of murder, back from the slippery slope where one is angry, back to edge of the hill where one is tempted to call names. One quenches conflict there, while the potential aggression is still a spark. Instead of dealing with war strategy while the improvised explosive devises are detonating or the missiles are launching, one deals with conflict when anger begins to simmer and insults start forming in the mind. Similarly . . .

Therefore if you are offering your gift at the altar and there remember that your brother or sister has something against you, leave your gift there in front of the altar. First go and be reconciled to that person; then come and offer your gift. (vv. 23–24)

In the way of Jesus, you are eager to resolve every interpersonal conflict, realizing that God prioritizes social reconciliation over religious ritual and observance. The same theme continues:

Settle matters quickly with your adversary who is taking you to court. Do it while you are still together on the way, or your adversary may hand you over to the judge, and the judge may hand you over to the officer, and you may be thrown into prison. Truly I tell you, you will not get out until you have paid the last penny. (vv. 25–26)

On an interpersonal level, while you still can, you need to work for reconciliation whenever conflicts arise. Otherwise, Jesus says, you will be sucked into a chain of events that you can't control, and you'll find yourself imprisoned, stuck in a place you don't want to be. Later, he summarizes: to imitate God and live in God's way means to shower your enemies with goodness—peacemaking with a preemptive kindness.

You have heard that it was said, "Love your neighbor and hate your enemy," but I tell you, love your enemies and pray for those who persecute you, that you may be children of your Father in heaven. He causes his sun to rise on the evil and the good, and sends rain on the just and the unjust. (vv. 43–46; author's translation)[5]

War is a force that gives us illusory meaning; Jesus offers a real alternative: love. Another word for *love*, in Jesus' vocabulary, is *neighborliness*. But that neighborliness, he makes clear, means crossing boundaries, something Jesus is continually doing—crossing the boundaries between men and women and between Jew and non-Jew (John 4:27), between religious and irreligious (Luke 15:1–2), between sick and healthy (Luke 18:40), and even between friend and enemy.

So Jesus says, "Yes, people have the freedom to define themselves as your enemies. Your job is not to deny the reality of their opposition or even hatred toward you. Your job is to meet that hatred with love, with acts of generosity and kindness. You should not take sides against your enemy, but instead you should seek to join with God, who is above your conflict, in an attitude of goodwill and love toward the person who self-identifies as your enemy. Your enemy may not choose to be your friend, but you can choose to be his."

Jesus' use of the term "enemy" is itself fascinating. He doesn't say, "You have no enemies if you are my disciple. Everyone is your friend and brother." Doing so, in spite of its appearance of enlightenment, would remove the "otherness" of the enemy; it would take away from the enemy the right to define himself or herself in opposition to the disciple. It would, in other words, be a subtle form of domination and colonization, melting his unique identity in a pot of absorption. That's no way to bring real peace, according to Jesus.

People who believe in Jesus' creative peacemaking strategy, then, are never bored, never complacent. The work of peacemaking is always urgent for them in peacetime as in wartime. Without people giving themselves to this important (and according to Jesus, blessed and rewarding) work, the entropy and gravity of war will exert their hellish, downward, destructive pull. It is hard for us sometimes even to imagine a world where this work of peacemaking would be taken seriously.

In the aftermath of Hurricane Katrina in 2005, my imagination got a small but real glimpse of such a world. Like millions of people around the world, I was glued to the television after the storm, wondering what could be done to help the people of New Orleans and its environs. Local, state, and federal agencies all had failed to anticipate the disaster and respond to it with appropriate dispatch. Then, in the midst of the chaos and despair, an army commander, Lt. Gen.

Russel Honore, landed near the Superdome in his Blackhawk helicopter. Suddenly, under his command, things began to happen.

This, I thought to myself, *can be the role of the military in a more peaceful world: preparing for and responding to natural disasters, intervening in crises, serving in times of great need as neighbors in the global neighborhood.* Instead of dividing the world into allies and enemies, this approach would unite the world against common enemies like storm, drought, earthquake, and disease.

THE SECURITY STRATEGY OF JESUS

The security strategy of Jesus clearly involved a radical break from that of Rome and of the various parties in his own nation, whether the violent Zealots, the accommodating Sadducees and Herodians, the blaming Pharisees, or the withdrawing and isolating Essenes. Rather than an aggressive and offensive empire, or a submissive or passive nation, or a fragmented and isolated subculture, Jesus envisioned a people actively dedicated to peacemaking—walking the second mile, turning the other cheek, giving freely to the enemy as well as the friend. This peacemaking work was not an expression of defeat or weakness at all, but rather, it required a courageous and confident commitment to transcend violence. Still today, Jesus' teaching challenges us to reject the deceptive, addictive emotions that forcefully drive us to war, and calls us to find new meaning in love, neighborliness, reconciliation, and the work of building vibrant, reconciled communities.

Nowhere is his message clearer than in his prophetic action on what we call Palm Sunday. One imagines Herod, two links down in Caesar's chain of command, coming into Jerusalem on one side of town.[6] He is attended by horses and chariots and guards armed with swords and spears. On the other side of town, Jesus also enters the city, not riding a white steed or a state-of-the-art chariot but a humble donkey, cheered by crowds of poor and humble people who wave not swords and spears but palm branches and colorful coats. They don't celebrate the one who comes in the name of Caesar and the empire of Rome, but the one who comes in the name of the Lord, proclaiming the kingdom of God.

The scene is all the more powerful in light of two passages from the Hebrew Scriptures that Jesus is obviously evoking in this entry that we can best compare to a political demonstration.

> Some trust in chariots and some in horses, but we trust in the name of the LORD our God. (Psalm 20:7)

> Rejoice greatly, Daughter Zion! Shout, Daughter Jerusalem! See, your king comes to you, righteous and having salvation, lowly and riding on a donkey, on a colt, the foal of a donkey. I will take away the chariots from Ephraim and the warhorses from Jerusalem, and the battle bow will be broken. He will proclaim peace to the nations. His rule will extend from sea to sea and from the River to the ends of the earth. (Zechariah 9:9–10)

Yes, Herod and Caesar trust in chariots and warhorses, but Jesus comes in a different manner: to proclaim "peace to the nations," which means the Gentiles, the other, the enemies.

WE HAVE A CHOICE

In defending the American "war on terror," former defense secretary Donald Rumsfeld summed up his, and the US government's, security strategy: "We have a choice, either to change the way we live, which is unacceptable, or to change the way that they live, and we choose the latter."[7]

In light of the security policy of Jesus, I would say it slightly differently: "We have a choice, either to change the unacceptable way we live, or to change the unacceptable way they live, which is impossible to do against their will—without stooping to ethnic cleansing so they don't live at all. So, we choose the former, in the confidence that a voluntary change in our behavior will precipitate an unexpected change in their behavior." The key, then, is to change the way we live not in capitulation to "them," not in fear or intimidation or surrender to "them," but in adjustment to the ways of God and the kingdom of God.

What would it look like to "change the way we live"—which, by the way, is another decent definition of the word *repentance*? What would it mean to trade the love of power for the power of love?[8]

Discovering good answers to those questions is not made easier by popular preachers who call for a violent strain of the Christian religion. For example, a popular conservative pundit, the day after the September 11, 2001, attacks, wrote a column called "This Is War," evoking the killing of innocent civilians in World War II in a call for retaliation: "We should invade their countries, kill their leaders and convert them to Christianity. . . . We carpet-bombed German cities; we killed civilians. That's war. And this is war."[9]

Three years later, referring to the Iraq war, a popular Christian preacher used similar language in a CNN debate with Jesse Jackson, moderated by Wolf Blitzer:

> . . . And the president's doing the right thing. He's looking for them, he's searching them out. He's killing them when he finds them. And that's the only cure for barbarians. . . . I'd rather be killing them over there than fighting them over here. . . . And I'm for the president to chase them all over the world. If it takes 10 years, blow them all away in the name of the Lord.[10]

These words starkly contrast with the words spoken by Jesus when he stood in that vulnerable and precarious position before Pilate, hours before his crucifixion: "My kingdom is not of this world. If it were, my servants would fight to prevent my arrest." His kingdom and his disciples could be characterized as "his" and not "of this world" precisely by their rejection of violence when under threat (John 18:36).[11]

In 1963, Dr. King chose between these contrasting kingdoms.

His countersuicidal logic, sanity, and rationality provide a fitting last word regarding the security options we face in our world today:

The ultimate weakness of violence is that it is a descending spiral, begetting the very thing it seeks to destroy. Instead of diminishing evil, it multiplies it. . . . Hate multiplies hate, violence multiplies violence, and toughness multiplies toughness in a descending spiral of destruction. . . . The chain reaction of evil—hate begetting hate, wars producing more wars—must be broken, or we shall be plunged into the dark abyss of annihilation.[12]

GROUP DIALOGUE QUESTIONS

1. Describe why war is compared in this chapter to a narcotic.
2. What would the "craving for justice" look like in your life? In your church or faith community? In your nation?
3. Share an experience you have had with name-calling—either being dehumanized through language or dehumanizing someone else, or both.
4. Think of a person or group who might consider you an enemy. What would it mean for you to practice the way of Jesus in relation to this person or group?
5. Describe Jesus' peacemaking strategy in your own words. How realistic is this strategy in comparison with the alternatives?
6. What are the strongest emotions you feel at this point in your reading of this book? How would you describe your reading experience so far for someone who is not in your reading group?

Part 6

THE
PROSPERITY
SYSTEM

Capitalism as God

Jesus' good news of the kingdom of God addresses the security system, as we have seen, in powerful and far-reaching ways. It offers not a prescription but a way, not a formula but an adventure of faith, hope, and love. It is not a matter of naive ignorance about the power of evil or of deluded romanticism about the good heart of the enemy; it is rather a loss of naïveté about the power of violence to cure violence. It is a dose of realism about the futility of seeking security through living "by the sword" (Matthew 26:52).

We know that the security system exists in large part to protect and support the prosperity system. So we can't think that the security system can be "fixed" in isolation from the prosperity system. How does Jesus' message speak to this powerful engine of the suicide machine?

Economist Herman Daly has much to say to this question. Describing the World Bank, he used language more typical of a theologian than an economist: "[The World Bank] is like the church—trying to do good in the world according to what its clergy learned in seminary. But the 'seminaries' are teaching bad theology. . . . Frequent academic advisers to the Bank . . . keep renewing a flawed theology."[1] Another man deeply interested in economics, Karl Marx, employed a similar analogy back in 1847: "Economists are like theologians. . . . Every religion other than their own is the invention of man, whereas their own particular brand of religion is an emanation from God."[2]

While to outsiders, economics may seem like an objective discipline of science, numbers, statistics, and other hard data, there are many reasons to look at the economic sector of the suicide machine—what we are calling the prosperity system—in a religious light. It is, after all, ultimately about the immaterial currency called *desire*.

THE THEOCAPITALIST RELIGION

When we reflect on desire, we quickly find ourselves asking the ultimate metaphysical and spiritual question—namely, what is of true value? What is worth desiring? No wonder Catholic theologian Tom Beaudoin offers the term *theocapitalism* to describe the contemporary prosperity system of the global suicide machine.[3] It is a system of seeking prosperity that functions like a religion, or perhaps a religious cult.

Seen in the light of theocapitalism, MTV and Fox become powerful forms of religious broadcasting, evoking fear and hope, love and hate, obedience and rebellion, forming souls under the guidance of famous spiritual directors. Malls become cathedrals; amusement parks, shrines of holy pilgrimage; celebrities and stars, saints, priests, idols. TV becomes an altar before which we don't kneel, but rather recline—entranced, enraptured, open-eyed and open-mouthed in speechless wonder, on pews called couches, eating our communion bread of potato chips and ice cream and sipping our holy wine of beer or Pepsi. Multinational corporations become denominations, world religions, and they know no separation of church and state.

This godlike "consumer media capitalism," Beaudoin says, does for us exactly what any religion does for its adherents:

1. It gives us *identity*, helping us find or create our true
selves—as the kind of man who wears cologne X, or the

kind of woman who wears dress Y, or the kind of teenager who buys music Z, or the kind of senior citizen who bonds her dentures and heals her hemorrhoids with Product Q or Product H.

2. It helps us belong to a *community* of kindred spirits who share our faith—whether that faith is in the power of a cosmetic to produce youth, or the power of a car to produce sex appeal, or the power of an investment firm to give us security.

3. It develops *trust* by making and keeping advertising promises, and thus reduces the anxiety of making choices, so when we purchase deodorant A, electric drill B, or computer C, we can do so with joy and anticipation.[4]

4. It helps us experience *ecstasy*—when we step out of a plane on vacation, when we bite a chocolate bar, when we sip a fine wine, when we click into an XXX website.

5. It communicates *transcendence* through sacred images and symbols—the mystical Nike swoosh that directs us toward transcendence through footwear, the holy cardinal red of a Coke sign that saves us through sugar, the iconic Target bulls'-eye that draws our concentration to the Center of All Things in the housewares aisle, or the heavenly Golden Arches that guide us to bliss through beef and cheese.

6. It promises us *conversion* to a new life if we try their product and join their brand "family."

7. Ultimately, theocapitalism promises *rest* for the restless heart—a rest that replaces Augustine's *Confession* with a thirty-minute infomercial featuring the testimonials of satisfied customers and believers in the product, complete with dramatic before-and-after photographs.[5]

Theocapitalism functions, Beaudoin says, as a kind of "anonymous spiritual discipline."[6] Like a religion, it attempts to unify all dimensions of life, absorbing and assimilating everything into the One, converting all of life into something new so that the profane and unprofitable can partake in the sacredness of profitability: sport is converted into the sports industry, art and music and drama are converted into the entertainment industry, and religion itself dies and is reborn as the religion industry.

Theocapitalism also displays godlike creative powers, Beaudoin says, constantly performing *creatio ex nihilo*, bringing into being powerful wants that previously didn't exist and then displaying a benign providence by providing just the product to meet that want. It fashions humanity in its own image, making a fetish of human creativity. We create worlds, maybe a Disney World or other amusement park, maybe self-contained environments of steel and glass, miraculous mixtures of weight and weightlessness, substance and transparency. And then within those worlds, we each create our own unique personal identity through buying, each of us being blessed with the hyperconformist freedom to choose our personalized, unique mixture of conformist and nonconformist products.

Having made ourselves and placed ourselves in our self-made Gardens of Eden, our struggle is not between good and evil, because here, within theocapitalism, it is precisely in yielding to temptation, in tasting every fruit, that we find life to the full. We struggle in a new test of free will, the daily and eternal choice between nonbeing and being: wear the wrong style, drive the wrong car, choose the wrong neighborhood, and you could unmake yourself into a nobody—but make the right choice, and you can be somebody. So, Beaudoin says, theocapitalism blesses us with "a perpetual unsolvable identity crisis . . . an unending process of adapting to the latest . . . clothes, cars, music."[7]

THE FOUR SPIRITUAL LAWS OF THEOCAPITALISM

We might say that the creed of theocapitalism has four spiritual laws.

1. The Law of Progress Through Rapid Growth
   I believe in one god: Progress, maker of all that is, through rapid growth.

In a kind of free-market fundamentalism (Cornell West's term[8]), this law requires us to believe in a speedy, literal six-day creation—because the Great God Progress always wants big results fast (so he can get to the weekend for rest and recreation). Beaudoin recalls the tragic story of Easter Island and its manic devotion to progress through rapid growth: "The people had been seduced by a kind of progress that becomes a mania, an 'ideological pathology,' as some anthropologists call it."[9]

The New Vision Group similarly describes the mania and pathology of the law of progress through rapid growth, calling it "untrammeled economic expansion":

> . . . if technological innovations can make the workplace more efficient, then we eliminate jobs. If unbridled competition obliges us to pursue the cheapest possible production costs, regardless of the consequences, then we shift production overseas to places of cheap labor and inadequate standards for employment and environmental standards. . . . Obsessed by an end (rising material prosperity), we have offloaded our responsibility and allowed various forces, means and powers in our society (such as untrammeled economic expansion) to become gods who dictate their will to us.[10]

These gods of progress—with names like Higher Consumption, More Growth, and Rising Productivity—inspire a hymn called, not "Holy, Holy, Holy," but "Faster, Faster, Faster." They may demand of us sacrifices, including, we might say, human sacrifices—but the sacrifices are worth it to all minds fixed and focused (or narrowed) on the first law: progress through rapid growth. Daley describes how these deities teach us to reinterpret the "rising poverty, increased stress, underfed people in the midst of overfed people, environmental deterioration and eroding care" that they cause. These realities are to be seen by the faithful not as tragedies but rather as inevitabilities and as "necessary sacrifices, essential for our progress."[11]

2. The Law of Serenity Through Possession and Consumption
I believe in happiness through owning and using more.

An errant religion often functions like the mafia, which promises security and protection for a fee; but if you don't pay the fee, it promises to destroy you. Instead of "protection rackets," religions often become "forgiveness rackets," creating guilt and anxiety and then offering forgiveness and comfort, but then creating more guilt and anxiety so that you'll need more forgiveness and comfort tomorrow, and so on.

Theocapitalism functions in exactly this way: it promises satisfaction and happiness through possessing and consuming, but always seeks to inflate your desire for happiness, so you'll always need to possess and consume more, creating an impossible satisfaction. It's not enough that you enjoy something: you actually need to own it, as Elaine Bernard, director of the Trade Union Program at Harvard, explained in *The Corporation*:

> One of the things I find very interesting in our current debates is this concept of who creates wealth. Wealth is only created when it's owned privately. What would you call clean water, fresh air, a safe environment? Are they not a form of wealth? And why does it only become wealth when some entity puts a fence around it and declares it private property? Well, you know, that's not wealth creation, that's wealth usurpation.[12]

But even owning can't produce theocapitalistic serenity: one must own *more*, and the *more* is what counts: it is a sum that never can finish being counted. Thus the clergy of theocapitalism can be seen as gangsters working a serenity and satisfaction racket, and business is good.

3. The Law of Salvation Through Competition Alone
By win-lose competition alone you have been saved.

One feels the dual joy of a winner and a true believer in the words of nineteenth-century magnate Andrew Carnegie in *The Gospel of Wealth*: Law #1 ("the progress of the race"—or the law of progress through rapid growth) and then Law #2 ("Peace on earth, good will to men"—or the law of serenity through possession and consumption) lead us to Law #3, which he calls the "law of competition":

> We accept and welcome, therefore, as conditions to which we must accommodate ourselves, great inequality of environment, the concentration of business, industrial and commercial, in the hands of a few, the law of competition between these, as being not only beneficial, but essential for the further progress of the race. . . . Such in my opinion, is the true Gospel concerning wealth, obedience to which is destined some day . . . to bring "Peace on earth, among men Good-Will."[13]

Even religious fundamentalists who reject Darwin in biology typically celebrate an economic or social Darwinism, which reveres inequality in order to reward the fittest—the most industrious, the hardest workers, the most task-oriented (as opposed to people-oriented). The poor, this law states, *should* and *must* be poor because they are unfit (individually or as a group); the rich, even though they concentrate great wealth "in the hands of a few," *should* and *must* be rich because they are the fittest competitors. To violate this law would be to work against the very structure of the universe, and would run counter to the will of God and his "gospel of wealth."

4. The Law of Freedom to Prosper Through Unaccountable Corporations

I believe in one, holy, catholic, and apostolic economy, and in the communion of unaccountable corporations.

In the tired and depressing world of the past, you belonged to a community, and you played your pathetic little role as a farmer, teacher, businessperson, tradesperson, or whatever, stuck in some dinky little community in the middle of nowhere. Being part of a community loaded you down with obligations. For example, you couldn't pollute the local stream because people would notice. You couldn't abuse workers because all your customers were their relatives, and if you abused one of them, all would stop doing business with you. If a disaster struck the community, you would be expected to do your duty and chip in to help. If your products were faulty or dangerous, word would get around and your reputation would be ruined. And in the ultimate insult, you were expected to pay taxes to cover your share of the costs for roads, sewage treatment, and other infrastructures that you depended on to make a living.

In today's dynamic and exciting world, communities can be bypassed completely. Corporations hover above any particular community, and "the big boys" can transcend nations as well. As a result, they can play fast and free with little or no accountability in the "one, holy, catholic, and apostolic" global economy. Here, the corporation is the temple; the corporate jingle is the hymn; the employee of the month is the newly canonized saint; CEOs are apostles and bishops; corporate goals and policies are sacred dogma; heaven is ungoverned trade; hell is taxes and other obligations to the community outside the corporation.

The problem, of course, is not the *corporation* itself, which simply is another word for a business entity, which is simply another term for a community of people who work together. Communities of people who work together, small and large, have a key role to play in the dismantling of the suicide machine and the construction of a better world. The problem is not the existence of corporations, nor is it (necessarily) their size. The problem is the unwillingness of some (again, not all) corporations to be accountable for damage they cause as they seek their own self-interest. While everyone celebrates what they contribute to the gross national product, nobody measures their share of the gross national destruction.

These sacred and unaccountable corporate entities, being legal persons who transcend mere human personhood, refuse to bow to the whims of any lowly state, or even of any standard moral code.

They are accountable only to themselves, as Joel Bakan, writer of the documentary *The Corporation*, says.[14]

The documentary describes corporations as "externalizing machines"—meaning that they seek to externalize any negative costs and consequences (like cancer, for instance, or pollution, or resource usurpation), so they can maximize profit without consequences or costs.

FBI consultant Dr. Robert Hare appears in the film to describe six characteristics of corporations.

1. They show a callous unconcern for the feelings of others—such as when a popular chain store sells brand-name shirts made by sweatshop workers, almost always women, in Honduras or China or Mexico. These corporations have minimized labor costs to perhaps .03 percent of retail price, which makes them, and American bargain-hunters, very happy. But what about the women who sit at sewing machines for seventy hours a week and make a pittance: about thirteen cents per hour in Bangladesh, forty-nine cents per hour in Haiti, or $1.69 per hour in the Dominican Republic? Yes, even these wages are better than unemployment, but is there no sense of compassion or fairness among the sellers and wearers of clothes for their neighbors across town or the globe who make them?[15]

2. They display an incapacity to maintain enduring relationships—so if workers in Honduras (or Ohio) organize to demand a more just wage, the corporation simply fires them and moves to another town, or country, as it also does after it has exhausted a resource or polluted the land.[16]

3. They show reckless disregard for the safety of others—such as people who might experience "human health implications" (a euphemism worthy of some sort of award) because of their products.[17]

4. They manifest habitual deceitfulness, lying and conning others when it is profitable to do so—even if they claim to be "fair and balanced" and devoid of spin.

5. They fail to conform to social norms with respect to lawful behaviors—even if that means taking the dubious path of using the law to legitimize the falsification of news.
6. In spite of these gross faults, they demonstrate an incapacity to experience guilt, and continue in the previous five behavior patterns indefinitely.[18]

Hare then explains that these six characteristics come from *The Diagnostic and Statistical Manual of Mental Disorders (DSM-IV)*, the psychiatric "bible," and together they constitute a unique diagnosis—*psychopath*.

Again, the problem isn't corporations themselves: the problem is this spiritual ideology of theocapitalism that drives many corporations to live for a single bottom line: profit for shareholders, without concern for three other essential bottom lines: the common ecological good, the common social good, and the ultimate good under the gaze of our Creator. Sadly, theocapitalism is running the show, driving the prosperity system to pursue progress through rapid growth, serenity through possession and consumption, salvation through competition, and freedom to prosper through unaccountable corporations.

The other day I saw two bumper stickers, spin-offs from the WWJD bracelet phenomenon of the 1990s—WWJB and WWJE: *Who Would Jesus Bomb?* and *Who Would Jesus Exploit?* Bumper stickers aren't a great venue for serious theological reflection, but they can raise some good questions that deserve deeper reflection after a hard day of shopping for bargains.

GROUP DIALOGUE QUESTIONS

1. Define *theocapitalism* in your own words.
2. The author makes a series of unusual comparisons in this chapter—FOX and MTV as religious broadcasters, malls as cathedrals, amusement parks as shrines, TVs as

altars, corporations as denominations. Reflect on these comparisons. Can you share experiences that would confirm or contradict these analogies?

3. Summarize "the four spiritual laws of theocapitalism" in your own words.

4. Bring some popular magazines to your meeting. Leaf through them, looking for connections between the advertisements and articles you find and the four laws of theocapitalism.

5. How would you define a positive and good kind of prosperity?

Obligations to Nonexistent Future People

The four spiritual laws of theocapitalism are seldom articulated overtly, but their covert influence is pervasive. Wherever you see appeals to progress through rapid growth, serenity through possession and consumption, salvation by competition, and freedom to prosper through unaccountable corporations, you can be sure you are in the territory of this nearly omnipresent god.

If Jesus has anything to say to our current global crises, this is a false deity he must confront. And he doesn't have much time, because evidence accumulates daily that theocapitalism has progressed beyond chronic psychopathic tendencies to become acutely suicidal. Robert Monks, a corporate governance adviser, said it like this: "It was more or less as if we created a doom machine. In our search for wealth and for prosperity, we created something that was going to destroy us."[1]

Interface CEO Ray Anderson puts it even more strongly, using a parable of sorts. He describes a man "going off a very high cliff in his airplane." The man feels good to be flying, feeling the wind in his face. However, Anderson continues, "this poor fool thinks he's flying but in fact he's in free fall and he just doesn't know it yet because the ground is just so far away."[2]

"That's the way our civilization is," Anderson explains. "Every living system of earth is in decline. Every life support system of earth is in decline. And these together constitute the biosphere" . . . ours and the home we share with perhaps thirty million other species. "We're leaving a terrible legacy of poisoning and diminishment of the environment for our grandchildren's grandchildren." Anderson calls this legacy "intergenerational tyranny—a form of taxation without representation," because we're taking from our ancestors without giving them a voice.[3]

Before 1994, Anderson seemed to be a typically faithful devotee of theocapitalism. But then, having been asked to give a speech about sustainability, something he knew nothing about, he read *The Ecology of Commerce.*[4] The book had a profound impact on him.

One day early in this journey it dawned on me that the way I've been running Interface is the way of the plunderer, plundering something that's not mine, something that belongs to every creature on earth, and I said to my self, my goodness, the day must come when this is illegal . . . when plundering is not allowed. Someday people like me will end up in jail. . . . Really, really, the first industrial revolution is flawed. It is not working. It is unsustainable. It is the mistake. And we must move on to another and better industrial revolution and get it right this time. . . . I visualize an organization of people committed to a purpose and the purpose is doing no harm. I see a company that has severed the umbilical cord to earth for its raw materials, taking raw materials that have already been extracted and using them over and over again, driving that process with renewable energy.[5]

David Rischard, author of *High Noon*, agrees with Anderson's assessment. Just as airplane passengers in free fall feel that they're flying (for a while), theocapitalism can produce a prosperity high in the short-term. But eventually, the flight becomes a crash: "The market's own mindless expansion, effective as it is in the short-term, inevitably brings its own long-term problems as it further taxes the planet's carrying capacity beyond the already bad overload coming from the population increase. It's not a question of ideology, but of physical limits."[6]

The suicidal unsustainability that Monks, Anderson, and Rischard describe can be detailed in a thousand ways. For example, one-fifth of our planet's tropical rainforests have been cleared since 1960, and rainforests are currently receding at 1 percent per year. According to Worldwatch.org, we are currently operating at one hundred to one thousand times the normal extinction rate, which means that today, one in four mammal species, one in ten bird species, one in four amphibian species, one in five reptile species, and half of all primate species are threatened with extinction, with 5 to 20 percent more in each category falling to near threatened status. In our lakes, rivers, and oceans, fisheries are being depleted at twice their replacement rate. And speaking of water, by 2020, one in three people will suffer from fresh water shortages. As I hinted at earlier, many of these shortages will be exacerbated by global warming, the aptly named "inconvenient truth" powerfully communicated by former US vice president Al Gore.[7]

THE IMPENDING APOCALYPSE OF THEOCAPITALISM

Herman Daly joins Monks, Anderson, Rischard, and Gore in a devastating critique of unsustainable theocapitalism. Its adherents, he says, choose to believe the impossible. They see "the economy receiving inputs from nowhere and exporting wastes to nowhere." They ask "how to make the economy grow as fast as possible by speeding up the flow of energy and materials through it."[8] In other words, they believe that the more resources we use and the more waste we produce, the better off we'll be. And we'll never have to deal with consequences—either of shortages in resources or toxicity from waste.

Daly can be seen as a heretic who denies all the essential doctrines of theocapitalist faith, or he can be seen as a prophet warning its satisfied adherents of an impending apocalypse. It's not just that we face economic collapse from resource depletion, poisoning from waste buildup, or disruption due to environmental instability. Before these crises hit with full force they will face the dark horsemen of war: "high-consuming countries, whether their high consumption results from too many people or from high consumption per capita, will, in a finite and increasingly integrated world, more and more be at each other's throats."[9]

If nations want to avoid war over diminishing resources—whether we're talking about oil, clean water, or arable soil—Daly says, they "must both consume less and become more self-sufficient." Yet the priests of theocapitalism give the opposite advice: " . . . we should become less self-sufficient and more globally integrated as part of the overriding quest to consume ever more." Daly concludes, "That is the worst advice I can think of."[10]

The insanity of believing that growth—the consumption of "ever more"—is the solution to all problems must eventually become obvious even to those who currently defend it as orthodoxy, Daly suggests:

> One only need try to imagine 1.2 billion Chinese with automobiles, refrigerators, washing machines, and so on, to get a picture of the ecological consequences of generalizing advanced Northern resource consumption levels across the globe. Add to that the ecological consequences from agriculture when the Chinese begin to eat higher on the food chain—more meat, less grain. Each pound of meat requires diversion of roughly ten pounds of grain from humans to livestock, with similarly increased pressure on grasslands and the conversion of forests to pasture.[11]

To complement Anderson's free-fall image, Daly offers a building image: "It was as if we were building a skyscraper and, having reached the twentieth floor, some of us were pointing out that the whole structure was out of plumb and that if we were to go up another twenty stories it would fall."[12]

SCRIPTING A BETTER STORY

Thankfully, growing numbers of us are listening to dissenters like Monks, Anderson, Rischard, Gore, and Daly. We are losing faith in the words of "sophists who argue that we have no obligations to the future because future people do not exist, and rights cannot inhere in nonexistent people, and without rights there can be no obligations. Therefore we have no obligations to future people."[13] In our consideration of global crises, we see that there can be no crisis greater than this. This tragic turn in the plot—in which the powerful main characters forget their obligations to characters not yet born—creates the critical moment when heroes must arise with a new vision and a new way. Otherwise, our dominant framing story will become our obituary.

If Jesus is indeed a hero who can inspire others to heroism at this critical moment, then he must address this carelessness about future generations inherent in our contemporary societal narrative. He must expose the "intergenerational tyranny" and suicidal insanity of theocapitalist faith.[14] He must bring a better story.

Again, we come to the point at which Jesus stands up to the suicide machine—perhaps like a frail Chinese student confronting the tanks in Tiananmen Square in 1989. We might be tempted to watch from the sidelines with silent admiration, except for this: he is asking us to come stand with him.

GROUP DIALOGUE QUESTIONS

1. Respond to the idea of "intergenerational tyranny." Who speaks up for the as-yet unborn in our corporations, communities, and nations?
2. Which statistic in this chapter most stands out to you? Why?
3. How could resource consumption lead to war? Create

some scenarios that seem plausible to you. What would it take to avoid these scenarios?

4. Compare the images of a falling airplane and a skyscraper being built out of plumb. Which image is more fitting in your opinion, and why?

5. What would it mean to "stand with Jesus" in opposition to the current commitment to consumption that drives our prosperity system?

6. What word do you wish would describe us instead of *consumers?*

Quick Bliss Through Footwear, Palate Grease, and Skin Paint

Through his good news, his framing story of the kingdom of God, Jesus recruits heroes to join him in deconstructing the acutely suicidal machinery of theocapitalism. Then he inspires those heroes to build a new kind of prosperity system that we have called *God's love economy,* a new way of living as part of *God's sacred ecosystem.*

We can see how Jesus' gospel confronts each of theocapitalism's four laws:

1. The Law of Good Deeds for the Common Good

First, Jesus addresses the law of progress through rapid economic growth. In its place, he offers *the law of good deeds for the common good.* For Jesus, the economy isn't a bad thing at all. He frequently uses business images to describe the kingdom of God, and entrepreneurship symbolizes for him the work of God's kingdom (Matthew 25:14–30).

In Jesus' vision, the exchange of money expresses the exchange of trust, service, love, and even worship (Luke 19:11–27; 20:20–26; 21:1–4). So money isn't inherently dirty. It's the "love of money," one of his early followers will say, that makes money dirty. Jesus envisions a truly new economy that is guided by a different framing story and that is, therefore, sustainable and not suicidal. This economy is "bound" to justice and not "free" of duties to neighbor and community. It is patient like a farmer who waits for his crops to mature and not in a rush for quick but ill-gotten gain. In his economic system, the goal is fruitfulness, not consumption.[1]

Take, for example, Jesus' parable of "the rich fool" (Luke 12:13–21). The story comes in response to a family feud between brothers dividing an inheritance. Jesus says, "Watch out! Be on your guard against all kinds of greed; life does not consist in an abundance of possessions" (v. 15). The word "life" evokes the whole constellation of terms that serve as synonyms for "life in the kingdom of God"— eternal life (or life of the ages), life to the full, and "the life that is truly life" (1 Timothy 6:17–19).[2]

In the parable, Jesus doesn't even give the rich man credit for his wealth: it is "the ground of a certain rich man" that "yielded an abundant harvest" (v. 16). Jesus then conveys the man's social isolation through a monologue in which he *speaks only to himself.* Withdrawn into the world of his own self-interest, he neglects the common good.

What goal arises from his internal conversation? Exactly the goal of everyone in the theocapitalist economy: "Take life easy. Eat. Drink. Be happy," and store up savings for future enjoyment. God names this man, not as a shrewd businessman or captain of industry, not as a successful entrepreneur with a good portfolio of securities, but simply "you fool." This fool who only speaks to himself, neglecting the needs of others, proves incapable even of storing up things for himself, because at his untimely death, all he owns will be taken from him and given to the others he previously ignored. His economic system is, in the most ultimate sense of the word, unsustainable. Jesus offers this commentary: "This is how it will be with those who store up things for themselves but are not rich toward God" (Luke 12:21).

His phrase "rich toward God" is elaborated by one of Jesus' later followers with the phrase "rich in good deeds," by which the rich may "lay up treasure for themselves as a firm foundation for the coming age" (1 Timothy 6:18–19). Paul here seems to be recalling this economic language from Jesus in Matthew 6:19–21, where, as we have seen, Jesus urges his disciples to "store up for yourselves treasures in heaven" (v. 20). Focusing on earthly savings, Jesus implies, creates a dark outlook, which he contrasts with a healthy outlook. The passage climaxes with a kind of ultimatum: "No one can serve two masters. Either you will hate the one and love the other, or you will be devoted to the one and despise the other. You cannot serve both God and Money" (v. 24). Money with a capital M here translates Mammon, an idol in Jesus' day. Either *Mammon* or *Money* can serve as a handy alias for theocapitalism.

So, for Jesus, the goal is not amassing capital; the goal is amassing a portfolio of good deeds, good deeds particularly identified with care for the poor.[3] For Jesus, exclusive concern for one's own self-interest qualifies one as "fool."

The way of the kingdom of God calls people to a higher concern than self- or national interest: namely, concern for the common good. And for Jesus, achieving the bottom line of profit and financial success without concern for the common good qualifies one uniquely—not for the heaven of the Fortune 500—but for hell.

With no apologies to Martin Luther, John Calvin, or modern evangelicalism, Jesus (in Luke 16:19) does not prescribe hell to those who refuse to accept the message of justification by grace through faith, or to those who are predestined for perdition, or to those who don't express faith in a favored atonement theory by accepting Jesus as their "personal Savior." Rather, hell—literal or figurative—is for the rich and comfortable who proceed on their way without concern for their poor neighbor day after day. As Jesus also makes clear in the story of the Good Samaritan (Luke 10:25–37), they fail to love their neighbors as themselves and fail to follow "what is written in the Law," and therefore will not inherit eternal life.[4]

In case after case, Jesus calls people to repent and defect from the goal of growing their personal wealth portfolios, and instead he calls them to grow their good deeds portfolios for the common good, especially the good of the poor and marginalized. The result will be a qualitative improvement in the lives of everyone.

Herman Daly defines *sustainable development* in exactly these terms: "development without growth beyond environmental carrying capacity, where development means qualitative improvement and growth means quantitative increase." He says, "The path of future progress is development, not growth." He calls this new path, not merely an economic system, but "an art of living" and "an ethic."[5]

It is encouraging to note that increasing numbers of business leaders—including the leaders of many multinational corporations—are embracing this ethic, using terms like "sustainability" and "the triple bottom line."[6] They are defecting from the undercover religion of theocapitalism and embracing a creed of *economic sustainability* (rather than maximum short-term profit), *ecological sustainability*, and *social sustainability* (which takes into account the preservation of families, communities, cultures, and other non-economic dimensions of life). In so doing, whether they realize it or not, they are aligning themselves with concerns central to the message of Jesus, the kingdom of God.[7]

2. The Law of Satisfaction Through Gratitude and Sharing

Second, Jesus overturns serenity through possession and consumption. Instead, he envisions satisfaction through gratitude and sharing. The word *consumption* is both fascinating and disturbing in this light. In an archaic usage, it referred to a wasting disease (tuberculosis), but now wasting has become the moral duty of participants in the suicide machine—who are known as *consumers*.

It's interesting to consider the importance of consumption in the biblical narrative. When the crisis of human evil is introduced in a passage beginning in Genesis 1:29 and ending in 2:20, forms of the words "eat" and "food" are used about twenty times. Consumption is closely linked with human evil. Adam and Eve live in harmony with creation in a garden, surrounded by food-bearing trees. But to be a human being is to live within creaturely limits in God's creation—reflected in self-restraint in regard to eating the fruit of "the knowledge of good and evil" (Genesis 2:17). If they break the limits represented by the fruit hanging on that tree, they will taste death (or as we said earlier, they will *decompose*).

Eve exceeds the limit, drawn to consume a fruit that "was good for food and was pleasing to the eye, and also desirable for gaining wisdom" (3:6). Adam joins her. As a result, an avalanche of alienation crashes into the human story—alienation from God, alienation from one another, alienation from oneself, and alienation from creation.

In the following chapters, brother is alienated from brother and a form of class violence enters the story, as the class of pastoralists (symbolized by Abel) is exterminated by the class of agriculturalists (symbolized by Cain). Soon new forms of institutionalized violence arise in great cities, so horrible that they are swept away by a flood of judgment. Eventually empires emerge, reflecting the imperial dream of unifying people under one dominating language and culture in Babel. Genesis provides a genealogy for all the pain and evil in the whole social structure of humans on planet Earth: it all can be traced back to a problem of consumption beyond limits.

How ironic, then, that consumption itself would be prescribed by the prosperity system as a cure for the disease of consumption. It is as if the snake of Genesis 3 is still whispering to Adams and Eves everywhere: *Consume more! You will not die! One more bite and you will be wise, like gods, without limits!*

Ironically, today's headlines describe a global pandemic of morbid obesity, as the McDonalds-ization of the planet proceeds according to plan, with "billions and billions served." Equally ironic, anorexia and bulimia, now on the increase in China, become localized, individual symptoms of this diffuse, systemic, consumptive pathology, frail human beings seeking relief from pathological consumption.

Both obesity and eating disorders become evidence that the prosperity system's second law, expressed in the concise formula *consumption = happiness*, or *possession = happiness*, is simply not working—in China, America, or anywhere else. According to David Korten:

> Comparative international studies . . . report that once a nation has achieved a moderate level of per capita income, further increases in wealth bring only slight increases in per-

ceived well-being. . . . Beyond the minimum level of income essential to meeting basic needs, the authentic relationships of strong communities are a far better predictor of happiness and emotional health than the size of one's paycheck or bank account. . . . Over the last half of the twentieth century, inflation-adjusted U.S. gross domestic product per capita tripled, yet surveys indicate the self-reports of satisfaction with life have remained virtually flat.[8]

Over the last fifty years in the United States, for example, we have doubled household incomes largely through the addition of wives and mothers to the paid workplace. We have also doubled the ratio of cars to people, and we have doubled the frequency of eating out, but we are slightly less happy.[9]

According to a global survey, three out of four of the happiest people groups in the world are not rich consumers. Using a scale where 7 marks the maximum of happiness, *Forbes* magazine's richest Americans came in second (5.8), tied with the Pennsylvania Amish. Close behind them (5.7) were the Masai of East Africa, a tribe without electricity or running water who live in huts made of dung. Happiest of all—ahead of America's richest—were the Inuits of Greenland (5.9). All this research suggests that a climate of warm, cohesive community and its attendant values are more important than material comfort or other external factors (like climate—in view of the Inuits!) in producing happiness.[10] Even seeing the numbers, though, how many of us believe what they're telling us?

Ironically, a materialistic culture doesn't suffer from an overemphasis on material things, but rather on a strange process of their disappearance. For the man who owns twenty Rolls-Royces, it's not simply the cars, the physical objects themselves, that he gets pleasure from, but the *number* of cars. For the anxious middle-class fellow living next to the infamous Joneses, it's not that he gets pleasure from his green, weed-free lawn; it's that his lawn is *as good as* his neighbors', or maybe even *better than* theirs. For the teenager who downloads a song every day on the Internet, it's not the song itself that counts—he hardly has time to listen to the songs, much less enjoy them; it's that he's keeping up with *the latest*, so he can have "bragging rights" to his friends when the subject of music comes up. The middle-aged woman who spends a fortune on cosmetics seldom appreciates the quality of the products themselves; for the most part, she isn't after good skin-care anyway. She's after *youth, beauty, fashion*. The CEO making a six- or seven-figure salary can't enjoy his current salary or his huge investment portfolio: he's too busy working to double his salary and triple his investment portfolio. It's not about enjoyment for him; it's about *growth*.

Growth is an abstraction. And this is the irony of the prosperity system in the suicide machine. It is, in a sense, utterly Platonic. The material thing doesn't count in itself: what counts is the abstraction, the immaterial idea behind it—*number, status, coolness, youth, beauty, fashion, growth*. The things themselves—cars, cosmetics, companies, songs—are just means to the end, which is an abstraction that is by nature unattainable. After all, when have you reached the end of growth, or youth, or fashion, or status, or power?

Jesus' oft-quoted but seldom-considered words burst this bubble: "What good is it for you to gain the whole world, yet forfeit your soul?" (Matthew 16:26).

Catholic philosopher Josef Pieper remarks that happiness is indeed to be had from things, but only things that are contemplated, or appreciated. The pursuit of more things—to the point of "gaining the world"—distracts one from contemplating or appreciating what one already has, and therefore guarantees that one lacks happiness.[11] After all, what businessperson spends time contemplating his loyal and happy customers, appreciating the relationships of trust they share, expressed in an ongoing exchange of money for goods and services rendered? Doesn't the average businessperson forget his current customers almost entirely, focusing instead on an abstraction like *market share*? (Many modern pastors, I have noticed, do the same, focusing on *growth rates* in attendance and giving and other similar abstractions, rather than on the faces and names of real people they are serving.)

So in this regard, gratitude becomes an act of defiant contemplation, expressing rebellion against the thousands of advertisements a year that tell you to want what you don't have, and not appreciate what you already have. Instead, gratitude celebrates what you do have, an exercise in contentment. It turns possession-without-appreciation into possession-with-appreciation, which produces happiness. And in so doing, it bonds the heart to the ultimate source of the gifts—God— instead of bonding the heart to the purveyor of the unfulfillable desire for abstraction, whether that be shoes (the abstraction of *easy status* through footwear) or fast food (the abstraction of *quick fullness* through palate grease) or cosmetics (the abstractions of *affordable beauty and eternal youth* through skin paint).[12]

When you picture a family bowing their heads before a meal, then, you begin to see this kind of simple, grateful appreciation as an act of defiance against and defection from the suicide machine. Similarly, their slow, appreciative eating of homemade (i.e., slow) food similarly expresses a rejection of the fast-food mentality.

Jesus' own practice of fasting ("People do not live on bread alone," he says during one fast [Matthew 4:4]) speaks of his awareness of the need to discipline consumption.[13] But even more striking, his miracles of feeding become powerful signs and wonders of an alternative economy that is not desperately anxious about consumption.[14]

Mark's version of one such story (6:30–44) begins in a fascinating way: "Then, because so many people were coming and going that they did not even have a chance to eat"—a profile of today's busy pace of life, we might add—"[Jesus] said to them, 'Come with me by yourselves to a quiet place and get some rest.'" Their need for a vacation is quickly interrupted, though, by a huge crowd eager to hear Jesus, people on whom "he had compassion . . . because they were like sheep without a shepherd" (v. 34).

The disciples later tell Jesus to send the people away so "they can . . . buy themselves something to eat" (v. 36). Jesus' reply contradicts both the words "buy" and "they/themselves." Instead of "they/themselves," he says "you," and instead of "buy" he says "give." The disciples (as usual) are confused: they can only imagine providing food by spending a year's wages in local markets. Jesus replies, "How many loaves do you have?" and adds, "Go and see" (v. 38). He wants them to count what they already have, because what they already have counts, and is, in fact, enough through God's gracious provision.

The five loaves and two fish they come up with are divided and distributed to the crowd, and twelve baskets are left over after all the people "ate and were satisfied" (v. 42). When I was a child, these stories were explained to me as evidence or proofs of Jesus' supernatural power, and that was it. But now, as an adult, that level of interpretation seems to me to miss much of the point. I see now that Jesus is engaging in powerful prophetic drama, demonstrating through sign and wonder a radically different economy, one that doesn't depend on spending more and buying more, but on discovering what you already have and sharing. And at the decisive moment, just before the miracle occurs, we see Jesus "taking the five loaves and the two fish and looking up to heaven," to give thanks (v. 41).

This is a different economy, indeed—one based on contemplative gratitude and neighborly sharing, not consuming more and more, faster and faster. In the minds of some readers, at this point, I'm sure a thousand practical questions are coming to mind—legitimate questions, such as, "Is this guy a Communist?" (no, I'm not) and "How could this kind of economic system ever be put into practice? What kind of detailed policies would it take? Isn't the devil in the details?" But Jesus seemed unconcerned with those details; he left them up to people like us, I think, to work out.

I believe it was this addiction that concerned Jesus as he challenged people to believe that there could be a better, more human, more satisfying alternative to the four economic laws of the Roman Empire. And the same can be true regarding the theocapitalist empire in our own day. If we don't believe Jesus' message, then we won't even seek for better alternatives, and so of course we won't work out the details. If we do believe him, what seems impossible may—as in the story—prove possible, and even exciting. The Gospels dare us to believe.

GROUP DIALOGUE QUESTIONS

1. The author uses the word *heroes* at the beginning of this chapter and at the end of the previous chapter. How do you respond to this word? Is it appropriate to this situation? Why or why not?
2. Summarize Jesus' alternatives to the first two laws of theocapitalism. Do you affirm these alternatives? Why or why not?
3. What insights does this chapter offer you about gratitude, happiness, and materialism? How could these insights help you in your life?
4. Several episodes from the life of Jesus are recounted in this chapter. Choose one, and find connections between it and experiences in your own life.
5. In what ways is the picture of Jesus presented in this chapter similar to and different from the picture you have had of Jesus in the past?

Collaboration for Co-liberation

In the previous chapter, we saw Jesus confront the first two economic laws of the theocapitalist empire. First, we considered how Jesus replaces the law of progress through rapid economic growth with the vision of *good deeds for the common good*. Second, we considered how Jesus replaces the law of serenity through possession and consumption with *satisfaction through gratitude and sharing*.

We also noted how important the imagery of food and eating was in his ministry. We have yet to mention one of the most important uses of eating imagery, though. It occurs in Galilee, the region where Jesus concentrated his ministry. Jesus could have focused his efforts in Jerusalem, in debates with the religious scholars and temple professionals there. But instead, just as John the Baptist chose to baptize far from the temple precincts in the wilderness of the Jordan, Jesus chose the rural region of Galilee as an interesting—and strategic—context for his work.

Galilee had suffered disproportionately under the Roman Empire.[1] The Romans demanded costly tribute (taxes both in cash and in the form of crops) from the farmlands of the region, and in choosing it as a focus of his ministry, Jesus was choosing an area characterized by unrest and insurrection. It is in this context that he delivers his Sermon on the Mount, and in which he pronounces blessings on eight groups, and in particular, the central group: "Blessed are those who hunger and thirst for justice, for they will be filled" (Matthew 5:6).[2]

3. The Law of Salvation Through Seeking Justice

These words convey Jesus' response to the third law of theocapitalism: Jesus replaces salvation by win-lose competition with salvation through seeking justice.

A hunger to consume, a thirst for abstractions like *more* or *growth*, produces ceaseless competition and a world divided into winners and losers. Jesus advocates a different kind of hunger and thirst, a hunger and thirst for justice. Competition won't save us, Jesus is saying. Justice will.

The word *competition* has a strange and almost mystical appeal to some devotees of the prosperity system of theocapitalism. If by competition we mean a respectful struggle that brings out the best in all competitors, this appeal seems legitimate enough. But if the term suggests a system that creates a few winners and many losers, we will find it hard to square with Jesus' emphasis on concern for neighbors, a concern that extends to enemies and that singles out "the losers" (the last, the least, and the lost) for special care.

So it is not the hunger for domination through competition that will save us, Jesus teaches. We must grow beyond that crude level so that we hunger and thirst for justice. When we realize that justice is about the right use of power, it becomes clear how much Jesus has to say on the subject.

Take, for example, the fascinating story found in Matthew 20:20–28. James and John accompany their mother to ask something of Jesus. She asks if one of her sons may sit at Jesus' right hand, and one at his left—as his vice president and secretary of state, to put it in contemporary American terms. It's the typical question of people devoted to competition: those who are hungry to make it to the top, to attain the seats of power, who want a promise, a guarantee that they'll get what they want. Jesus' reply suggests that his movement will not bring the kind of victory that awards top positions to the winners, but rather, his kingdom will bring profound suffering to its leaders.

The other ten disciples hear about the attempt to gain top cabinet positions, and they're incensed, perhaps because they resent being treated as competitors rather than teammates by James and John, perhaps because they, too, were hoping for high positions in what they expected would be a rather typical new regime. Then Jesus calls the whole group together and says:

> You know that the rulers of the Gentiles lord it over them, and their high officials exercise authority over them. Not so with you. Instead, whoever wants to become great among you must be your servant, and whoever wants to be first must be your slave—just as the Son of Man did not come to be served, but to serve, and to give his life as a ransom for many. (vv. 25–28)

It's striking that Jesus refers directly here to the Roman dominance system. In a similar passage in Luke (22:24–30), this kind of competitive conversation happens (of all places) at the Last Supper where Jesus has just spoken of his body and blood being given for them. Jesus says, "The kings of the Gentiles lord it over them; and those who exercise authority over them call themselves Benefactors. But you are not to be like that" (vv. 25–26).

Here Jesus shows political sensitivity to the ways people use the verbal camouflage of words like *benefactors* to make competition and domination covert. He shows the same sensitivity shortly after the incident with James, John, and their mother (Matthew 23:1–12), this time regarding the abuse of power of the religious leaders of their nation. They have a position of power, Jesus says—they "sit in Moses' seat." Using this power, they "tie up heavy, cumbersome loads and put them on other people's shoulders, but they themselves are not willing to lift a finger to move them" (v. 4). To avoid their abuse of power, Jesus tells his disciples not to take on titles that would grant them competitive advantage—rabbi (religious domination), father (familial domination), or teacher (intellectual domination).

Sadly, too few of us who bear the name Christian today seem to have taken Jesus' message seriously in this regard. We seem to believe that the drive for competition and victory will satisfy, not the hunger and thirst for justice. Sadly, many of our theologies focus on the evasion of justice—which is what an obsession with being forgiven and avoiding hell begins to resemble when it is not accompanied by a desire to forgive others and pursue justice on their behalf. A gospel of hell-evasion provides a cheap, convenient, and fast alternative to the gospel of the kingdom of God.

But it is the gospel of the kingdom of God that Jesus preaches, and about which he makes one of his most startling promises: "Seek first [God's] kingdom and his justice, and all these things will be given to you as well" (Matthew 6:33). Here, "all these things" refers to exactly the things we would say constitute prosperity: having enough to eat, enough to drink, enough to wear, along with a lack of anxiety about having enough for tomorrow too. Seeking prosperity without justice, Jesus says, is fruitless, maybe even suicidal. But seeking justice for all—the justice of God's kingdom—will bring the best and truest prosperity too.

In light of Hebrew grammatical construction, it is highly possible that when Jesus says, "Seek first God's kingdom and God's justice," he is not saying two things, but one: God's kingdom is God's justice—both of which are included in another of Jesus' appositives for the kingdom, which he had stated a few moments earlier: God's will being done on earth as it is in heaven (6:10). When that happens, justice comes. And with it comes freedom, which brings us to Jesus' confrontation of the fourth economic law of theocapitalism.

4. The Law of Freedom to Prosper by Building Better Communities

Jesus offers an alternative path to freedom—not through unaccountable corporations (the gangs of the rich) linked together to become wealthy using the labor of the poor, but rather through the rich and poor joining their labor for the building of a better world by the building of better communities.

The twentieth century was, in many ways, a battle between two economic systems. My friend Rene Padilla offers an interesting analysis of the two systems from a Latin American perspective.[3] Communism, he says, specialized in distribution but failed at production. As a result, it ended up doing a great job of distributing poverty evenly. Capitalism, he says, was excellent at production but weak at distribution. As a result, it ended up rewarding the wealthy with obscene amounts of wealth while the poor suffered on in horrible degradation and indignity. Latin America is still waiting for a viable alternative, as is the whole planet.

The twenty-first century began in the aftermath of the defeat of Marxism. The story of the coming century will likely be the story of whether a sustainable form of capitalism can be saved from theocapitalism, or whether unrestrained theocapitalism will result in such gross inequity between rich and poor that violence and counter-violence will bring civilization to a standstill, or perhaps worse.

Marxist revolutionaries have tended to see the oppressed poor as morally good and the rich as morally unsalvageable. Where their revolutions put the proletariat into power, the revolutionaries generally prove themselves as corruptible as the elites they replaced.

Theocapitalists have done the opposite: they have tended to see the rich as morally good and the poor as morally culpable for their own poverty; the hard work and cleverness of the former have made them rich, and the laziness, irresponsibility, and looseness of the latter have made them poor. As a result, theocapitalists have tended to trust the rich, to believe that they deserve freedom and support, not accountability and oversight. They seek to bring the suffering rich "relief" from taxes, for example, and they speak of the "burden" of government regulations. If the rich profit more and more, they believe, benefits will trickle down to the poor. The best thing the rich can do for the poor, then, is make all the money they can, and the best thing the rest of us can do for the poor is to encourage the rich, to relieve them of their burdens so they can, like profitable prophets and priests, mediate economic salvation to the world.[4]

Whatever the merits of trickle-down economics, Jesus offers a different plan. For him, both the poor and the rich need saving; one needs liberation from addictive wealth and the other, liberation from oppressive poverty. Part of the work of the kingdom of God is to turn them from their ideologies of exploitation and victimization to a vision of collaboration in the kingdom of God—a kind of kingdom *co-liberation*.

Jesus' encounter with a height-challenged tax collector named Zaccheus (Luke 19:1–10) illustrates his response to the law of freedom through trust in elites. As a tax collector, Zaccheus represents the Herodian compromise: try to make a quick and lasting profit from the Roman Empire's occupation. He is a short man who made it big by hitching his wagon to the elite Roman train. Jesus surprises Zaccheus by inviting himself to the man's home for a meal. His desire to associate with Zaccheus surprises the crowd as well, who are scandalized that Jesus would show acceptance for a collaborator of this sort. But Jesus obviously has a plan: his connection with Zaccheus will make space for Zaccheus to repent, to defect from the system of progress through rapid growth, and instead to care for the common good: "Look, Lord! Here and now I give half of my possessions to the poor, and if I have cheated anybody out of anything, I will pay back four times the amount" (Luke 19:8).[5]

Jesus' reply is striking. He pronounces that this man has received *salvation* (from, we could say, greed, from a dark outlook, from the hell of being under God's condemnation, from self-centeredness, from spiritual bankruptcy, and from a loss of identity as a Jew through participation in the empire of Rome rather than the kingdom of God). Jesus then explains that his very purpose in coming is to save people in exactly this way.

Capitalists are right, or at least partly so: many rich people are good people—hardworking, clever, dedicated, disciplined, and exactly the kinds of people who should prosper. But unless they use their prosperity for the common good, they find themselves working for a theocapitalist prosperity system rather than the love economy of God. In the theocapitalist system, all that is expected is the single bottom line of return on investment, but in the love economy of God, the stakes are higher and success is more meaningful: the bottom line of economic profit is exchanged for the top line of the common good.

Jesus explores this theme using a business story about a manager (Luke 12:42–48). Jesus pictures God as a landowner for whom the manager works. The manager is put in charge of some of the landowner's employees "to give them their food allowance at the proper time" (v. 42). Here, the "bottom line" is not return on investment or profits compared to losses. It is, rather, caring for one's employees in a way that will please God. First, Jesus paints a picture of a manager doing a good job, but then he describes a manager who doesn't take his accountability to the landowner seriously. Instead, he "begins to beat the other servants, both men and women, and to eat and drink and get drunk" (v. 45). The outcome for that fellow, Jesus says, will not be pretty. Then he says, "From everyone who has been given much, much will be demanded; and from the one who has been entrusted with much, much more will be asked" (v. 48). In this light, wealth and power become not a carte blanche for unaccountability, but instead a matter of responsibility and accountability.

As we've seen, the global economy, as a collaboration among corporate elites, currently lacks both accountability and responsibility to local communities. Meanwhile, those local communities (where they still survive) are bound by a primal human bond: neighborliness. In Jesus' teaching, from the Great Commandment to the story of the Good Samaritan, neighborliness is a duty that cannot be escaped or avoided. Even the stranger and the enemy, in Jesus' vision, must be treated as a neighbor.

So for the global economy to be liberated from service to theo-capitalism and connected instead to God's love economy, it needs to replace the fourth law of freedom through global corporate elites with a vision of co-liberation for neighborliness and community building.

Herman Daly again expresses the challenge well:

> The true road to international community is that of a federation of communities—communities of communities—not the destruction of local and national communities in the service of

a single cosmopolitan world of footloose money managers who constitute not a community, but merely an interdependent, mutually vulnerable, unstable coalition of short-term interests.[6]

U2 front man and rock-prophet Bono also understands the challenge: "Distance does not decide who is your brother and who is not. The church is going to have to become the conscience of the free market if it's to have any meaning in the world—and stop being its apologist."[7]

Economics need not be a dismal science or the study of so-called filthy lucre. It can instead be the story of human beings working together for the common good in God's love economy. Each person, using the gifts she has been given, through trial and error, success and failure, struggles to become the best she can be at what she is gifted to do. She brings into the world her own unique good works or good deeds—well-grown vegetables, well-made clothing, well-written computer programs, well-administered offices, well-performed surgeries, well-designed airplanes, well-taught classes, well-governed nations, well-crafted poems—each an expression of her uniqueness as a person created in the image of God and as a citizen in the kingdom of God. Through the medium of money, she exchanges the fruits of her labors with others who bring different goods and services to the economic table.

Together they are deeply grateful for all they earn and have, and they are careful to share with those who are in need. Where there are systemic injustices that privilege some and disadvantage others, they work for justice so the system becomes more of what it can and should be. Those who are more prosperous, believing that more is expected from them, seek to use their advantages to help those who are less prosperous, and together rich and poor seek to build better communities that, in turn, build a better world. This collaborative pursuit, they discover, brings the co-liberation of true prosperity.

It's a grand dream, far from reality in many ways, but closer than we may think. It's the kind of dream that can turn the prosperity system from suicide to hope.

GROUP DIALOGUE QUESTIONS

1. Summarize Jesus' response to the final two laws of theocapitalism in this chapter.
2. Share some insights about *competition* as used in this chapter. Share an experience from your life where competition was positive, and share an experience where it was negative.
3. Share some insights about *verbal camouflage* as used in this chapter. Share an experience from your life where you heard or used verbal camouflage.
4. Read Matthew 6:33, and discuss what this statement promises. How does this relate to your life?
5. Summarize what this chapter says about theocapitalism and its relation to communism.
6. How do you respond to the word *co-liberation*?
7. If you are well-off, how many poor people do you know? If you are poor, how many well-off people do you know? Why do you think it is normally rare for rich and poor to socialize with one another? What benefits would come to you from knowing more poor (or rich) people personally? How could you experience co-liberation with them?
8. What is the dream the author closes this chapter with? Put it into your own words. Is it your dream too?

Part 7

THE
EQUITY
SYSTEM

On the Side of the Rebel Jesus

I came of age in the late 1960s and '70s. Like most people, I have a special affinity for the music of my coming-of-age years. I love all kinds of music, but I have a special place in my heart for the singers and songwriters of those years: Joni Mitchell, Carole King, James Taylor, Bob Dylan, and Jackson Browne. One of my all-time favorite songs comes from Jackson Browne; it's called "The Rebel Jesus."

The song begins with a Christmas scene, streets full of light and laughter and Christmas music. People gather to celebrate the season . . . "the birth of the rebel Jesus," Browne says. Of course, the word "rebel" interrupts this peaceful holiday scene; the jarring intrusion is not accidental, and the tension it creates runs like a tight strand of barbed wire through the song.

Browne continues reflecting on happy Christians celebrating Christmas, singing about Jesus as Prince of Peace and Savior. But all is not well, because these very people fill up his churches with pride and gold. Not only that, but they turn the temple of creation—mountains, streams, valleys, and fields which are for Browne God's true sanctuary of worship—into a "robber's den." The arrogant pursuit of wealth and the careless plundering of creation, Browne knows, are the kinds of things "the rebel Jesus" would have spoken against strongly.

Browne can't help being cynical even about holiday charity. The seasonal giving of gifts among relatives contrasts with the locks and guns with which people guard their personal assets the rest of the year. Browne allows that, during the Christmas season, people may indulge in a little holiday generosity for the poor among us. But he quickly adds that our charity goes only skin-deep, because if we go farther than charity—to the realm of justice—and deal with the systems that make and keep poor people in poverty, we will get "the same as the rebel Jesus." The song climaxes with Browne self-identifying as "a heathen and a pagan," but then comes the dramatic punch line: "on the side of the rebel Jesus."

Browne's use of disturbing religious language—"heathen" and "pagan"—is significant. He suggests that there is a kind of economic orthodoxy that may allow or even encourage us to throw some dollars toward the poor, but this orthodoxy commands us never to question the systems that create and reinforce poverty. Anyone who interferes—anyone who refuses to accept the locks and guns, the pride and gold, the meager generosity, the carelessness about the environment, and the obliviousness to economic justice for the poor—will be banished from the inner circle of the pious and respectable, and will "get the same as the rebel Jesus."[1]

THE DYSFUNCTIONS OF THE SOCIETAL SYSTEM

In recent months, I have walked the streets of some of the poorest places on earth . . . muddy or dusty, trash-strewn and crowded, edged with open sewers, narrow passageways crowded with barefoot children, skinny dogs with vacant eyes and ribs like picket fences, sandaled and unemployed adults trying to scrape by somehow. Slums and barrios, squatter areas and informal settlements . . . from Khayelitsha in South Africa to Nueva Suyapa in Honduras to Kibera in Kenya, from the seemingly endless slums in Mexico City to poor neighborhoods in downtown Baltimore and Washington, DC, where I live. I have talked with desperately poor people in their homes, in community centers, in overcrowded buses, on the street, in homeless shelters and refugee camps, in jail, in local churches. These experiences have converted me, like Jackson Browne, into "a heathen and a pagan" in regard to the dominant system, because I can no longer "give a little to the poor" without interfering in the business of why they are poor, an interference that I believe Jackson Browne is right to associate with Jesus.[1]

Equity System

These are concerns of the equity system of our societal machinery. But the equity system is plagued by dysfunction. First, the equity system is programmed by the dominant framing story; how can it get leverage to deal with inequities caused by that narrative's own deficiencies and pathologies?

Second, the equity system is rigged by both the dominant framing story and the dysfunctional prosperity system to work for the insiders—the aggressive, the dominant, the hasty, and the historically advantaged. So, even if it can handle small problems of inequity among the insiders, it is blindly biased against the inequities of outsiders, no matter how big those problems may be.

Third, all existing equity systems were developed to deal with environmental assumptions and economic realities of the modern nation-state in the industrial age; they move too slowly to deal with fast and expansive problems emerging in a postindustrial digital age and global economy in an era of global warming.

Fourth, since the equity system depends on the prosperity system for its funding and therefore its survival, nobody should expect the equity system to be authorized to change the rules of the game by which the prosperous insiders prosper. For these reasons and more, the equity system is rendered incapable of dealing with the growing inequities of today's world. As a result, the equity system spends more and more of its energy on comparably less and less significant issues, thereby trivializing itself, producing the status quo: political and corporate and military entities working for their own self-interest, with decreasing restraint, increasingly oblivious to the common good, callous or numb to the needs of the desperately poor.

Prosperity System

The prosperity system, as we've seen, can determine neither its own limits nor its own purpose, so in their absence it works obsessively in the pursuit of two abstractions: growth and speed. These abstract obsessions drive it mindlessly and relentlessly toward "more," "bigger," and "faster," but never allow us to ask "More what?" "Why bigger?" and "Faster to where, and for what purpose?" Driven in this mindless way, the prosperity system is guaranteed to exceed our environmental limits as soon and as extravagantly it can, and to produce intolerable and unsustainable inequity along the way.

As it rewards the aggressive, the dominant, and the hasty, the prosperity system withholds rewards from the peaceful, the humble, and the morally sensitive. Those who arrive first to a field of competition, especially those with either needed tools or weapons to commandeer resources from others, are given an insurmountable unfair advantage. As we've seen, then, the prosperity system produces some insiders who prosper quickly, leaving others farther and farther outside, falling farther and farther behind.

As I've suggested already, this ever-widening gap between extremely prosperous insiders and intractably poor outsiders produces a kind of double hatred. The poor first envy, then resent, and eventually hate the rich, who take up more and more of the space in the world—physical space, but also environmental, economic, and cultural space. The rich sense this hatred and respond with fear, which eventually becomes a form of hatred too.

Security System

So the societal machine sputters. An incoherent and self-destructive framing story programs it. An aggressive prosperity system drives it, pedal to the metal, ignoring speed limits and lane markers. An increasingly trivialized and co-opted equity system tries to regulate it, but fails, so the gap between rich and poor grows wider and deeper.

As a result, the security system is continually pumped up with high-octane jet fuel—combustible resentment from the poor and fiery fear from the rich. These security tensions go off the scale as the global prosperity system reaches and exceeds environmental limits, throwing the environment into radical instability. The ensuing desertification, increasingly intense catastrophic storms, rising ocean levels, and spread of human and agricultural epidemics send millions of people into a new status as internally displaced persons or international refugees—or corpses. Add to this unstable equation nuclear weapons. Then add chemical and biological weapons. Then add terrorism. Finally, add the fact that many sectors of the security system augment their income by manufacturing and selling weapons.

Taken together, these rising international tensions guarantee that the marginalized poor will become more and more resentful, more and more tempted to violence, more and more desperate, while the rich insiders will become more and more afraid and obsessed with security. Here we have a perfect recipe for frequent outbreaks of violence and catastrophic war. It's a suicidal scenario.

WHAT ARE WE FREE FOR?

That's why so much depends on the equity system's ability to intervene, recalibrate, reorder. But we're living in an age of "free markets," and the word *free* suggests that the equity system should be in handcuffs, if not a straitjacket so as to not interfere.

One naturally asks, What are markets to be free from? What are they freed for? For what purpose? Are markets freed from government regulation so that the rich can achieve luxurious levels of wealth, leaving the poor to starve or barely survive in degradation and indignity? Are markets free so that inequity can reach its apogee, providing liberty and justice for a very few? Are markets free so that those who plunder the environment can do so without accountability, or so that those who exploit the labor of the poor can do so without impunity? Is there no equity system that seeks to redress these injustices? Are the powerful free for the purpose of pursuing prosperity and security without equity?

The answer to the final question, it appears, is yes. In an essay titled "Democracy Matters Are Frightening in Our Time," African-American scholar and activist Cornell West assessed the economic and political landscape in the United States. His tone is not conciliatory, but perhaps you'll agree stiff rhetoric is appropriate in this case:

> The first dogma of free-market fundamentalism posits the unregulated and unfettered market as idol and fetish. This glorification of the market has led to a callous corporate-dominated political economy in which business leaders (their wealth and power) are to be worshipped—even despite the recent scandals—and the most powerful corporations are delegated magical powers of salvation rather than relegated to democratic scrutiny concerning both the ethics of their business practices and their treatment of workers. This largely unexamined and unquestioned dogma that supports the policies of both Democrats and Republicans in the United States—and those of most political parties in other parts of the World—is a major threat to the quality of democratic life and the well-being of most peoples across the globe. It yields an obscene level of wealth inequality, along with its corollary of intensified class hostility and hatred. It also redefines the terms of what we should be striving for in life, glamorizing materialistic gain, narcissistic pleasure, and the pursuit of narrow individualistic preoccupations—especially for young people here and abroad.[2]

If West's use of the term "obscene" seems extreme, consider the facts globally.

The richest 1 percent of the world's population owns almost 40 percent of total wealth, and the richest 5 percent owns 70 percent of the wealth. Take the assets of the world's three richest individuals and you have wealth that exceeds the combined gross domestic product (GDP) of the world's forty-eight poorest countries.[3]

According to the United Nations Development Program, "In

today's world, deepening impoverishment and increasing enrichment appear to go hand in hand. In 1969 the incomes of the wealthiest 20 percent of the world's population were 30 times higher than those of the poorest 20 percent of the earth's people. By 1990 that gap had doubled: the incomes of the wealthiest 20 percent were 60 times higher than those of the poorest 20 percent. The difference factor is now 83."[4] In Africa, where half of the population suffers in extreme poverty, the statistics have "actually grown worse over the past two decades as the world has grown more prosperous."[5]

In the year 2000, the world's developed nations contributed aid and foreign investments to the developing nations that amounted to 3 percent of their GDP. But in that same year, developing nations paid the developed nations 6.3 percent of their GDP in debt repayment, more than twice what they received. The result? The developed nations profited and the developing nations lost ground. In 2005, the G8 nations cancelled some debts for developing nations— 2 percent of those debts, to be exact. Meanwhile, the conditions that lead to increasing indebtedness remain unaddressed.

It is no surprise, then, that six million children under the age of five starve each year—an annual unacknowledged holocaust. The progress we were making in eliminating childhood starvation in the past has reached a standstill. Current projections indicate that over one billion people now face a decline in their current living standards, which are *already poor.*[6]

Since 1950, global economic output has increased by 600 percent, but 80 percent of this increased income was shared by 20 percent of the world's people, leaving the other 80 percent of people living virtually unchanged lives.[7]

People living in the United States might feel that their situation is better, but the United States is, in this respect, a microcosm of the world—although it is a much richer microcosm: the gap between the rich and poor is growing greater and greater, with the rich becoming richer at a rapid rate, and the poor improving only slightly, if at all. The United States is in the bottom 25 percent of all nations in terms of wealth distribution, and runs dead last among industrialized nations.[8] In 1998, the richest 1 percent of US house-holds held 47 percent of all household financial assets. There are, of course, strong racial correlations to this inequity: the average Anglo household has a net worth that is 5.5 times the average African-American household.[9]

In terms of annual income, the richest 1 percent of Americans receives 15 percent of the nation's annual income, more than the com-bined income of the bottom 40 percent. In other words, less than three million Americans earn more than the combined income of one hun-dred million of their fellow Americans. Their share has increased by nearly 90 percent in less than twenty years. If you take the top 20 percent of wage-earners and compare them to the bottom 20 per-cent, the ratio jumped from 18:1 in 1990 to 24:1 in 2000.[10]

The skyrocketing inequity is even more striking among CEOs. The ratio of the average CEO salary to the salary of the average American worker (after taxes) was 12:1 in 1960, 35:1 in 1974, 151:1 in 1995, and reached 301:1 in 2003.[11]

To Cornell West, these trends are downright un-American, denying the primal, revolutionary American belief that "the consoli-dation of elite power was the primary object of democratic revolt." The American Revolution that decried taxation without representa-tion has sold itself to another form of nonrepresentative tyranny: "At this moment our imperialist elites are casting themselves as the defenders of our democracy. . . . Our business elites have cloaked themselves in the rhetoric of the unfettered free market and of the inevitable juggernaut of corporate globalization, justifying an obscene exacerbation of wealth inequality."[12]

THE "R" WORD

Some readers may be thinking, *What's wrong with a growing gap between rich and poor? Isn't it a good thing that rich people are being rewarded for their hard work?* People who ask such questions often haven't seen what I've seen: huge factories where people—mostly women, and often, mostly young girls—work harder than any CEO has ever worked, running sewing machines for eighteen hours a day, seven days a week, earning pennies an hour. They are glad for these jobs because they are much better than having no work and no income at all. But their labor enriches, not them, but already-rich people in New York, Los Angeles, Paris, London, or Hong Kong. This kind of inequity can only lead in one direction: *revolution.*

The "R" word brings to mind a conversation I had a few months ago in South Africa. I was having dinner with a man who had spent several years in prison for participating in revolutionary activities against the apartheid regime in his country. His methods in those days were violent, inspired by Marxist revolutions in other parts of the world. While in prison he became a believer in Christ, and then after his release, a pastor, and eventually, a denominational official. As he rose in the religious world, he distanced himself from politics and economics.

He had heard me speak on these matters a few days before our dinner. "I went home the other night after you spoke," he said, "and picked up *Das Kapital* by Marx. I hadn't read it in over twenty years. Your lecture made me realize that we have to think about economics again. Marx's prescription was faulty, but at least he diagnosed the problem: the exploited and excluded poor won't abide their marginalization forever. We escaped a bloody revolution in 1994 when we peacefully dismantled apartheid. But if we can't dismantle the inequity of our current economic system, we will have an explosion of violence that nobody can imagine. The streets will run red. I feel it. I feel it when I walk in the slums. It's like a volcano, ready to explode—the anger of the poor, the hopelessness of the poor."

The word *explosion,* of course, is apt. Terrorism and violence tick like a time bomb where inequity has a free market. We seem to have our choice made clear: the way of "the rebel Jesus," or the way of the violent revolution.

GROUP DIALOGUE QUESTIONS

1. Respond to the terms "heathen" and "pagan" in the Jackson Browne song. If possible, listen to the song together two or three times.

2. Share any experiences you have had in places of extreme poverty. If you haven't had any experiences, consider watching a movie as a group that will give you a feeling for life in a slum or refugee camp—*Tsotsi, City of God,* or *Blood Diamond,* for example.

3. This chapter provides a kind of summary of what's wrong with the societal machinery. Try to summarize these dysfunctions in your own words.

4. Which statistic in this chapter most struck you, and why?

5. How does this chapter help you understand terrorism?

6. Imagine you are a poor person living in a slum in a desperately poor nation. Would you be hopeless? If you had hope, what would that look like? What would the word *revolution* mean to you in those circumstances?

Beyond Blame and Shame

Whenever the subjects of inequity and poverty come up, many rich and middle-class people feel they are being blamed and shamed for the poverty of others, when all they have done is taken advantage of their advantages, worked hard, and reaped good consequences. True, some rich people are corrupt, hard-hearted, and careless; they very much deserve blame and scorn for their behavior. But blaming the rich for the poverty of the poor can be another expression of inequity. It assumes that the relationship is linear and works like this:

But a more accurate diagram would work like this:

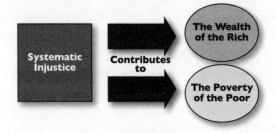

Whether the poor blame poverty on the rich, or the rich blame poverty on the poor—an economics of blame and shame is blind to the reality of systemic injustice.

JESUS' MESSAGE ABOUT SUBVERTING THE SYSTEM

Jesus, though, was not blind to this reality. For Jesus, the societal system often needed to be subverted because it was riddled with injustice.

Consider, for example, his thinking in regard to the so-called justice system of his day. It's best, he suggests, to avoid society's justice system when possible—to seek reconciliation outside of the courts (Matthew 5:25–26). The justice system has a mechanistic quality to it that grinds away, producing "fair" punishment while failing to produce true reconciliation. This level of just punishment might satisfy "the justice of the scribes and Pharisees" (Matthew 5:20; author's translation), but it is not the justice of the kingdom of God, which is not satisfied until there is true reconciliation.

Or consider Jesus' sensitivity to the systemic injustice of the economic system of his day. In Matthew 18:23–35, Jesus tells the story of a servant—probably a poor tenant farmer—who owed the landowner (or master) a huge debt. The landowner requires justice: "The master ordered that he and his wife and his children and all that he had be sold to repay the debt" (v. 25). The servant then asks for patience and promises to repay, and the master—going far beyond the request—actually cancels the debt. Then the servant goes out and demands repayment from a peer who can't repay and who also asks for mercy. But the recently forgiven servant responds in a merciless and unforgiving way, throwing his neighbor into jail—demanding a penal justice that is devoid of mercy. His peers are incensed and report his behavior to the master, who replies, "Shouldn't you have had mercy on your fellow servant just as I had on you?" (v. 33). For Jesus, clearly, penal fairness that requires punishment by the book but lacks mercy isn't the kind of justice desired by God.

Jesus' approach to subverting the economic system of his day is even clearer (yet more unsettling) in another parable, in which a landowner agrees to hire day laborers for a full day's work, at the wage of one denarius—around twenty dollars in today's currency (Matthew 20:1–16). Day laborers in Jesus' day, as in our own, are already vulnerable people: landless, jobless, living hand-to-mouth. As the day progresses, the landowner hires on more workers at midday, at midafternoon, and late in the afternoon. At day's end, he pays them all one denarius. Those hired at the beginning of the day feel slighted and complain, but the master again responds with a question: "Didn't you agree to work for a denarius? . . . Don't I have the right to do what I want with my own money? Or are you envious because I am generous?" (vv. 13, 15).

Interestingly, the workers' complaint is about equality: "You have made them equal to us who have borne the burden of the work and the heat of the day" (v. 12). They resent the equality of reward for an inequality of burden and work, but God's justice goes beyond mathematical equality. It seeks a kind of healing equity that takes into account, not just burden borne and work accomplished, but also the unequal opportunity faced by the various workers at the beginning of the day. The fact that there wasn't enough work (or opportunity) for everyone seems to be a factor in the mind of the employer.

By including that inequality in his equation, Jesus creates an economy of care for the common good. In this light, the justice of God is not unfair; it goes beyond fairness to include a concern for social sustainability, healing, and transformation; it doesn't fall short of fairness, but its fairness includes a grace (my friend David Anderson calls it "gracism"[1]) that can heal society and undermine systemic injustice, not just maintain its status quo.

Something similar occurs in Luke 16, which we considered briefly in chapter 12. My old King James Bible inserted a title for the parable found there: "The Parable of the Unjust Steward"—but the word "unjust" revealed more about the presumptions of the Bible translator than about the teaching of Jesus. Again, Jesus uses the common economic situation in Galilee, where Roman taxes forced many small farmers to sell their land to rich landowners, reducing them to the status of tenant farmers. As we've already noted, landowners would frequently hire managers, or stewards, to be the middlemen, demanding a portion of crops from all the tenant farmers and saving the landowner from this unpleasant task . . . a task that would bring landowner and tenant face to face.

The middleman/manager in Jesus' story has been accused of poor management and waste, so the landowner demands an account. Jesus conveys the man's inner dialogue: "What shall I do now? My master is taking away my job. I'm not strong enough to dig, and I'm ashamed to beg—I know what I'll do so that, when I lose my job here, people will welcome me into their houses" (vv. 3–4). He goes to all the tenant farmers and cuts their debts: a debt of nine hundred gallons of olive oil is reduced by half, a debt of a thousand bushels of wheat is reduced to eight hundred.

To many modern readers, this move sounds like injustice, because we view it from the detached and privileged perspective of the landowner class. But Jesus sees the entire system as unjust. And so in his story, the man isn't condemned for malfeasance. By reducing an unfair debt that would further advantage the rich and further oppress the poor, the steward is actually decreasing injustice by assisting the disadvantaged tenant farmers, so he is praised for being shrewd. In essence, he has defected from the systemic injustice of the dominant system and has switched sides, seeking to help the poor instead of making a profit for himself by assisting the rich.

Jesus follows up the parable with words we've already heard from him: "No one can serve two masters. . . . You cannot serve both God and Money" (v. 13). Interestingly, Luke offers this epilogue to the parable: "The Pharisees, who loved money, heard all this and were sneering at Jesus" (v. 14). Obviously, they like the current system and see no injustice in it; the societal system is "working" for them in a way it isn't "working" for the tenant farmers. But Jesus tells them their concept of justice is skewed: "You are the ones who justify yourselves in the eyes of others, but God knows your hearts. What people value highly is detestable in God's sight" (v. 15).

Even if the conventional "justice" of the current economic system is "detestable in God's sight," these religious leaders act (recalling Bono's diagnosis) as the system's apologists. And their own religious system is similarly critiqued by Jesus, with rhetorical flourish: "You have a fine way of setting aside the commands of God," he says, letting the word "fine" sting with irony (Mark 7:9). Then he details the system, where people could discharge their duties to their parents by making a gift to the temple establishment instead. "Thus you nullify the word of God by your tradition that you have handed down. And you do many things like that," he says.

"Tradition" here is another word for system. Whether we're dealing with a dietary system ("Nothing outside you can defile you by going into you" [Mark 7:15]), the temple system ("A time is coming when you will worship the Father neither on this mountain nor in Jerusalem" [John 4:21]), or the Sabbath system ("The Sabbath was made for people, not people for the Sabbath" [Mark 2:27]), Jesus is acutely aware of the systemic injustice each may perpetuate. Just as Jesus judges as insufficient those punitive or penal justice systems that reward and punish without healing and reconciling, he notes how religious systems frequently work against the good and just purposes for which they were intended (Matthew 19:1–9, for example). Systemic injustice must be exposed and confronted wherever it occurs and replaced with a higher justice—one that "surpasses that of the Pharisees and teachers of the law" (Matthew 5:20), one that reflects the kingdom of God.

Similarly, Jesus constantly confronts and transgresses social systems or traditions of inequitable exclusion. In fact, one of Jesus' favorite images for the kingdom of God is a party to which "the wrong people" are invited. On one occasion, Jesus, himself a guest at a dinner party thrown by a Pharisee, offers this teaching: "But when you give a banquet, invite the poor, the crippled, the lame, the blind, and you will be blessed. Although they cannot repay you, you will be repaid at the resurrection of the righteous" (Luke 14:13–14).

He follows up with a parable that makes his meaning clear: the kingdom of God creates equitable space where the "lower classes" are treated with high dignity and respect, and where no advantages are given to the "higher classes." In other words, where the kingdom of God is, class distinctions and elitism disappear (Luke 14:15–24), the lost and excluded are recovered and given a place (Luke 15 demonstrates this with three stories), and a new inclusive equity appears. Jesus demonstrates this equity wherever he goes, breaking social convention by welcoming outcasts (a woman with a gynecological disorder, prostitutes, lepers, Samaritans, tax collectors, and others) as equals.

Jesus' treatment of women is especially striking. He rejects the chauvinism and eroticism that typically team up to reduce women to inferior status. He includes women among his traveling entourage (Luke 8:3; 23:55), honors them, and protects them from critique (Matthew 26:10). He defends the right of a woman to "sit at his feet"—which (contrary to its contemporary sound) suggests not dishonor but honor, as this is the place of a disciple, an identity normally held exclusively by men (Luke 10:38–42). When he extends extraordinary respect to children (Luke 18:15–17), when he rejects typical terms of status (Matthew 23:1–12), and when he washes his disciples' feet (John 13:1–17), he further sabotages the systemic inequities of class and hierarchy and models a radical new kind of equity where little ones are honored, class distinctions disappear, and leaders stoop to serve.

AN INCREDIBLE, SHRINKING GOSPEL

Through history, some adherents to the Christian religion, though not enough, have shared Jesus' perspective. Methodist pastor and activist Duane Clinker recalls John Wesley's deep sensitivity to systemic injustice.[2] For Wesley, "The gospel of Christ knows of no religion, but social; no holiness but social holiness."[3] Reflecting on Wesley's term "social holiness" and his integral approach to mission, Clinker observes, "As humans we inherit a certain history. We inherit sin caused by decisions made in previous eras. We inherit a sort of sin 'frozen' into the institutions and social arrangements within which we are birthed."[4] With this understanding of social holiness, no wonder Wesley was an early convert to the cause of abolishing slavery.

Sadly, like many concepts in the modern era, the concept of holiness did not retain the profoundly social dimension it had for Wesley, but over time shrank to a matter of personal rule keeping. David Lowes Watson and Douglas Meeks articulate the danger of shrinking or flattening Jesus' social message to personalized, privatized dimensions:

> Only a fraction of our sins are personal. By far the greater part are sins of neglect, sins of default, our social sin, our systemic sin, our economic sin. For these sins Christ died, and continues to die. For these sins Christ atoned, and continues to atone. . . . As long as evangelism presents a gospel centered on the need for personal salvation, individuals will acquire a faith that focuses on maximum benefits with minimal obligations, and we will change the costly work of Christ's atonement into the pragmatic transaction of a salvific contract. . . . The sanctifying grace of God in Jesus Christ is meant not just for the sinner but also for a society beset by structural sin.[5]

About a hundred years ago, Walter Rauschenbusch expressed a similar sensitivity to systemic injustice in *A Theology for the Social Gospel*: "Individualistic theology has not trained the spiritual intelligence of Christian men and women to recognize and observe spiritual entities beyond the individual."[6] In other words, many of our religious institutions have taught us to see no horizon for the message of Jesus beyond the soul of the individual.

Jacques Ellul, a twentieth-century French Christian scholar in the Reformed tradition, agreed:

> A major fact of our present civilization is that more and more sin becomes collective, and the individual is forced to participate in collective sin. Everyone bears the consequences

of the faults of others. This becomes particularly poignant when nations are at war, for instance, but is true of all social situations.[7]

We must take seriously the full dimensions of collective sin, as contemporary Pentecostal theologian Eldin Villafane has said: "Our spirituality, and the very gospel that we preach, needs to be as big and ubiquitous as sin and evil. We will falter in our spirituality and thus grieve the Spirit if 'our struggle with evil' does not 'correspond to the geography of evil.'"[8] When, in the words of David Korten, "ordinary people find their choices controlled by the hierarchies of big business, big government, big education, big unions, big media, and big religion," a small gospel will seem pathetic and incredible.[9] Because sin and evil are so "big and ubiquitous," and because "the geography of evil" extends so far beyond the dimension of the individual soul, any gospel capable of confronting today's global crises must be correspondingly expansive.

Sadly, in too many quarters we continue to reduce the scope of the gospel to the individual soul and the nuclear family, framing it in a comfortable, personalized format—it's all about personal devotions, personal holiness, and a personal Savior. This domesticated gospel will neither rock any boats nor step out of them into stormy waters. We have in many ways responded to the big global crises of our day with an incredible, shrinking gospel. The world has said, "No thanks."[10]

In this big world of "collective sin" and complex, collective realities "beyond the individual," Duane Clinker realizes that "specific evil action is not required to wipe out vast sections of humanity, but simple apathy."[11] To appropriate the words of nineteenth-century statesman Edmund Burke, all that is necessary for our contemporary global crises to destroy us is for enough good people to do nothing.

WHAT CAN BE DONE?

Aided and abetted by a shrunken gospel and widespread apathy, the gears of "big business, big government, big education, big unions, big media, and big religion" will grind on in systemic injustice. All compassionate efforts to help victims of injustice—as essential as they are—will be overwhelmed by these big systems that constantly create and renew more injustice as a by-product of every transaction.

What can be done to deal with this gross and growing inequity that is being produced by our societal machinery? Many claim that the invisible hand of free markets will resolve these problems naturally, over time. But to reiterate J. F. Rischard's analysis:

> Whether from intellectual laziness or from single-minded pursuit of ideology, what these free-market fundamentalists fail to see is that while central planners were either cretins or fools, the market is a moron. An effective moron, but a moron nevertheless: left to its own devices, it will churn away mindlessly. . . . [If we are complacent,] if we leave all problem-solving to the market, emerging social problems will be left unattended. . . . We'll end up with scores of unnecessary social stresses over the next twenty years—and a lot of protesters on the street.[12]

If we have confidence in the message of Jesus, how will we deal with these big problems and collective stresses? It's clear, for starters, that we will not be complacent and trust the fox to guard the hens. Instead, we will tell the truth about systemic injustice, as Jesus did, and we will defect from it at every opportunity. We will seek "God's kingdom and God's justice" as our first priority (Matthew 6:33). This will require us to face, admit, and repent of what Jesus called "hypocrisy." We will have to acknowledge, again and again, how we ourselves are living by a dual narrative, wearing a mask of piety while being complicit in our world's inequitable system. (The term "hypocrite" clearly has these more social and economic connotations, as we saw in Luke 16:14–15; see also 11:39 and 20:47.) Taking the story of Zaccheus as an example of "salvation" from greed and hypocrisy, we will then seek to heal the system, beginning with our own role in it. Our actions will, I imagine, have at least three dimensions:

First, we will seek to help the poor through generosity—feeding the hungry, clothing the naked, visiting the imprisoned, showing hospitality to the homeless. In so doing, we must be careful to avoid a dehumanizing and demoralizing paternalism.

Second, we will call the rich to generosity, as Jesus frequently did. We will call the comfortable to turn from their own endless enrichment and to instead invest their energies for the good of their poorer neighbors. In today's world, this would often involve using their entrepreneurial skills to create good jobs, since unemployment is at the core of so many of the sufferings of the poor, including substance abuse, violence, and disease.

And third, we will work to improve the system, to detect and remove systemic injustice, so that the equity system of the societal machinery would indeed be equitable.

A CHALLENGE TO "DO JUSTICE"

An African-American friend recently challenged me in this regard. He was referring to efforts of suburban churches like the one I served to help poor people in the inner city. "I hope you don't mind me saying this," he began, "but sometimes I have mixed feelings about you folks in the suburbs coming down to teach poor urban kids to read."

He paused for a minute, then continued, "Look, we know how to read, and we should be teaching our own kids. What I wish you would do is something we can't so easily do for ourselves. I wish you would get organized and go down to Congress, and go to the White House, and go to other branches of government, and get them to change the laws and policies that keep our people so poor and our schools so ineffective. If we go in there, they don't listen to us. We have no power, no clout. We don't wear the right clothes, and we don't write letters and speak with the kind of English they respect. But you could do all those things, to try to confront systemic injustice. You could use your power and privilege on our behalf. That's what I wish you would do."

While neither he nor I want to squelch any generous impulse to tutor children, I think my friend had a point. With the Old Testament prophet Micah's words in mind (6:8), we might say that all Christians and churches believe in *walking humbly with God*. More and more Christians and churches, thankfully, are also showing a concern to show *kindness* or *compassion*—helping the victims of injustice through mission trips, giving to social needs, and so on. But the number of individuals and churches focused on *doing justice* remains disproportionately low.

Depending on how you look at it, that could be an indictment or an opportunity.[13]

GROUP DIALOGUE QUESTIONS

1. The author recounts several episodes from Jesus' life. Which episode most struck you, and why?
2. Respond to the terms *holiness* and *social holiness*, as used in this chapter.
3. Respond to the idea of *collective sin*, as presented in this chapter. Look over today's news headlines and relate them to the idea of collective sin.
4. What forces promote apathy among us? What would it take to overcome apathy in your life?
5. The author speaks of *big religion* and a *small gospel*. How do you relate these two terms?
6. Do you see the lack of attention to justice as more of an indictment or opportunity? How can we seize the opportunity?
7. Is there any issue of social justice or collective sin that you feel a special concern about? How could this reading group become an action group around that issue?

A New Kind of Question

I scan the colossal (and avalanching) failure of the equity system. I ponder how far the barefoot poor are falling behind the riding-in-style rich. I sense their corresponding resentment and fear intensifying as the distance between them grows. At those times I feel the grey noise of hopelessness hissing in the back of my brain.

I have a delicious dinner with a group of "normal" friends in the United States, all of us far wealthier by global standards than we can possibly fathom, eating food that is good beyond description—its only flaw being, perhaps, that there is too much of it. And then a few days and a few airplane tickets later, I sit on a dented old folding chair in a slum in Africa or Latin America, surrounded by the smell of sewage and the noise of barking dogs, eating simple bread, beans, maybe a little dark, greasy chicken, and the contrasts crush in on me. Our societal machinery seems to be humming along, perfectly calibrated to drive us along in this inequitable trajectory.

I think about where the path of gross inequity leads—globally, nationally, locally. I think about the streets of Latin America and Africa, where every window must be protected by iron grates and every wall topped with razor wire or broken glass to keep out desperately poor people who have found robbery the only way to survive.

I think about the United States, growing ever more conservative because it has so much to conserve, spending larger and larger per-centages—obscene and irrational percentages—of its unbalanced budget on an elusive abstraction called *security* (which is as elusive and abstract as *growth*). I think about our crowded prisons. I think about our failing urban and rural schools. I think about terrorism and counterterrorism, locked in a death match to defeat each other through violence, and I remember the old Buddhist proverb that when two elephants fight, the grass gets trampled—and I know that the poor people of the world are the grass.

I recall the words of Kofi Annan in December 2003: "We should have learned by now that a world of glaring inequality—between countries and within them—where many millions of people endure brutal oppression and extreme misery—is never going to be a fully safe world, even for its most privileged inhabitants."[1]

Then I think of Jesus and the beauty of his teachings, and there's a brief glimmer of hope, but then comes the realization of what hap-pened to him, what (recalling Jackson Browne's song) he "got" from those who profited from the inequitable equity system of his day. And then I ask myself, "Do I believe in resurrection?" and suddenly that question matters a very great deal.

Occasionally, I hear hopeful news. For example, in an article by Jeffrey D. Sachs I read that $25 billion could improve health care so as to save eight million poor people per year.[2] Then I read this:

> In the year 2000, the top four hundred US households earned a combined income of sixty-nine billion dollars. (This is annual earnings, not assets.) So the four hundred richest Americans, if they chose to do so, could save eight million lives a year and still be able to live on forty-four billion dol-lars a year, or 101 million dollars of annual income for each household on average.[3]

My mind starts calculating. America's share of $25 billion, pro-portional to our 32 percent share in the world's economy, would amount to about $8 billion. Seven billion of that $8 billion could be raised in one easy step: by reversing the so-called tax relief recently given to four hundred households by our government. Surely those four hundred families would agree that they need "relief" less than the desperately poor?

Then I read that according to the United Nations, $80 billion could provide all the poor people in the world with clean water, basic health care, basic education, and basic nutrition. With global income at $8 trillion per year, this represents only 1 percent of the world's income, and less than 10 percent of the world's military budget (without including US costs for the war in Iraq).[4] Suddenly, equity seems almost . . . doable.

Then I think about the US investment in the war in Iraq—over $200 billion as I write, with the total cost predicted to exceed $1 trillion—and I think that if my government had made different decisions, just two years of the war's costs could have taken care of the world's poor for five years.[5] And I wonder—how much more secure would my country be if it had made that kind of investment instead? Suddenly, the impossible doesn't seem so impossible.

And I also gain hope when I hear popular Christian leaders like Kay and Rick Warren, Lynne and Bill Hybels, Kristen and Rob Bell, Andy Stanley, Don Miller, Rick McKinley, Chris Seay, Joel Hunter and Richard Cizik express an increasing level of concern for the world's poor, or when I hear bold statements about equity from groups like the World Alliance of Reformed Churches:

> The material wealth of the wealthy has grown enough. Their trees are now mature and should leave space for new trees to develop and blossom. Our alternative is an orchard of blossoming economies each bearing its own kind of fruit. The time has come for radical change if total catastrophe is to be prevented and all creation is to enjoy fullness of life.[6]

And my hope grows more when I recall the unquenchable commitment to equity of many of my heroes—displayed over decades—prophetic Christian leaders like John Perkins, Ron Sider, Tony and

Peggy Campolo, Bart Campolo, Barbara Williams-Skinner, Jim Wallis, Steve Chalke, Adam Taylor, Rudy Carrasco, Mary Nelson, David Batstone, Shane Claiborne, and so many others. I think back to the words and example of Anglican theologian John Stott:

> What will posterity see as the chief Christian blind spot of the last quarter of the twentieth century? . . . I suspect it will have something to do with the economic oppression of the Third World and the readiness with which western Christians tolerate it, and even acquiesce in it. Only slowly is our Christian conscience being aroused to the gross economic inequalities between the countries of the North Atlantic and the southern world of Latin America, Africa and most parts of Asia. Total egalitarianism may not be a biblical ideal. But must we not roundly declare that luxury and extravagance are indefensible evils, while much of the world is undernourished and underprivileged?[7]

I am additionally encouraged when I meet increasing numbers of businesspeople seeking to use their business skills for the cause of equity. They are creating and supporting microenterprise projects to help potential entrepreneurs in poverty-stricken areas. They are addressing unfair trade policies and bonded labor, and they're seeking to motivate large corporations to decrease their negative "social footprint" along with their "ecological footprint." They are developing fair trade projects and finding ways to make ethical buying more convenient and widespread.[8] And along with businesspeople, I am beginning to hear politically involved people speaking meaningfully about campaign finance reform, seeking ways for the voices of the poor themselves to be heard in the political process, which is too often controlled by elites with big-budget backroom influence.

Then I see how budding movements such as the ethical buying movement and the green movement are beginning to affect people's behavior. For example, last month I met with a friend who is developing a website where people can buy fair trade gifts—meaning that the people who made these gifts in Africa or Latin America or Asia were paid a fair wage for their labor. Through his site (www.tradeasone.org), you can order a gift knowing that your purchase helps promote equity in the world. Or last week, I found websites where I could identify my ecological footprint, which helps me be sure that I don't use more than my share of the earth's resources (myfootprint.org and coolingcreation.org).

When these encouraging signs move me beyond both naïveté and despair, I become confident that, even though the current equity system is too often dysfunctional to the point of being counter-productive, it can be changed if enough of us are determined to change it. True, our current politicians and religious leaders, as those in Jesus' day, seem hell-bent on trivial matters ("straining out gnats" and "swallowing camels," to use Jesus' terms in Matthew 23:24) and oblivious to weightier matters (*justice, mercy, and faithfulness*, according to Jesus). But perhaps we are the ones we have been waiting for: perhaps we—especially those of us who have confidence in Jesus—will finally take the sage counsel of John Stott, that more and more of us

> . . . should gain the economic and political qualifications to join in the quest for justice in the world community. And meanwhile, the development of a less affluent lifestyle, in whatever terms we may define it, is surely an obligation that Scripture lays on us in compassionate solidarity with the poor. Of course we can resist these things and even use (misuse) the Bible to defend our resistance. The horror of the situation is that our affluent culture has drugged us; we no longer feel the pain of other people's deprivations. Yet the first step toward the recovery of our Christian integrity is to be aware that our culture blinds, deafens and dopes us. Then we shall begin to cry to God to open our eyes, unstop our ears and stab our dull consciences awake, until we see, hear and feel what through his Word he has been saying to us all the time. Then we shall take action.[9]

All of our initiatives for social justice will require courage, creativity, and above all, persistence. It is a mistake to imagine that inequity can be solved once for all. True, there are times (like ours) that demand creative, bold, and dramatic breakthroughs. But the struggle for a healthy equity system, like the struggle for a wise prosperity system and a sane security system, is perpetual: it is as much a part of the ongoing social task of being human as eating, drinking, and sleeping are part of the physical task. As long as you're alive, you're not finished.

ASKING THE RIGHT QUESTIONS

The struggle must begin with education, supported by persuasion, leading to the development of faith-inspired movements for social justice around the world. Wherever these movements are successful, their struggle will be institutionalized and preserved through improvable legislation and evolving social custom. My writing and your reading of this book, in a sense, can be seen as our joint attempt to encourage this struggle, to educate and to persuade and to foment, so that the prophetic social justice movement that is trying to be born can be born. If we follow the educational and persuasive strategy of Jesus, one of our first and most important activities will be to ask a new kind of question, because the right questions cause people to think rather than react.

Perhaps questions like these can dislodge us from our conceptual ruts and ideological reactions—and inspire some creative imagination: *What benefits will come to the rich if the poor are better off? What dangers and negative consequences will follow for the rich if the poor are not better off?*

And we can extend the frame of reference for these questions beyond ourselves to future generations, recalling the Great Law of Peace of the Iroquois Nation: "Look and listen for the welfare of the whole people and have always in view not only the present but also the coming generations."[10] *What kind of world will we who are comparatively rich and powerful bequeath to our children and grandchildren if we do not redirect our energies from accumulation, and self-protection toward compassion, service, and equity? And what kind of world will we bequeath to future generations if equity becomes our sacred passion and personal ambition?*[11]

Questions like these can liberate our imagination from its captivity and domestication within the closed and depressing narrative of the suicide machine. And that is no small thing, according to Brian Walsh and John Middleton:

> It is only when we can imagine the world to be different than the way it is that we can be empowered to embody this alternative reality which is God's kingdom and resist this present nightmare of brokenness, disorientation and confusion. . . . A liberated imagination is a prerequisite for facing the future. . . . If we cannot have such a liberated imagination and cannot countenance such radical dreams, then the story remains closed for us and we have no hope.[12]

Dr. Martin Luther King Jr., of course, is remembered for his imagination, his dream, and that dream extended beyond racial reconciliation in the United States to economic equity around the world. In his last book, *The Trumpet of Conscience*, he wrote:

> The developed industrial nations of the world cannot remain secure islands of prosperity in a seething sea of poverty. The storm is rising against the privileged minority of the earth, from which there is no shelter or isolation and armament. The storm will not abate until a just distribution of the fruits of the earth enables people everywhere to live in dignity and human decency. We may now be in only the initial period of an era of change as far-reaching in its consequences as the American Revolution. . . . If we do not act, we shall surely be dragged down the long, dark, and shameful corridor of time reserved for those who possess power without compassion, might without morality, and strength without sight. A true revolution of values will soon cause us to question the fairness and justice of many of our past and present policies. A true

revolution of values will soon look uneasily on the glaring contrast between poverty and wealth.[13]

It is clear that Jesus' framing story of the kingdom of God calls for this kind of revolution of values and hope.[14] It is not clear how many believers in Jesus today will open their hearts to this revolution. But there are at least two of us, right?

GROUP DIALOGUE QUESTIONS

1. The author relates being known as *conservative* to *having much to conserve*. How do you respond to that understanding of *conservative*? What might a corresponding definition of *liberal* mean?

2. Go online and download the entire statement of the World Alliance of Reformed Churches mentioned in this chapter. Read it aloud and respond to it together. (wave.ch/24gc/index.html)

3. The author suggests that those having business skills can use those skills to help those suffering from poverty. Take the skills of the members of your group (and add the skills of friends and family members if needed) and imagine how they could be used in this way.

4. Respond to the author's statement, "We are the ones we have been waiting for."

5. Discuss the "new kind of questions" the author proposes. What kinds of questions could you use in the coming week to stimulate good conversation among your friends outside this reading group? Try to use some of these questions this week, and share your experiences next week.

6. How did you respond to the last sentence of this chapter?

7. Describe Jesus as a *values revolutionary*. What values does he stand for?

Organized Religion or
Religion Organizing for
the Common Good?

As I become more aware of the way the dominant system works, and as the message of Jesus provides a new framing story through which I see our world and its possibilities, I become eager—even impatient—to know how I can make a difference on the side of equity. A few years ago, as my two preoccupying questions were beginning to move to the front burner of my thinking, I had a chance to ask a veritable herd of experts for their advice.

I had just performed a wedding ceremony and was mingling at the reception, looking for my assigned seat. I found my name neatly printed on a folded card, and it was soon clear that my six or seven tablemates, already seated, all knew each other. So after introductions, I asked how they had met. "I was the PhD supervisor for everyone here at the table," a middle-aged fellow replied with a laugh. They responded with a lot of jokes about being brought together through misery, having survived the same slave driver, and so on. "In what field?" I asked. "We're all economists," the senior PhD replied, "but we promise we won't bore you by talking shop."

"I'm actually interested in economics," I replied. "As you know, I'm a pastor, and I believe that God has a special concern for economic equity—for social and economic justice for the poor. So I'm especially interested in understanding how we can help poor people around the world. Can you guys teach me anything about that?" At that, the entire table again broke into laughter. Those issues, it turned out, were exactly the specialties of my tablemates. All of their research had focused on what interventions make a difference in helping the poor. The next two hours passed swiftly as I received a crash course in development economics.

SEVEN CATEGORIES OF DEVELOPMENT ECONOMICS

Building on that introduction, I began reading everything I could find on the subject. It was no surprise that experts disagreed on a thousand details, but it was surprising to see the degree to which they agreed that overcoming extreme poverty requires concerted action in seven basic categories: trade, aid, debt, limits, wages, justice, and community. This list of areas for action should stand alongside our earlier lists of global crises in chapter 6.

Trade

Without a thriving prosperity system, an equity system can only distribute poverty. So the experts tell us we need three kinds of trade reform to encourage the prosperity system to thrive equitably.

First, of course, we need to adjust our economic philosophy to live within environmental limits, as we've already seen. Exceeding environmental limits will always eventually cause environmental collapse somewhere and will only increase the disproportionate vulnerability of the poor.

Second, we need to integrate free trade with fair trade. In particular, the United States must hear the world's rising anger about the unfair advantages it demands in world markets. This anger has already turned to hatred, as Ziauddin Sardar and Merryl Wyn Davies make clear in *Why Do People Hate America?*:

> The US has simply made it too difficult for other people to exist. . . . The US has structured the global economy to

perpetually enrich itself and reduce non-Western societies to poverty. "Free markets" is simply a euphemism for free mobility of American capital, unrestrained expansion of American corporations, and free (unidirectional) movement of goods and services from America to the rest of the world.[1]

What would happen, I wonder, if followers of Jesus and other people of faith in the United States decided that they didn't want to support, explicitly or implicitly, this kind of national behavior? What would happen if millions of people of faith and conscience became as committed to fair trade as they are to free trade?[2] What if, in the spirit of Philippians 2:4, we determined to look out not only for our personal or national economic interests, but also for the interests of others? What if we pursued, with integrity, the both/and of free *and* fair trade?

Third, we need to make it easier for people to grow small businesses. This will often involve both *deregulation* (cutting red tape for poor but aspiring entrepreneurs and for small-business owners who are expanding their businesses and thus providing more employment) and *regulation* (restraining powerful, large corporations—especially transnational ones—from crushing local entrepreneurship while exploiting local resources and cheap labor).

Economic conservatives are at their strongest when it comes to trade. Guided by Jesus' message of God's global love economy, they have the capacity to leverage their commitment to free and fair trade in ways that can increase equity and decrease the suffering and vulnerability of the poor across town and around the world.

Aid

Economic conservatives and economic liberals agree: aid is absolutely essential. Yes, poorly planned and administered aid can unintentionally increase corruption and hurt local economies. But the alternative to unwise aid is not *no* aid, but *wise* aid.

In this light, the call of groups like the One Campaign, Bread for the World, and the Micah Challenge to achieve the Millennium

Development Goals seems modest and reasonable, as does their call for the prosperous nations of the world to give an additional 1 percent of their income in aid to the world's poor. This amount invested in advance to compensate for and reverse current failures in the prosperity and equity systems will be a tiny fraction of the escalating costs of doing less, which include the costs of crime and conflict combined with an inflating, bloated security system of police, border patrols, military and intelligence institutions, counterterrorism bureaucracies, and jails.

We shouldn't be surprised that living by the good news of the kingdom of God is a wise financial decision, and that refusing to let it frame our lives—including our economic lives—would prove to be costly.

Debt

We've already seen how current aid from rich countries is being swallowed by debt payments from poor countries, and how the net balance currently favors the rich countries. As with aid, poorly administered debt relief can have unintended negative consequences.

However, if debt relief is implemented wisely—linked with needed steps of political reform in the nations receiving the relief, for example, steps that will strengthen the nation's economy long-term—then debt relief has an essential role in helping the poor.

Limits

Human beings must recognize that as finite and responsible creatures in a finite creation, we must live within biological limits—both in terms of consumption/pollution and population. Herman Daly summarizes the situation well:

> While all countries must worry about both population and per capita resource consumption, it is evident that the [global] South needs to focus more on population, and the North more on per capita resource consumption. . . . Why should the South control its population if the resources saved thereby are merely gobbled up by Northern overconsumption? Why

should the North control its overconsumption if the saved resources will merely allow a larger number of poor people to subsist in the same level of misery? . . .

The critical issue is for the North to attain sustainability in the sense of a level of resource use that is both sufficient for a good life for its population and within the carrying capacity of the environment if generalized to the whole world.[3]

It is well known that for population growth to stay within the carrying capacity of its local environment, nations must invest in four initiatives: improving the health and education of children, improving the health and education of women, expanding the availability of contraceptives or natural family planning, and developing social security systems for the elderly. These four actions, taken together, give poor parents good reasons (and means) to have fewer children.[4]

What is less known is how to curb consumption in the North, although the sustainable development movement is focusing needed attention on this essential question. The efforts of this movement, among others, are helping us realize that to have a 10 percent growth in gross national product is not desirable if it is acquired at the cost of a 20 percent growth in gross national *destruct.*

Perhaps, in the interests of sustainability, we should speak less of an *environmental crisis* and speak more of an *overconsumption crisis.* That way, we'd focus our attention on the source of the problem, not its victim—the source being human beings, particularly in the global North, who are living an unsustainable life, oblivious to limits, destroying their natural wealth in pursuit of financial wealth.

Again, it is clear how the wrong framing story teaches people they have the right to live without limits. It is equally clear how a wise framing story situates us in God's world, living within the limits of creatureliness and mutual responsibility.

Wages

As an element of fair trade, to protect poor workers from exploitation, many experts are calling for an international minimum wage.

Such a wage would have to be context-specific, related to the local cost of living and other economic conditions.

Some economists, including Herman Daly, also recommend a kind of maximum wage, but not the "invidious, forced equality" of the old, failed centralized planning economies. Instead, they recommend a ratio-based arrangement in which the salary of the highest-paid worker in a corporation would be limited by its relation to the salary of the lowest-paid worker. So, if the relation was a factor of fifty and the lowest-paid worker earned $20,000 per year, the highest-paid worker could earn up to $1,000,000. Beyond that level, his salary could not increase without a corresponding increase among the lowest-paid workers. Daly actually recommends a factor of ten or twenty, suggesting that the "bonds of community break at or before a factor of one hundred."[5]

Within a framing story that provides no moral context, this kind of ceiling may sound ridiculous, but within a framing story that takes bonds of community seriously, the lack of a ceiling sounds even worse.

Justice

My tablemates at the wedding reception listed an effective justice system as the key element in breaking free from poverty. But, they said, there is a kind of vicious cycle in effect. A good justice (or equity) system is expensive and therefore depends on the taxes of a healthy prosperity system. But a nation can't achieve a healthy prosperity system without a good equity system. So a society must have integrated, incremental, ongoing growth in both systems—requiring, in my terms, not my tablemates'—a framing story that treats both as essential. Without such a framing story, every effort to increase equity will be undermined at every turn by corrupt politicians, unethical businesspeople, and other criminals who value their own prosperity more than equity for all.

So governments, regulatory agencies, journalists, artists, religious leaders, and other cultural influencers need to turn the social tide against corruption and for wise governance, especially among the most powerful. The most comprehensive way to turn the tide in this way is through a coherent framing story that calls for *integrity*— meaning, prosperity and equity integrated together.

This fight for integrity and against corruption can't be reduced to abstractions like "democracy" or "freedom." In fact, assuming that a single political change will solve these problems has proven disastrous on repeated occasions.[6] Instead, cultures around the world must engage in the painstaking work of naming and fighting corruption day after day, year after year, whether the source of the corruption is a freewheeling transnational corporation or a violent gang of local drug traffickers. And societies seeking equity must immediately replace corrupt systems with improvable systems and institutions of wise governance, bearing in mind Jesus' words that one can't expel an evil spirit without replacing it with something better (Matthew 12:43–45).

This work is an essential part of what David Korten calls "the public oversight" of democracies. He suggests there is an equitable alternative to a failed, centralized socialism and an equally (but differently) centralized capitalism:

> There is a democratic, market-based, community-serving alternative to the unappealing choice between a socialist economy centrally owned and administered by government and a capitalist economy centrally owned and administered by an elite class of wealthy financiers and corporate CEOs. . . . a proper market-economy operates with rules, borders, and equitable local ownership under the public oversight of democratically accountable governments.[7]

Where will this public oversight come from, if the governments of nation-states are proving incapable of providing it? Echoing the proposals of J. F. Rischard in *High Noon*, Jim Garrison says, "In an integrating world, governance, not government, is the key to effective management of the global system because networks, not nations, are the emergent powers of the future."[8] He calls for the strengthening of governance networks beginning with the United Nations, for radical reform of the World Trade Organization, and then for a group of peer network organizations to be created, operating along the lines of the International Atomic Energy Commission—including a World Labor Organization, a Global Environmental Organization, and an International Reconstruction Fund (to help failing states rebuild).[9]

Along with these new network organizations, the emerging judicial structures of the civil society movement will also provide accountability by molding public opinion and, when necessary, bringing people into the streets. Some societal narratives—whether they're imperial, nationalistic, tribal/ethnic, or theocratic—will oppose the development of these needed networks. But a framing story that envisions an interdependent, mutually committed, global community of communities is a hospitable environment in which these needed networks can develop and flourish.

Community

Philosopher and author Wendell Berry introduces two helpful concepts that can aid us in our attempts to strengthen the equity system: communities and publics. Communities are families of families linked together in a local environment of land, water, air, and climate. Publics are larger networks of people whose influence spreads over many communities, such as governments, political parties, multinational corporations, institutions, cartels, and media.

Systemic injustice generally works on the level of publics, and publics often weaken or destroy communities as they seek more power or profit. For example, a corporation may sell food that makes individuals obese, or a drug cartel may sell drugs that cause addiction, or a media company may produce movies that stimulate people to be promiscuous, or a political party may promote loose gun-control laws that increase violent crime, or a religious institution may inspire adherents to be hateful against members of other sects. Obesity, addiction, promiscuity, violent crime, and hatred harm local communities, but the publics that promote them don't have to pay the price of dealing with that local harm. Instead, they keep making more money and garnering more contributions. The publics can prosper at the communities' expense.

Whenever communities are weakened in these ways, so are families, because by nature families and communities are interactive and interdependent. And when families are weakened, so are individuals. So if we try to build or sustain communities and families without dealing with inequity on the public level, we will feel like we're trying to build or preserve a house in a hurricane. If we deal with injustice among publics by addressing the previous six factors, yet fail to rebuild damaged communities and families, we will feel like we have survived a hurricane but are still living in the rubble.

Local churches, local schools, local government, and locally rooted businesses and other civil organizations and associations have a pivotal role in this regard—strengthening families and communities through celebrating virtue and training people to practice it. And again, one of the most powerful ways to strengthen families and communities through virtue development begins with teaching, celebrating, and modeling a coherent, transforming framing story—like the one found in Jesus' message of the kingdom of God—translated, perhaps, into the language of God's sacred ecosystem or God's global love economy.

THE POWER OF ORGANIZING RELIGION

The hard work of rebuilding community and family is essential—through community organizing, through moral instruction in local churches, through support for women and children through community centers and health clinics and schools, through microenterprise projects and drug rehabilitation programs to help people develop employment or become employable.

In my travels, whether in the inner cities of the United States or in slums around the world, the vast majority of these programs are overtly or implicitly faith-based, often drawing inspiration from Jesus' good news of the kingdom of God. For all the obvious failures of "organized religion," in these organizations I see the power of *organizing religion* . . . people of faith organizing for something truly beautiful and good. As they promote a vision for the common good resourced by Jesus' good news of the kingdom of God, they promote the seven components of equity: trade with integrity (both free and fair), wise aid, wise debt relief, respect for environmental limits in terms of both resource consumption and population growth, fair wages, the development of justice systems, and community and family development.

If there is a force in the world powerful and good enough to overcome the grinding, destructive momentum of the suicide machine, it is to be found, not in organized religion seeking institutional self-preservation, but in religion organizing for the common good.

GROUP DIALOGUE QUESTIONS

1. Review the seven action areas described in this chapter. Which one of these is most interesting to you, and why?
2. Why do some people hate America?
3. Discuss the relationship between overpopulation and overconsumption.
4. What difference would it make to rename the *environmental crisis* as the *overconsumption crisis*?
5. Respond to the idea of minimum and maximum salaries. Do you think this is a crazy proposal? Why or why not?
6. Contrast *organized religion* with *religion organizing for the common good.* How would you relate your faith community in this regard?

Part 8

A REVOLUTION
OF HOPE

The Most Radical Thing
We Can Do

Can the suicide machine really be stopped? Can the earth really be liberated from the destructive framing story that drives it? Is Jesus' healing and transforming framing story really powerful enough to save the world?[1]

The simple answer is that nobody knows.

My friend Jim Wallis offers a powerful image to convey the challenge we face. If we look back, we realize that political systems (not to mention business, military, and even religious systems) have, in spite of their high ideals and noble ambitions, frequently been driven by the winds of expediency, self-interest, fear, greed, and pressure. So, looking around today, we see politicians wetting their fingers and raising them to see which way the political wind is blowing—to see what voters want so they can remain popular, raise donations, and secure reelection. Wisdom and honesty tell us that we aren't going to change politicians much in the future. They're always going to be wetting their fingers and testing the wind. So, Jim says, there's only one hope: we're going to have to change the wind.

Changing the wind would mean changing public opinion, which requires changing the values that guide people individually and as groups, which in turn requires changing the vision of what is both possible and desirable, which ultimately means changing our framing story. In other words, changing the wind means doubting, rejecting, and defecting from our old framing stories, and instead, discovering and adopting—in a word, *believing*—a new framing story. That, once again, is exactly where I believe Jesus steps into human affairs, challenging us simply to believe his good news (Mark 1:15), and to believe him as the bearer of that good news (John 6:29, 35; 7:38; 10:37; 14:1).

A WILD AND RADICAL BELIEVING

If the word *believing* seems too soft a strategy for confronting global crises, I would reply that believing seems like a soft or weak thing only when it is a domesticated belief. Tame believing *for* and *within* the dominant system may be easy, but wild believing *against* and *beyond* it turns normal people into heroes and history changers. Martin Luther, Martin Luther King Jr., Galileo, Nelson Mandela, Gandhi, Mother Teresa, Saint Francis . . . they all showed this heroic courage to believe against and beyond the dominant systems of their day.

So we must realize this: the suicidal framing story that dominates our world today has no power except the power we give it by believing it. Similarly, believing an alternative and transforming framing story may turn out to be the most radical thing any of us can ever do. (If I were preaching, I would repeat the previous sentence twice, the second time, in a whisper.)

Jesus proclaims that simply believing his good news brings salvation. This is "salvation by grace through faith" in a planetary sense: if we believe that God graciously offers us a new way, a new truth, and a new life, we can be liberated from the vicious, addictive cycles of our suicidal framing stories. That kind of faith will save us. If we don't believe, we will persist in trying harder and harder, again and again, to achieve our own salvation through our existing narratives and the techniques they inspire. Even if Jesus' good news is true, our failure to believe it will keep us from experiencing its saving potential, and so we'll spin on in the vicious cycles of the Casear.

What's more, if believing seems like too easy an answer to you, I'd remind you that believing isn't the whole strategy, but it is the essential first step. Unless we deprive the dominant system of our confidence and consent, it will absorb and neutralize all our attempts at reform because we will still be part of its framing story; we will not be different enough to change it, because our very efforts to change it will draw on its own logic and values. But if we transfer our trust from the way of Caesar to the way of Christ, our actions will draw their power from another source. We will have a new leverage point; we will be independent of the system, so our energies can no longer be co-opted by this system that has now become pathetic and pathological to us.

So the revolution we need starts in us—in our minds, our hearts—as an act of faith, a transfer of trust from the dominant system to a new way of seeing, believing, and living.

Our dominant societal machinery does not make this defection easy. It entices us to keep faith in its current program by making big promises: to increase wealth, cure depression, create constant sexual excitement and fulfillment, stop oppression, increase security, end poverty, overcome injustice, end discrimination, liberate the oppressed, educate the stupid, entertain the bored, and defy or reverse entropy. It never keeps these promises. Instead, it faithfully does the opposite: it increases the cost and decreases the value of prosperity, spreads depression, creates constant sexual frustration, institutionalizes oppression, universalizes terror, widens the gap between rich and poor, popularizes injustice and discrimination, oppresses the liberated, stupefies the educated, makes the entertained boring, and sucks everything into a vortex of entropy. Yet so many of us keep on believing its false promises.

JESUS' RADICAL HOPE

Jesus challenged people in his day to stop believing the empire's empty promises and stop fearing its threats through a brilliant strategy. First he lured its dark machinery into the light, so to speak, so it could be seen for what it was, exposed, named, rejected, and defected from. After praying "Your will be done" in the Garden of Gethsemane, after choosing self-sacrifice over self-protection, he walked like a lamb into the middle of the forest, so the wolves would come out of the shadows and circle around him. Then he stretched out his neck, as it were, inviting them to pounce, and they did. Ironically, though, as he exposed his own neck, he also exposed their vicious wolfishness, and in that way he sabotaged them, defeated them, rendering them ugly and incredible. After all, they could no longer claim to be agents of peace and promise after torturing and killing a good and peaceful man.

Just as the wolfish powers breathed a sigh of satisfaction at nailing yet another challenger to a cross, Jesus' quiet but real resurrection validated to his disciples that the liberating king was not defeated, but rather was on the move, quietly, at the margins, where all revolutions begin. His resurrection told them that Caesar's muscle couldn't conquer God's vulnerability, that Caesar's spears couldn't conquer God's heart, and that Caesar's whips and nails and crosses couldn't overcome God's way of love and reconciliation.

So in the shadow of Caesar's ruthless kingdom, witnesses of Jesus' resurrection could never live by Caesar's framing story again. It had become disgusting to them, despicable, pathetic, exposed. Liberated from Caesar's false promises and fear, they chose to live in the framing story of a new Lord, in his "in-but-not-of-this-world" kingdom, as citizens in his "kingdom from another place," with headquarters not in Rome but in the heart of God. They withdrew their trust from the domesticating and domesticated narratives and counternarratives that energized the empire, and they chose instead to believe Jesus' wild, untamed good-news story about the kingdom of God—as a story of hope that could frame and transform a better future.[2]

Perhaps now, with them, we can begin to envision what it would mean for us to confront the suicide machine of our world in the way of Jesus, to expose it and deconstruct it, to intercept its trajectory and turn it to a better way, to reclaim its potential for ends more in line with their original creation. Perhaps we can see ourselves in a new light too, not armed with an ideology but infused with a new imagination, part of a peaceful insurgency seeking to expel a suicidal occupying regime, gardeners working with God to tend the holy ecosystem so it continues to unfold anew day after new day, members of a secret insurgency of hope, a global movement unleashing coordinated, well-planned acts of unterror and healing, producers in a new economy of love—an economy so radical that old terms like *capitalism* and *communism* seem like two sides of a Confederate coin left over from a fading and discredited regime. This new vision requires of us one irreplaceable thing: *faith*—faith that the old narrative of domination is suicidal, and that a new story (good news) of liberation and reconciliation is available if we will only rethink everything and believe it.

OUR GREAT CHOICE

So far in these pages, I have asked you to disbelieve a number of things: That our current societal machinery is working fine. That we can seek prosperity without regard to ecological limits. That we can achieve true security through military dominance, and peace through violence. That we have already achieved equity, or that equity is an unachievable pipe-dream. That our religious systems are standing up to the societal machine and providing it with a transforming framing story. That our current understandings of Jesus are sufficient and accurate.

And I have asked you instead to believe a number of other things:

1. *We live in a societal system or machine.* It consists of three subsystems (prosperity, security, and equity), situated in a finite environment, guided by a framing story.
2. *The system goes suicidal when driven by a destructive framing story.* Destructive framing stories employ narratives of domination, revolution, and withdrawal, all of which are ultimately self-destructive.
3. *Jesus saw these dynamics at work in his day and proposed in*

word and deed a new alternative—neither conforming to the suicidal framing story, nor reacting in a violent counternarrative or defeatist withdrawal narrative.

4. *Jesus' creative and transforming framing story invited people to change the world by disbelieving old framing stories and believing a new one:* a story about a loving God who, like a benevolent king, calls all people to live life in a new way, the way of love.

Our great choice is whether or not we will dare to believe against the suicide machine, and believe Jesus, toward a different world. Believing is the most radical thing we can do. No wonder Jesus, when performing his healings and exorcisms, would often say, "Your faith has saved you."

GROUP DIALOGUE QUESTIONS

1. Respond to the metaphor of "changing the wind."
2. In what way can the teachings of Jesus be seen as *saving poetry*?
3. The author says that believing is the most radical thing we can do. Do you agree? Talk about the role of believing in your life right now.
4. What does it mean to believe in the death and resurrection of Jesus, according to this chapter?
5. The author summarizes what he has asked you as a reader to disbelieve and believe. Are you a believer? Where do you still have doubts? What questions remain for you?

An Unfolding, Emergent, Spiraling Process

I hate easy answers. They are attractive in the short run, but they exhaust and disappoint and create cynicism in the long run. So it is with some ambivalence that I conclude this book by repeating this answer—which is actually far from easy, but may appear to be so.

There is one great step we can take to dismantle the suicide machine and the framing stories that legitimize it: to stop believing in it, and to believe, in its place, a different story, the story of the kingdom of God.

This is the story articulated on Palestinian beaches and hillsides by a carpenter's son two thousand years ago, a story that has echoed through history in the dreams of our best and brightest—from Saint Francis to Martin Luther King Jr., from Saint Patrick to Nelson Mandela, from Harriet Tubman to Mother Teresa, from Oscar Romero to Mahatma Gandhi, from Saint Claire to Jane Goodall.

The way to dismantle the suicide machine is to deny it the fuel on which it runs: confidence—confidence in its framing story. The way to create a generous, generative, and humane alternative society in place of the suicide machine is to believe the good news of the kingdom of God.

If that sounds like an easy answer, then you've never tried to believe the impossible or see the invisible.

By "seeing the invisible," I don't mean practicing make-believe where you try to see things that aren't really there. Instead of *delusion,* I mean *vision:* seeing things that aren't there *yet.* The kingdom of God is one such thing—truly real, truly there (or here), but not fully manifested *yet.*[1]

The Unfolding, Agonizing, Upward Process

Clare Graves, a key thinker in systems theory, said, "The psychology of a mature human being is an unfolding, emergent, oscillating, spiraling process marked by progressive subordination of older, lower-order behavior systems to newer, higher-order systems as man's existential problems change."[2] In other words, as human beings mature, they go through predictable stages in a kind of ascending spiral. Each time they go around the cycle of stages, they do so at a higher level and in a wider way, grappling with new problems and embracing more reality. Jesus' message of the kingdom of God, I propose, points to a higher-order system that continually invites humanity to move upward in the "unfolding, emergent . . . spiraling process." It is a "beautiful whole" that integrates partial things, and, like a work of art, can even bring beauty from darkness and pain.

It is like a bridge that is partially built. We who believe in the destination to which that bridge leads, we who can "see" the promised land on the other side, walk out on the unfinished bridge, carrying building materials, and through our faith and work, we extend it farther and farther out over nothingness day after day. That might sound simple, but it's not easy.

In fact, *agonizing* is often the word for it. I picture Jesus, a stone's throw away from his sleeping friends in a garden near Jerusalem. It's Thursday night. He has seen the suicidal trajectory of his society. He has done his best—in word and deed, through parable and sign, in example and instruction—to proclaim an alternative framing story and to stop the suicide machinery before it's too late. But now, he knows that there is one more step he must prepare to take: he must stand, like that Chinese student in Tiananmen Square we mentioned earlier, staring down the suicidal machinery of his society. He must lay down his life in the track of destruction.

You don't do that sort of thing unless you really believe two things; first, that the machine is truly dangerous, and second, that sacrificing your life will make a difference. For Jesus' followers, to believe in him meant—and means—not only that we have faith *in* Jesus, but also that we share the faith *of* Jesus: that our world is on a suicidal trajectory, and that our lives can make a difference.

While most of us won't be called to sacrifice our physical lives (but many may), having faith *in* Jesus and sharing the faith *of* Jesus will lead all of us to make what an early disciple called "a living sacrifice." We will give up the life we could have lived, the life we would have lived—pursuing pleasure, leisure, treasure, security, whatever. And instead, we will live a life dedicated to replacing the suicide machine with a sacred ecosystem, a beautiful community, an insurgency of healing and peace, a creative global family, an unterror movement of faith, hope, and love.

ENCOUNTERING AN OUTRAGEOUS HOPE

I'm writing these words at the end of a five-week journey through Latin America. On one level, it has been a speaking and teaching tour—I have had the honor of joining Latin American theologian Rene Padilla in engaging young leaders in seminaries, local churches, and universities, from Mexico City to Buenos Aires. On another level, it has been a listening and learning tour, part of my research for this book—encountering both Latin American poverty and Latin American attempts to understand and address poverty and the deeply embedded social and spiritual dysfunctions that produce it. (I have had similar pilgrimages through Africa as well.)

On the deepest level, it has been a series of personal encounters with amazing people who are doing amazing things, including an encounter early this afternoon in a small farming town in northern

Argentina. I sat at the kitchen table of a middle-aged woman named Graciela and her daughter Leticia as they told me about an adventure that has consumed their lives for the last sixteen years. It began with a family vacation, visiting Graciela's sister in Southern Argentina. They decided to drive up into the mountains to visit a community of indigenous people—a tourist trip, really, nothing more.

But as they left the green and fertile fields of the valley and ascended the rocky, inhospitable mountains to the west, Graciela somehow realized that she was encountering her own history—the history of colonization that drove the indigenous people farther and farther from their ancestral homelands, down from temperate north to frigid south, up from the fertile lowland valleys into inhospitable mountains, until they found their last option for survival at this cold, high, rocky margin—literally on the edge of existence. All of this hit her, and she began to weep and couldn't stop weeping. When they reached the village—a town of just a few hundred people—her heart and the hearts of her whole family bonded with the villagers, and Graciela promised they would return, which they did, many times over the ensuing years.

Graciela, her husband, Luiz, and their family were careful not to do what too many well-meaning "whites" do ("whites" being what the indigenous people call the European descendants of the conquistadores): they didn't want to "assist" the people in paternalizing ways that would only wound their dignity even further, fostering dependence and humiliation. So instead, they asked the people what their biggest problem was, and then they offered to join them as helpers in solving it. The biggest problem? They needed a school so their children would have a place in their own community to learn and grow.

So over the coming years, Graciela and her family rounded up help—an architect, volunteers from their local church, mostly young people who paid their own way. Eventually, even the mayor of their town heard about the project and asked if he could join them. They made the thirty-plus hour trip by car and train season after season. In the coming years, over many visits, they not only built a school, but in the process, they showed honor and respect and love to the indigenous people who had been, for so many centuries, treated with scorn and neglect and so much worse.

As this mother and daughter told me their story and showed me pictures and video of their visits, I realized that the simple action of one family—not a big NGO, not a huge government program, but a simple family project of neighborliness and humanity—illustrated the kind of subversive faith and action that can stop the suicide machine and build, in its place, a better world.

But a question wouldn't let go of my attention: "Why," I asked her, "didn't the people try to build a school before?" My experience in many slums and depressed areas in the previous months had brought this question into focus. In so many cases, thousands, millions of people scraped by day after day. Often, they sank into alcoholism or they turned on one another in violence and crime. If they had only organized themselves and combined their efforts, they could have made a profound difference.

This paralysis, this complacency, this self-sabotaging behavior were not just problems of slums, I had come to realize: they also were typical of my own country, of the so-called civilized world in general, and its failures to address our critical global crises—politically, environmentally, economically, socially, spiritually. What holds us back? Why do we continue to persist in ways of living that are so complacent, so pathetically counterproductive, so obviously suicidal? Our apathy, our complacency, our paralysis simply *don't make sense*, a sentiment affirmed by mega-venture capitalist George Soros:

> We have become aware how precarious our civilization is. It does not make sense to devote all our energies to improving our relative position in a social system when the system itself is drifting toward disaster.[3]

Graciela didn't hesitate a second when I asked her what held the indigenous people back: "The people had no hope," she said. She continued, "When people have no hope, all they think about is scraping by for one more day. There is no tomorrow, there is no creativity, there is no will to organize, people can't even think straight, because they have no hope.[4] Then she paused, seeming to recall something she had almost forgotten.

"You know, when we first came to the village, the people would never speak their native language in front of us. They were ashamed of their native language and would only speak Spanish. So we began to ask them to teach us words in their native tongue. They couldn't believe that white people were interested in learning their language. That simple act of curiosity seemed to tell them that we weren't there just to help them as some superior people helping inferiors. No, we were there because we genuinely loved them—no, not just that—we liked them. . . . It wasn't the resources we brought that made a difference. It was our presence. We were simply among them as people with hope, among them as people with love, and that made the difference. They caught our hope."

As she spoke, I pictured Jesus, wandering through the villages of Galilee, walking among his own oppressed and dominated people, people who, like the people of this indigenous village, had lost their hope. Their hopelessness left them paralyzed and powerless between two primary schemes of despair—the violent despair of terrorist resistance or the resigned despair of capitulation and collaboration with their powerful oppressors. He didn't fix all their problems, even though many of them wanted him to and hated him when he didn't. He didn't organize an army or hatch a plot or design liberal democracy or create a new get-rich-quick business plan. He didn't scapegoat anybody—if anything, he kept letting scapegoats off the hook, taking their side to the consternation of their hyperreligious critics.

Instead, he simply let the people know he liked them—and so did God, that he was interested in them, that they didn't have to be ashamed of who they were. He came close to them in their illnesses, wept with them at the graves of their loved ones, ate at their tables, drank their wine, listened to their words, let himself be injured by their pain—and, although it isn't recorded in any of the Gospels (canonical or otherwise), I imagine he laughed at some of their jokes too.

And he did one other thing: he told the people something, something outrageous, something so familiar to us, so familiar to me that it is only in rare moments that I get a glimpse of how wild it really was. It wasn't an if/then statement—*if you do this and this and this and this, then you'll get that result.* That would have been more pressure, another chance to fail.

No, all he did was tell them that something was already true: *the kingdom of God is here.* Already. Here in its full flower, no, but here in reality, yes. Whether you believe it or not, whether you notice it or not, whether you like it or not. And all that he invited them to do was to believe it. And somehow, some of them did.

There was an interesting twist in Graciela's story. When the school was finished, the members of the village did not want it to be a private school: they wanted it to be donated to the government of Argentina. The government didn't know what to do with this: they had never been offered a school before. It actually took some persuasion to get them to accept it. Why was it so important to the indigenous people for the school to be a public, government-funded school? Because if the government was responsible for the school, it would, in effect, finally be recognizing that this little indigenous community exists and is part of the society. By owning the school, the government would be acknowledging that this little village was not just a village of "poor Indians"—it was a village of *genuine Argentinean citizens.* In this way, the people of the village showed how great their hope really was: not just that their children could be educated, but that their nation could be changed as well, converted from its racism and exclusion, and they would be given a place of respect and value in it.

There in Argentina, in this little farming village earlier this afternoon, sitting at a kitchen table listening to Graciela and Leticia, I felt the beautiful rush of wonder and hope: that if we dare to believe today, schools can be built, economies can be turned around, the rich and powerful with all their talents and advantages can defect from selfish pursuits and instead invest their energies on behalf of their poor neighbors, that old injustices can be acknowledged, and new relationships born. If we believe, the poor can organize and use their own labor and intelligence to build their own communities and economics instead of letting the best years of their lives be exploited by selfish corporations with headquarters and bank accounts half a world away.

If we believe, the decadent and self-indulgent West can be converted from overconsumers to creative stewards, from empire builders to community builders, from sex-obsessed and self-indulgent couch potatoes to people like Graciela, Luiz, and Leticia and their family—who along their way through life, discover a magnificent vision and a sacred mission that give their lives unimagined meaning.

If we believe, we can be transformed into agents of something beautiful that is trying to be born in our world. We can be caught up in the unfolding, emergent, spiraling process of God giving birth to a beautiful whole, the kingdom of God.

GROUP DIALOGUE QUESTIONS

1. Respond to the phrases "seeing the invisible" and "believing the impossible" as used in this chapter.
2. The author uses the word *agonizing* to describe belief. Has belief ever been agonizing for you?
3. Do you believe your life can make a difference in our world? How big a difference? In what ways? How can you help one another believe more?
4. Respond to some specific detail in Graciela's story.
5. The author speaks of the conversion of "the decadent and self-indulgent West." What might this look like? Which is harder to imagine, the conversion of the West in this way, or the improvement of the lives of the world's desperately poor?
6. Your group is nearing the completion of your reading. How do you feel about your progress so far? What have been the high and low points of your dialogue so far? What do you hope happens after you finish reading this book?

Exposing the Covert
Curriculum

A revolution of hope is not just a matter of reading a book or hearing an inspiring sermon. True, a book or sermon or personal encounter may be the vehicle through which hope wins our hearts. But a revolution of hope makes radical demands of us. It requires us to learn new skills and habits and capacities: the skills of a new way of seeing, the habits of a new way of thinking, the capacities of a new way of living. This kind of learning is less like mastering material for a test and more like evolving from a burrowing or crawling creature into a new species that can walk upright or learn to fly. It is less like switching political parties and more like growing from an aquatic larval stage to a new mature stage with wings. As we have said before, it is not a new system of belief patched into an old way of life; it is a new way of life that changes everything.

It is no wonder, in this light, that the early movement started by Jesus did not have the name *Christianity*. That name never occurs in the Bible and has a much more recent history, one that evokes a highly developed doctrinal system or a list of richly storied denominations. The original revolution of hope was simply called "the Way," evoking a new way of life (Acts 9:2; 22:4; 24:14). Jesus' second-generation disciple Paul called it "the way of love" and repeatedly used the metaphor of walking to describe it (1 Corinthians 13:1;

14:1; Ephesians 5:2; Colossians 2:6; 3:7; Romans 6:4), as did another of Jesus' earliest disciples (1 John 1:7). It is also no wonder that the earliest followers of this way were called *disciples*, which means students and apprentices. As disciples, they would learn to practice, to live, to walk this new way, which would also require them to unlearn old ways.

So, faith communities that seek to form disciples of this sort today will have a dual task. First, they must recognize that the dominant societal system, the collective reality we have called the suicide machine, has its own covert curriculum, a curriculum that must be unlearned. Second, they must develop their own creative counter-curriculum to teach people the art of living in this new way. As they do so, they discover the subtle but pervasive power of the dominant system's covert curriculum.

Everywhere they look, they see the system infusing its values, teaching its skills, domesticating all dissent, reinforcing desired behaviors. They see the covert curriculum at work in TV commercials, in political speeches, in video games, in sitcom plots, in movies, in popular songs, in what gets taught in educational institutions and, more subtly, in how it gets taught, in so-called news reporting, in business practices, in sporting events, and even in churches.

Yet those who are being malformed by the dominant system's covert curriculum are generally unaware of what's happening to them; after all, the system's curriculum has become the unconscious, precritical lens through which they see everything else. It takes a kind of enlightenment or conversion to become aware that there is a covert curriculum by which one already has been formed or shaped.

The subtlety and pervasiveness of this covert curriculum can become more visible when we realize that in our world today, *both sides* of most arguments between groups and ideologies are arguing by the same logic, working from within the bounds and values set by the curriculum itself. By and large, these arguments between ideologies or parties are, no matter how loud and strident, only intramural squabbles because both sides rely on the same assumptions and the same methods of argument to make their differing points.

They are a kind of professional wrestling: useful for releasing tension, dramatic enough to hold attention, profitable for the participants and sponsors, but rigged from the start and therefore not real sport. Or perhaps better put, they are part of the spectacle of today's Coliseum, which substitutes Rome's debased circuses with 167 channels of cable television playing out today's death-matches between political, religious, and entertainment gladiators. The more intensely the contestants struggle, the more they reinforce the assumptions and methodologies and habits of the dominant framing story that they share.

I'm suggesting that if we go deep enough, we will realize that Democrats and Republicans, left and right, even "terrorists" and "free world" are generally playing by the same rules and part of the same system—in much the same way as in Jesus' day, complacent Herodians and Sadducees and activist Pharisees and Zealots were, for all their squabbles, playing within the same system: defining their lives in relation to Caesar. On one level, they disagreed about how to respond to Caesar, but on a deeper level, they agreed that Caesar was the reality in relation to which people had to define themselves. No wonder they also agreed that Jesus must be killed: he had defected from their whole system, their whole reality, because he taught that we should begin to define our lives in relation to God and God's kingdom, not Caesar and his empire. Jesus simply walked away from the emperor, declared Caesar passé and irrelevant—naked, if you will. Instead, Jesus chose to live in relation to the God who cares for birds of the air and flowers of the field, the God who welcomes runaway children home, the God who cares about the worst of us as a good shepherd cares for a wandering sheep.

Which side wins—Democrat or Republican, East or West, elite or bourgeois or proletariat, Herodian or Zealot—may be considered *news* within the system, but until someone brings into the system resources from outside it, unless someone kicks a hole in the wall of the system so we aren't trapped within it, there is no real *good news*. There is only more information, most of which isn't that new at all, nor is it that good. The dominant system is at its most powerful when its covert curriculum has taught us that it is all there is; there is no outside.

A SIMPLE THOUGHT EXPERIMENT

I think I can make the dominant system's covert curriculum more visible by playing out a simple thought experiment, showing how two contentious and polarizing issues are actually expressions of the same "doctrine." Let's consider how the practice of abortion, a long-standing moral touchstone of the so-called Right, expresses the same underlying lesson plan as global warming, which has until recently been seen (by many on the Right) as an issue of the so-called Left. Through this one example, I hope readers will be sensitized to see others, and become more aware of how the conventional language of *culture war* between Left and Right (or between socialist and capitalist, or even between terrorist and free world) has become a smokescreen, a distraction, or camouflage under which a more dangerous battle of values is waged covertly.

Nobody, as far as I know, thinks abortion is good. By that I mean that not even the most committed pro-choicer sets out to have an abortion. You might hear people defend abortion as a legal right, but you never hear anyone say, "I can't wait to get pregnant so I can have an abortion!" the way they would say, "I can't wait to get a raise so I can buy a new car!" Some might say that abortion is harmless, morally neutral, or not a lot different from cutting off an overgrown fingernail. More would say that abortion should be available as the lesser of two evils or the better option among other undesirable choices. But nobody says, "The more abortions, the better!"

Putting rape-induced pregnancy aside, abortion is considered necessary because some people contract a pregnancy they don't want in the process of seeking pleasure, intimacy, or other consequences of intercourse that they do want. They know what causes pregnancy, so in that sense, they don't get pregnant by accident, but the pregnancy feels accidental because it was not the goal of their sexual activity.

They could have chosen abstinence. They could have used birth control. They could have chosen a better partner with whom they would have wanted to raise a child, or they could have waited for a more auspicious time to have sex. But in spite of the many pre-pregnancy options at their disposal, they chose to engage in life's only pregnancy-causing activity while hoping to avoid that outcome. Then, when they discover themselves pregnant, abortion presents itself as a way of "fixing" the undesired consequence of their desired behavior.

Similarly, nobody, as far as I know, thinks global warming is good. By that I mean that not even the most committed industrial-ist sets out to emit greenhouse gases and raise the global tempera-ture. You might hear people defend free markets and free trade as a right, but you never hear anyone say, "I can't wait to start a mega-corporation so I can destabilize the global environment!" the way they would say, "I can't wait to get my MBA so I can afford to live in Silicon Valley!" Some might say that global warming is part of a natural cycle, not human-induced, simply another chapter in the process that brought us the Ice Age. More would say that global warming should be tolerated as the lesser of two evils or the better option among other undesirable choices. But nobody says, "The hotter the earth, the better."

Global warming is currently considered inevitable because some people produce it without intending to produce it in the process of seeking profit, which is something they do want to produce. They now know what causes global warming, so in that sense, they don't create an atmospheric greenhouse by accident. But what they desire is not global warming; they want the quick profit and high return on their investments without having to be environmentally conscious, so the unintended consequence of global warming feels like an accident.

They could have chosen another line of business. They could have used other more environmentally friendly means of produc-tion. They could have waited for cleaner technologies or invested in carbon abatement. But in spite of the many preproduction options at their disposal, they chose to engage in one of humanity's primary greenhouse-gas-producing activities while hoping to avoid global warming. Then, when they discover the world is heating up, they look for a way of "fixing" the undesired consequence of their desired behavior, although no satisfactory fixes currently have presented themselves.

These two "productions"—the production of unwanted pregnancies and the production of greenhouse gases—both follow from a script taught by the covert curriculum in a thousand ways: namely, *we can engage in pleasurable or profitable behaviors with undesired consequences and either avoid the consequences or clean them up later.* Or put otherwise, if something feels good or makes a profit, do it now and deal with consequences later. The professors who teach this lesson, of course, are the people who profit from our indulgence in short-term pleasure and profit without regard for long-term wisdom. Their enticements—we call them "advertisements" or "sales pitches" or "campaigns"—synergize like a mega-weather system, bringing small storms together to create the dominant system of our world.

Jesus comes onto the scene, and what does he say? For starters, he says that the fulfillment of your desires can destroy you—that you'd be better off (speaking no doubt by hyperbole) plucking out your eye or cutting off your hand if your hand or eye (symbolizing your desire to take something that you see) causes you to do something foolish or evil (Matthew 5:29–30). He asks *what good it would be to gain every possible desire—sexual, financial, political—but to lose your soul in the process?* (Mark 8:36)

So, today, he might raise a series of questions to a culture that engages in pregnancy-producing and greenhouse-gas-producing behaviors but doesn't want pregnancies or a warmer global environment: What kind of world do you want? Do you want a world full of consequences that you don't desire? What kind of life do you want? Do you want to be creating crises today that you must solve tomorrow? What kind of people do you want to be? Do you want to be the kind of people who think only of short-term gain? In so doing, he would be pointing out how arguing about effects—from abortion to global warming—can keep you stuck in the dominant system, straining at gnats and swallowing camels (Matthew 25:24).

Before we move on, please notice what I am not saying about abortion and global warming. I am not saying these two problems are morally equivalent. Nor am I saying that they can be solved the same way, through legislation or whatever. But I am saying that the two productions (unwanted pregnancies and unwanted greenhouse gases) are related, because each is sustained and legitimized by the same narrative that teaches us we can live without limits in a care-free pursuit of what we want.

I am saying if you want to reduce the number of aborted fetuses or the tonnage of greenhouse gases produced by humanity, you'd be wise to realize that a common script or lesson plan invigorates them both, a script of individual pursuit of happiness without concern for the common good. I'm saying that if you want to inhibit one and permit the other, you are working against yourself because they run on the same rationale. I am saying that without dealing with that deeper script or lesson plan and, deeper still, the framing story from which it derives, you're not going to make much difference. And I am saying that whatever changes you wish to see in our world, you would be wise to uncover the covert curriculum that opposes your efforts and sustains the status quo at every turn.

Looking at the Covert Lesson Plan

The covert curriculum has many other lessons that it teaches in many other ways. The common lesson plan that underlies forty thousand commercials tells us we can eat desirable foods and not get fat, or if we do get fat, we can surgically remove the unwanted tissue. We can drive a new car every year or two and not go into debt, or we can titillate our sexual appetite and not hurt ourselves or our families. The common script that underlies our most popular movies shows us that the way to defeat bad guys is through violence, violence that, the movies teach us, will bring a happy ending with no negative consequences. The lesson plan that informs our video games gives us the same message; after all, the next time we play, the children and grandchildren of our last game's casualties aren't waiting to inflict revenge. We get a fresh start each time we turn the game on. No consequences of the last game's violence follow us. We live by the sword but never have to die by it, and so Jesus is proved wrong game after game after game.

The covert curriculum teaches us what matters and what doesn't by strategically ignoring certain things. So our public schools overtly teach our children that math and reading deserve years of practice. But patience, self-discipline, conflict resolution, gratitude, interpersonal communication, contemplation, or reconciliation have little or no visible part in most curricula I know of. You can get an A in math and an F in contemplation and self-knowledge, and you are still judged a success, because there is no course called "contemplation and self-knowledge" in the curriculum. That fact itself is a key element of the covert lesson plan.

Similarly, popular songs and TV shows covertly teach teenagers (and their parents) that sexual behavior is a matter of personal choice between two individuals, with no community ramifications—even though the spread of STDs, the rise in teen pregnancy, the epidemic of divorce, and the prevalence of fatherless households have huge community costs. Those costs simply are invisible in nearly all popular media. This invisibility is not an accident; it is a major learning objective in the covert curriculum. Meanwhile, grocery stores teach us that it doesn't matter where your food comes from; food magically appears shrink-wrapped in plastic and Styrofoam, disconnecting us from the land and rendering farming and land management invisible to nearly everyone who depends on them. What is the covert curriculum teaching us, say, about the relative importance of farming, land management, and soil conservation by this consistent invisibility? And the racks of celebrity news magazines at the checkout counter—what are we being taught covertly by their existence and placement?

What is the covert curriculum in our culture regarding aging and death? What are we taught about gray hair, wrinkled skin, changing body shape, and failing health—except that these facts of life are embarrassing and to be feared or covered up in some way?

What use does this denial of death and aging serve in our dominant system? Could it be that if we were to think more deeply about our mortality, we would see how silly so many of our culture's obsessions really are? Would the covert curriculum and the framing story in which it is situated become ridiculous?

What's the covert curriculum these days about marriage? How have so many people been taught—covertly, of course—to postpone marriage later and later, and to do the same with childrearing? What are the long-term personal and social costs of this postponement? Who writes the unwritten "marriage course" in the covert curriculum, and who profits from it?

What is the covert curriculum of the news industry? Why are some things considered newsworthy and others not? Who decides and why? Who makes money from selling us too much sugar and fat and too many new cars? Who profits from making us fear aging, death, celibacy, fidelity, marriage, parenthood, or wearing last year's hot brand name or hairstyle? Who profits—in money or in votes— from teaching us to fear terrorism caused by others, but not fear the consequences of wars we ourselves start? What are we taught about our emotions, when our teenagers take illegal drugs to numb their pain or replace their boredom, and their parents take legal drugs to do the same thing?

What are we being taught each day, covertly, about prosperity? About equity? About security? About the story we find ourselves in? About what human beings are worth and what human life is for?

A GROUP OF PEOPLE WHO COULD CHANGE EVERYTHING

A community of people who begin to wake up to the covert curriculum in which they swim each day would want to band together to share their insights about it. They would help one another not be sucked in, not be massaged into passivity, not be malformed by this powerful educational process occurring in a multimedia classroom without walls or vacations. They would remind one another of the alternative framing story they had come to believe was good, beautiful, and true, and they would seek, together, to live by this alternative framing story, the radical good news.

They would develop practices of spiritual formation so they and their children for generations to come would be able to learn, live, and grow as part of the solution, not part of the problem; as agents of healing, not as carriers of the disease; as revolutionaries seeking to dismantle and subvert the suicidal system, not as functionaries and drones seeking to serve and preserve it.

They would understand that at every moment, their identity as revolutionaries remains under assault; the gravity of compromise pulls and drags to hunch their backs, slacken their step, and lower their gaze. They would be on guard for ways that they themselves could sabotage themselves—by becoming preoccupied with trivia, or by working from the system's logic and values when trying to fight the system, or by slipping into dual narratives as the Pharisees and religious scholars in Jesus' day did, or by substituting talk for action or activity for fruitfulness.

So through word and deed, song and ritual, holiday and daily practice, they would seek to be the revolution they wished to see in the world, and they would work to spread their vision and extend the invitation to others to join their revolution in every way they could.

A group of people like this, functioning in a difficult environment dominated by a hostile system with a covert curriculum, would make lots of mistakes and need continual renewal. But it would be worth the effort and sacrifice—as long as it understood its sacred and unique role as the bearers of the revolutionary good news, the message of the hope: *another world is possible, available now for all who believe.*

This kind of group would be the current expression of Jesus' original band of disciples. It would be the church as Jesus intended. It would be an exciting thing to be part of: a community that forms disciples who work for the liberation and healing of the world, based on Jesus' good news of the kingdom of God.

Groups like this wouldn't need buildings, pipe organs, rock bands, layers of institutional structure, video projectors, parking lots, and so on . . . although having these things wouldn't necessarily be a bad thing, and could possibly be useful. What they would need would be simple: a passion to understand Jesus and his message and a commitment to live out that understanding in a world in which everything must change.

GROUP DIALOGUE QUESTIONS

1. The author says that a revolution of hope makes radical demands of us. Where do you feel these radical demands touching your own life?
2. The author creates an analogy between abortion and global warming in this chapter. Summarize what he's trying to say through this analogy, and how you responded to it.
3. Can you think of some similar analogies?
4. Discuss some examples of "covert curriculum" you and other group members experienced in your daily life this week—perhaps from an advertisement, the way a news story was reported, or a movie or popular song.
5. Respond to the title of this book in light of your reading so far.

Moving Mountains

If we disbelieve the dominant societal system, and if we transfer our trust from its covert curriculum and framing story to the good news of Jesus, a radical and transforming hope begins to happen to us. Just as a fearful vision reshapes the world according to that which it fears, the hopeful vision of the kingdom of God will surely begin to reshape our world in its own hopeful image. We could say that a hopeful change in our "inner ecology" will inevitably manifest itself in a hopeful change in our global ecology.

We might picture the change like this:

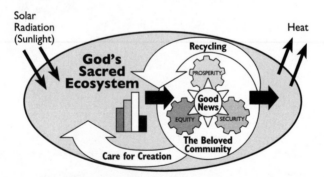

Now the machine has been transformed into a beloved community. It has lost its hard edges and its impervious boundaries. It has once again become part of God's sacred ecosystem. It is no longer careless about its consumption and waste, but it seeks to live with a sense of stewardship in God's world. And the beloved community expresses not only its need for creation's resources, but also its care for creation as a whole—human and nonhuman, living and nonliving.

The prosperity system now lives more humbly and responsibly within creaturely limits. It works in cooperation with the equity system, investing the community's energy for the common good, never forgetting the community's weakest and most vulnerable members. The transformed prosperity and equity systems in turn transform the security system—whose resources are focused less on the proliferation and use of weapons in conflict and more on the alleviation of human suffering. The less we have to fight to be safe from each other, the more we can concern ourselves with safety from disease and epidemic, safety from natural disaster, and safety from our own lack of virtue and wisdom.

At the center of the beloved community is good news—a framing story that calls humanity to creativity, harmony, reconciliation, justice, virtue, integrity, and peace, because these values reflect the character of the Creator whose world is our home and in whose presence we live and move and have our being. In short: we are all part of one kingdom, one beautiful whole, with one caring Creator, who is faithful to us even in our stupidity and sin. God calls us to reconcile with God, one another, and creation, to defect from the false stories that divide and destroy us, and to join God in the healing of the world through love and the pursuit of justice and the common good.

This process of healing is described by Jesus through a variety of metaphors. It works like a seed that germinates under the soil, eventually—against all odds—bringing forth an unimaginable harvest (Matthew 13:18–32). It works like yeast that transforms a huge, sixty-pound lump of dough (13:33). It works like a pearl or treasure hidden in a vacant lot, a treasure that gives the land previously unimagined value (13:44–46). It works like a net, hidden under the surface of the water, that quietly gathers a huge catch of fish

(13:47–50). In each metaphor, the forces of injustice are defeated and justice reshapes and transforms the world for the common good. The end is a hopeful one for all who love justice.

A VISION OF EU-TOPIA

Many believe the apocalyptic vision of the New Testament is not intended to give us this kind of hope within history. They might point to the vision of the new Jerusalem (Revelation 21), which, they say, is intended to give us a vision of the destruction of our dynamic space-time universe and its replacement, beyond history, with a timeless, static state called "eternity"[1] or "heaven" where everything is absolutely perfect. Increasing numbers of us disagree with this assessment.

As we discussed in chapter 18, more and more of us see this eschatology of abandonment and despair to be an example of the biblical story being rewritten to aid and abet the dominant system. We believe the vision of the new Jerusalem, like all prophetic visions, seeks to inspire our imaginations with hope about what our world can actually become through the good news of the kingdom of God.

In this emerging view, the "new heaven and new earth" (Revelation 21:1) means, not a different space-time universe, but a new way of living that is possible within this universe, a new societal system that is coming as surely as God is just and faithful. The lack of an ocean (v. 1) doesn't mean the planet becomes a literal desert, but rather the chaos that the sea represented to ancient people would be gone—including the chaos of war and rumors of war, which are part of the "old order of things" (v. 4) that is passing away. Similarly, the lack of night (v. 25) suggests that the time of fear is over.

The new Jerusalem represents, then, a new spirituality, a new way of living in which the sacred presence of God is integrated with all of life and not confined to temples (v. 22)—a vision which Jesus saw as real in his day (John 4:21–24). We haven't evacuated the dark earth for the light of heaven or eternity; no, the light of heaven has come down, come down to us, down to earth.

The extravagant language doesn't describe a utopia (meaning a no-place) but a eu-topia, meaning a good place, a new-topia, meaning a renewed place. The message of the apocalypse is that the empire of Caesar, including the religious apparatus that sustains his system, will not last for ever, but that the empire or kingdom of this world (earth's integrated political and economic and social systems, its principalities and powers, its societal machinery) will ultimately be transformed so it becomes "the kingdom of our Lord and of his Messiah, and he will reign for ever and ever" (Revelation 11:15). This is the coming of a new generation of humanity that Jesus embodied, demonstrated, proclaimed, and invited us to believe.[2]

Yes, this is the *end* of the world—but not *end* in the sense of the discontinuation of our story; rather, it is the *end* in the sense of the goal toward which we move. Yes, it is the end of the world *as we know it*—a world dominated by suicidal machinery driven by a suicidal framing story. But it is the beginning of the world *as God desires it*, a new story, a new chapter, a new way.

OUR CALL TO ACTION

Jesus' invitation to his original disciples was to begin living into this new way now. And it is, I believe, his ongoing invitation to us today. This is our call to action.

As I said, believing is the indispensable first step in this process, but it is not the only step. Without it, we don't go anywhere, but with it, an exciting journey begins—a journey that leads us to action on four levels.[3]

Personal Action

First, there is personal action. If we disbelieve the dominant framing story and instead believe Jesus' good news of the kingdom of God, we will suddenly find ourselves making new personal decisions—not because we have to, as a duty, but because we want to, because we are now liberated from the cramped possibilities of the old framing story, free to move toward the eu-topia. "Saved by our faith," we will pray differently. Prayer will cease to be a technique for enlisting God to help us "make it" in the dominant system; it will instead become a way of bathing our inner world in the transforming presence of God, a way we seek to be shaped by the new framing story, the new reality, the good news, so that we can be catalysts bringing transformation to the dominant system.

If we disbelieve the old framing story and believe the good news, we will also work differently. When we realize that the most powerful world-changing work we can do is simply to believe, as Jesus told his original disciples (John 6:29), we experience liberation from panicked, frantic, desperate, incoherent, and often fruitless or counterproductive action. We rediscover Sabbath and rest and even play, and we come to our work with a new sense of energy and purpose. We will no longer be "just" anything—just a homemaker, just a laborer, just an accountant, just a kindergarten teacher. No, whatever our work, we will do it as agents of the kingdom of God, builders of a new world.

We will also buy differently. For example, when faced with a choice between an inexpensive pair of pants produced by a corporation that exploits workers (whom we now see to be our neighbors), we will choose a more expensive pair produced by a corporation that treats its workers fairly. Maybe we'll own fewer pairs of pants, but we'll feel better wearing them. We will vote differently, drive differently, invest differently, eat differently, volunteer differently, treat our neighbors differently, and so much more. Multiply all these kinds of daily personal decisions by the increasing numbers of people for whom they make sense, and you begin to see the power of personal action inspired by a new kind of faith.

Community Action

Second, there is community action. This level of action should perhaps come first in our list, because individuals can't learn a new kind of faith to inspire new personal action without a faith community to teach the faith and model the action. Sadly, it's painfully obvious the degree to which many if not most of our churches are currently co-opted, living by dual narratives, domesticated by the dominant system and domesticating the next generation as well. Rather than providing an alternative, they serve as the religious chaplains of the dominant system, purveyors of religious goods and services to keep its supporters spiritually preoccupied and thus pacified. Probably, when people disparage "institutional religion" or "organized religion," they are expressing disappointment in forms of religion that function in this emasculated and emasculating way.

But new kinds of faith communities are emerging, and more will emerge—virile, courageous, nurturing communities that center their theology on Jesus' revolutionary message of the kingdom and that center their lives on living out that radical message.[4] These are communities of profound spiritual formation leading to liberating social transformation, and their continuing emergence is one of the most important developments in our time.[5]

These faith communities, large and small, are indispensable for the spiritual formation of individuals, but they are also powerful expressions of combined personal effort. Already, literally millions of people are being mobilized by faith communities to make a difference—through mission trips and mission groups, community involvement projects, faith-based initiatives, and other expressions of faith-based community action.

Public Action

Third, there is public (or social) action. In the tradition of Martin Luther King Jr., Desmond Tutu, and others, individuals and faith communities—whose normal work is done "in secret"—begin to go public, linking together in larger social movements, employing the full range of nonviolent methods of social change—from education to civil disobedience, from rallies and festivals to political organizing, from artistic expression of the new vision to coalition-building and public demonstration.[6]

Global Action

And fourth, there is integrated global action. When personal, community, and public actions are integrated in synergizing ways, what was previously impossible happens. This dynamic is signified powerfully by something Jesus says in the course of performing a miracle for a man and his boy. As the scene opens, the disciples have been asked by a father to expel an evil spirit from his son—an evil spirit that, not insignificantly, drives his son to suicidal behavior (Matthew 17:14–20). The disciples try to help but cannot. Jesus himself intervenes, and the disciples ask, "Why couldn't we drive it out?" (v. 19).

Jesus replies, "Because you have so little faith. Truly I tell you, if you have faith as small as a mustard seed, you can say to this mountain, 'Move from here to there,' and it will move. Nothing will be impossible for you" (v. 20).

Jesus is not interested in the geographical rearrangement of mountains. It is the societal map of greed, lust, arrogance, fear, racism, domination, oppression, revenge, and injustice that he wants to redraw. He wants his disciples to move mountains of injustice and make new rivers of creativity and compassion flow. He wants them to uproot the fruitless fig tree of dual-narrative religion and plant in its place a spiritual vineyard of joy and transformation. He wants his followers to do the impossible: to label as *unacceptable, unnatural,* and *changeable* a world where homeless children beg outside the sprawling estates of the super rich, whose luxuries are protected by walls and fences topped with razor-wire and patrolled by vicious dogs, dogs that eat better than the street children from whom they serve as protection . . . a world where families subsist as scavengers on garbage dumps while the producers of the garbage drink cocktails and watch reality shows on TV . . . a world that could tithe its weapons budget and so feed, clothe, and shelter the poor.

It's interesting—astonishing, really—that Jesus doesn't simply say, "Nothing will be impossible for me," or "Nothing will be impossible with God." Instead he says, "Nothing will be impossible *for you.*" This is our call to action, our invitation to move mountains and so reshape the social and spiritual landscape of our world. Yes, change is impossible through human effort alone. But faith brings

God's creative power into our global crises, so the impossible first becomes possible and then inevitable for those who believe.

Mountains can be moved and everything can change, beginning with our stories, beginning with faith, beginning now, beginning with us.

GROUP DIALOGUE QUESTIONS

1. This last chapter begins with a revised diagram of our world. Use it to summarize the message of this book to one another.
2. The author uses the phrase "end of the world" in two different ways. Explain them, and give your personal reaction.
3. What personal action do you want to take as a result of reading this book and participating in this dialogue group?
4. What community action would you like to pursue?
5. What public action could you imagine planning in response to the message of this book?
6. Imagine some global action that could arise from the message of this book.
7. Write (or spontaneously compose) a prayer that expresses your faith response to this book.
8. What are this world's top global crises?
9. How do the life and message of Jesus address these crises?
10. So what? Now what? Will your group end now, or have a future together?
11. Would you like to recommend this book to some friends? Whom?

Notes

CHAPTER 1: HOPE HAPPENS

1. Brian McLaren, *The Secret Message of Jesus: Uncovering the Truth That Could Change Everything* (Nashville: W, 2006).

CHAPTER 2: THE *AMAHORO* FLOWING BETWEEN US

1. For example, in 1992, a group of scientists including Carl Sagan invited religious leaders to join them for a summit on the environmental crisis, believing that science could describe the crisis, but only religion could motivate people to address it.
2. World religion statistics in these paragraphs are taken from http://en.wikipedia.org/wiki/Major_religious_groups.
3. I'm not making any distinctions here between "true" Christians and nominal ones. That's not because there is no distinction, but because the distinction isn't necessary to my point here.
4. For more statistics on world religions, see religioustolerance.org.
5. For more about Claude's work, see amahoro-africa.org.

CHAPTER 3: EVERYTHING MUST CHANGE

1. To learn more about this group, go to amahoro-africa.org.
2. In the United States, immigration has again become a critical issue. For contemporary reflection on colonialism from a Latino-Christian perspective, see the work of Fernando Segovia, Ada Maria Isasi-Diaz, Benjamin Valentin, and Gabriel Salguero. See also latinoleadershipcircle.typepad.com.
3. This subject of the kingdom of God is the theme of my book *The Secret Message of Jesus: Uncovering the Truth That Could Change Everything* (Nashville: W, 2006). It should be seen as a companion volume to this one.

CHAPTER 4: NOT WHAT JESUS INTENDED

1. Just the other day I received an e-mail from this health-care worker. The pastor who hosted the gathering that day has now created office space for the health-care worker and his organization in the church building where we met. Communication happened that day. Things began to change.
2. Of course, the missionaries could not have addressed these issues without issuing the call to their fellow white Europeans to love black Africans as neighbors and equals. Doing so would have called the whole project of colonization into question.
3. For more information on these kinds of outreaches, see lareddelcamino.net and read C. Rene Padilla and Tetsunao Yamamari, *The Local Church: Agent of Transformation* (Buenos Aires: Karios, 2004).

CHAPTER 5: SECOND THOUGHTS HAD COME TO STAY

1. By global North, we loosely mean the former colonizers, and by global South, we mean the formerly colonized. See Philip Jenkins, *The Next Christendom* (New York: Oxford UP, 2007). For a thoughtful critique of some of Jenkins's perspectives by a Catholic priest and scholar from the global South, see Emmanuel Katongole, *A Future for Africa* (Scranton, Penn.: University of Scranton, 2005).

2. For more on this image, see Gabe Lyons and David Kinnaman, *UnChristian: What a New Generation Thinks About Christianity and Why It Matters* (Grand Rapids: Baker, 2007), and Dan Kimball, *They Like Jesus But Not the Church* (Grand Rapids: Zondervan, 2007).

3. Walker Percy, "Notes for a Novel About the End of the World," *The Message in the Bottle* (New York: Picador: 1954, 2000).

4. I don't mean to imply that any of us have found and articulated a "pure" form of Christianity, or that we ever will, only that we all need the freedom to name and address the "viruses" that had become apparent in our system.

5. Like an alcoholic who wants to put his last lost job, last broken marriage, and most recent auto accident behind him without diagnosing the disease that was a major factor in each, most people were eager to move on without this kind of painful reflective and diagnostic work.

6. Some portion of this excessive confidence arose no doubt in reaction to the humiliation the nation had suffered in World War I, and earlier, and to the relatively small successes Germany experienced in colonization when compared to the British, French, Spanish, and Portuguese. One could argue that this expression of excessive confidence was actually a kind of overcompensation for an even deeper insecurity or inferiority.

7. Dee Brown, *Bury My Heart at Wounded Knee* (New York: Bantam, 1974).

8. To learn more about the tragic story of how "Christian" white colonists and settlers treated the Native Peoples of North America, see the brilliant and important work of Richard Twiss (wiconi.org) and Randy Woodley (eagleswingsministry.com).

9. Rene Descartes, *A Discourse on Method* (1637) (New York: Oxford UP, 2006).

10. Defenders of foundationalism today distinguish between "hard" forms, which they admit are potentially malignant, and "soft" forms, which they believe are benign.

CHAPTER 6: SIMMERING ON THE BACK BURNER OF MY MIND

1. Brian McLaren, *A New Kind of Christian* (San Francisco: Josey-Bass, 2001).

2. I had been prepared for this insight when I identified conquest and control as prime characteristics of the modern age. Once, while speaking on the subject, the word *conquistadores* came to mind. I realized that colonial conquest by Europeans (and more recently, by the United States) was indeed a (if not *the*) dominant historical theme of the last five centuries. This realization may be ridiculously obvious to some readers, and shockingly new to others.

3. Conservative critics of postmodernism—including many critics of my work—rightly realize that one can so successfully undermine a culture's *excessive* confidence that it eventually lacks *sufficient* confidence. Unfortunately, they often warn of the dangers of insufficient confidence without demonstrating awareness of the terrible effects of their own culture's past and present hyperconfidence. As a result, we end up with some "postmodernists" backing away from the dangers of colonialism, but falling backward into opposite dangers associated with amoral relativism, nihilism, consumerism, and what Ken Wilber calls "boomeritis." (Boston: Shambhala, 2003) And then we have many modernist defenders backing away from the dangers of relativism and nihilism, only to fall backward into an immoral defense of cultural chauvinism, colonialism, and empire. One hopes we can all work together in more balanced, both-and ways in the future.

4. Archbishop Desmond Tutu, quoting Jomo Kenyatta, available at thinkexist.com.
5. Lomborg explains the rationale behind the Copenhagen Consensus: "There are a lot of problems confronting humanity, and we have a tendency just to focus on one of these at any one time. . . . But the issue is to realize that there are a very large number of different things confronting us: 800 million people starving, 1 billion people lacking clean drinking water, and several billions of people who will be affected by global warming. So the issue here is to say: if we can't do it all, what should we do first? . . . If the world decided to spend another, say, $50 billion over the next four years, where should that extra money be spent? . . . Where should we focus extra effort?"

This kind of prioritization isn't easy, Lomberg explains. For every item that is included in a "top ten" list, many more are excluded, and each of them is significant to large numbers of people. For example, if your child lies in a bed, paralyzed by spinal cord injury, the need for spinal cord research is the most significant problem in your world. If you live on the edge of an expanding desert in the Sahel region of Africa, desertification is the top problem in your world. If your spouse has just relapsed in an ugly addiction, or if your daughter has been trapped in the sex slave trade, there's no question what the top problem in your world would be.

Even though prioritization of global problems is difficult, Lomberg says, still it is necessary: "Not prioritizing doesn't make prioritization go away; it doesn't mean we don't do it. It simply means we put it back in the shade, that we don't talk about how we spend our money most wisely, and that means that we end up doing less good than we could otherwise have done" (www.cceis.org/resources/transcripts/5090.html).
6. There has been quite a bit of confusion regarding the Copenhagen Consensus' position on climate change. In their cost-benefit analysis of potential solutions, they ranked climate change solutions low. Many erroneously interpreted this low ranking to mean the economists didn't think climate change was a serious problem. To the contrary, their low ranking meant that the proposed solutions were not yet strong enough to reduce the strong impact of climate change. The *proposed solutions*, not the *seriousness of the problem*, were given a low ranking.
7. For more information on the Copenhagen Consensus, see copenhagenconsensus.org.
8. See wikipedia.org/wiki/15_global_challenge for more information and links.
9. The Millennium Development Goals have inspired the One Campaign (one.org) and its affiliates, including the Micah Challenge (micahchallenge.org) and Data (data.org).
10. Some believe that any list coming out of the United Nations or the World Bank will be so politically determined as to be suspect. For example, any emphasis on human rights issues might be minimized by China, or any emphasis on global climate change may be marginalized by the United States. Even so, the MDG's and Rischard's list of twenty problems have awakened more people than ever before to begin grappling with global problems. *High Noon: 20 Global Problems, 20 Years to Solve Them* (New York: Basic, 2002).
11. Rischard's emphasis on regulation is important because of two trends unique to the twenty-first century. First, he predicts that we will reach our maximum population for the planet by century's end, rising to 9 or 10 billion from our current 6.7 billion. Closer to the present, he predicts a global population of 8 billion by 2025, which represents a 30 percent increase in less than one generation. This 2-billion-person growth would be significant enough (it took until 1930 for the planet to ever reach a total population of 2 billion), but a full 95 percent of the new births will come to the world's developing countries. Coping with the stress of this kind of growth among the less prosperous countries (combined with actual population decreases among some of the most prosperous) will create huge political and economic problems.

No less significant, Rischard explains, the earth's multiplying population increasingly participates in a single unified global capitalist economy. Over the last twenty years, as the experiment of communism was universally judged as a failure, the number of people living in capitalist economies rose from 1.5 billion to over 6 billion. But increasingly, fueled by technological (especially digital) advancement, these 6 billion people aren't simply competing in the old local or national capitalist markets known to our economics textbooks, legal structures, and charitable organizations. Instead, they participate in a single, integrated global market.

These demographic, technological, and economic changes provide many opportunities, including what he calls "catch-up opportunities" for some of the poorer countries: "Never have there been such massive opportunities for improving the human condition" (199). But these rapid changes also bring many new challenges, especially if we place a naive trust in capitalism to solve all problems:

"With the central planning model [communism] gone for good, more politicians and other players see the market as the solution to all problems, sometimes dumping on government while they are at it. Whether from intellectual laziness or from single-minded pursuit of ideology, what these free-market fundamentalists fail to see is that while central planners were either cretins or fools, the market is a moron. An effective moron, but a moron nevertheless: left to its own devices, it will churn away mindlessly." (34)

In particular, he warns against capitalism's "mindless expansion," which will inevitably exceed "the planet's carrying capacity" already overloaded because of rapid population increase (34). Rischard says that minor, incremental improvements of existing systems will not suffice in the face of these dangers, because of "the basic, undeniable failure of the *entire* international setup and the world's nation-states at the task of fast and effective global problem solving" (201). Instead, we must think in radically new ways in order to imagine and create radically new kinds of non-hierarchical partnerships between business, government, and what he calls civil society (charities, advocacy groups, associations, trade unions, religious communities, and other NGOs).

12. Rick Warren, *The Purpose-Driven Life* (Grand Rapids: Zondervan, 2002).
13. See purposedriven.com/peaceplan.htm.
14. Quote from Rick Warren: The first Reformation, led by Martin Luther, Warren explains, "was about belief. This one will be about deeds. It is about what the church should be doing in the world."
15. See http://www.acunu.org/millennium/issues.html.
16. Duane Clinker, in his excellent but as-yet unpublished manuscript *Social Holiness: Experiments in Prayer and Other Subversive Acts in the Local Church and Community*, identifies three dominant global problems that resonate strongly with the other lists: degradation (environmental), disparity (between rich and poor), and depravity (the utter complacency and carelessness among the rich and powerful about the first two problems). Dr. King, in *Where Do We Go From Here* (Boston: Beacon, 1968), identified racism, war, and poverty as the big three. For Bill Clinton's work on global crisis, see clintonglobalinitiative.org.
17. I encountered their work through an early manuscript of a book that has been released as *Hope in Troubled Times: A New Vision for Confronting Global Crises* (Baker, 2007).
18. Specifically, they identify four sick ideologies that fuel societal ill health:
    Resistance Ideologies. Some ideologies focus on the systematic resistance of all exploitative and oppressive powers that prevent the arrival of a better society. (However, to resist exploitation and oppression, they often inflict equal or greater violence and oppression, and even if they succeed in bringing down corrupt systems, they either leave a vacuum or replace old systems with new systems that do an even worse job of achieving peace, sustainability, and prosperity.)
    Survival Ideologies. Some ideologies focus on the survival of one's people, culture, group, or religion. (However, to assure that survival, a threatened group may begin to threaten or savage others. That threat may in turn energize the others with the same

self-preservation ideology, so that more and more groups find themselves locked in an escalating life-or-death cycle of offense and revenge with one another.)

Wealth Ideologies. Some ideologies specialize in pursuit of ever-increasing material wealth or prosperity. (However, they may do so at the expense of the environment, or they may use means to increase or maintain their wealth that impoverish or do violence to others.)

Safety Ideologies. Other ideologies seek to guarantee the protection of oneself, one's children, and one's fellow human beings against any attack from outside. (However, that legitimate desire for self-defense may be used to legitimize the destruction of others. And as more and more groups invest more and more money and energy in self-defense, fewer and fewer resources remain to be invested in overcoming poverty and environmental destruction.)

CHAPTER 7: THREE INTERLOCKING SYSTEMS

1. I decided to use the phrase *suicide machine* only after considerable soul-searching. As a former pastor, I can't use this disturbing term casually, because I have presided at the funerals of too many suicide victims over the years and I have "talked off the ledge" too many people who were leaning over the abyss of despair. Yet I believe the problems we will consider together in these pages are themselves so dangerous that the use of the disturbing word is justified.

2. Jared Diamond, in *Guns, Germs, and Steel* (New York: Norton, 2005, p. 411)

3. David Korten, *The Great Turning,* (Washington DC: Berrett-Koehler, 2006), 13.

4. Leonardo Boff, *Cry of the Earth, Cry of the Poor* (Mary Knoll, NY: Orbis, 1997), 1. In full, the latter two quotes read, "[We must] overcome the anti-ecological paradigm of dominating power that has the effect of a killing machine spreading destruction" (74), and "The Earth is crying out under the predatory and lethal machinery of our model of society and development" (112).

5. For example, without a metaphor like "laws of nature," we wouldn't "see" gravity, entropy, thermodynamics, momentum, and inertia as we do. Without speaking metaphorically of God as "our Father in heaven" or "our shepherd" or "our guiding light," we wouldn't be able to see God as we do.

6. Governments and religions do the same kind of metaphor manipulation when they render fellow human beings as "the axis of evil" or "the great Satan" or "collateral damage." It's much easier to drop a bomb on an axis of evil than it is to kill a kindly grandmother named Washida and her five-year-old grandson with Down's syndrome named Abdul. It's much easier to fly a plane into a building full of people metaphorically reduced to "the great Satan" than it is to kill moms and dads, kids and siblings, friends and lovers with names like Robert, Jasmine, Charlotte, Daniel, Jen, or Timothy.

   We also get in trouble when we lean too heavily on a single metaphor and ask it to support more weight than it can bear. For example, if we are limited to the familiar metaphor of "falling in love," we will miss what could be learned from an alternative metaphor like "growing in love" or "rising in love." Or if we think exclusively of God as judge, we may minimize our consciousness of God's parental care or kind disposition, and so we will need to rediscover and reemphasize metaphors like shepherd or father. Of course, if we then think excessively of God as father or shepherd, we may overly masculinize or personalize God, and then we'll need to rediscover and reemphasize metaphors like mother, light, or wind. If God becomes a nurturing pal or indulgent genii who wants our happiness above all, unconcerned about whether we become just and good, we'll need to come full circle and rediscover the metaphor of God as judge—the one who tells the truth about us without partiality. (Far better, I think, to live with many metaphors simultaneously in dynamic tension, at once enriching and deconstructing one another.)

7. Where people turn from modern to postmodern perspectives, they tend to prefer organic

or social metaphors over mechanistic ones. Take, for example, David Korten's *The Great Turning: From Empire to Earth Community* (Washington, DC: Berrett: Koehler, 2006).

8. Gary Haugen, founder of International Justice Mission (IJM.org), says that sometimes the poor and vulnerable need food, water, shelter, or medicine. But sometimes they need a good law. (Personal Communication, June 7, 2007).

9. In the English legal system, Equity Courts developed to transcend a perceived rigidity and inflexibility in the traditional courts. Their development reflected the belief that human wisdom was an essential factor in justice, and that justice could not be achieved simply through an unthinking dependence on legal precedent.

CHAPTER 8: THAT COULD NEVER HAPPEN TO US

1. Perhaps someday, human society will colonize other planets, enlarging the context for the machine. Even now, certain aspects of the machine are situated outside the earth's atmosphere—communication satellites, for example, which serve all three systems in ways you can easily imagine. But for the foreseeable future, it's safe to say that both human society and its supporting systems happen within the atmosphere of earth, or if not that, within its gravity.

2. This diagram is derived from the groundbreaking work of Herman Daly, *Beyond Growth: The Economics of Sustainable Development* (Boston: Beacon Press, 1996). Reprinted by permission of Beacon Press, Boston.

3. It's hard to overestimate how important solar energy is. The earth's ecosystem long ago achieved a delicate balance, which is quite amazing, when you think about it—where the amount of energy (in the form of heat) that radiates out from the earth into space each night is almost perfectly balanced with the amount of energy coming in through sunlight (or solar radiation) each day. The result is a climate stable enough for a long enough period of time so that life can develop and continue.

Solar radiation—conveniently for us—can be converted by photosynthesis in plants into many useful, storable, portable forms—from foods (which provide the only source of energy for our bodies) to coal and petroleum (which, as you probably know, are petrified or liquefied forms of concentrated, decayed plants). Even the water that we use to produce some of our electricity (through dams and related machinery) becomes useful to us because of solar energy, which causes heated ocean water to evaporate and rise high in the atmosphere where it condenses as rain and is drawn downward by gravity in streams and rivers. It is that downward motion that we convert (through turbines and magnetos) into electricity. Similarly, the wind, which we currently use to produce a small but growing fraction of our electricity, moves because the sun heats some parts of the atmosphere more than others; the heated parts expand and rise, producing the dynamics of wind and weather.

While solar energy is by far the most important source of energy for the earth's ecosystem, plate tectonics and volcanoes can make available to the societal machine some resources and energy—such as precious metals and minerals, and some geothermal energy, for example. But even the movement of the earth's tectonic plates is dependent on the dynamics of superheated layers beneath the earth's crust, and their heat was originally derived from the sun.

CHAPTER 9: THE STORIES WE TELL OURSELVES

1. I decided not to use the term *metanarrative* because of the negative connotations associated with it, as explained in chapter 5. Some framing stories would qualify as metanarratives because of their tendency to dominate or eradicate competing stories. Other framing stories, though, would seek to save, reconcile, fulfill, and redeem alternative stories rather than destroy them. Some are using an alternative term *meganarrative* to describe these redeeming framing stories.

2. In their book *Hope in Troubled Times: A New Vision for Confronting Global Crises* (Grand Rapids: Baker, 2007), Goudzwaard, Vander Vennen, and Van Heemst do not use the term *framing story*, but their terms *worldview* and *the deeper dimension* refer to the same reality:

> . . . almost every current diagnosis of the crisis of our time lacks something fundamental. Many observers neglect how deep desires can coalesce into a modernist perspective, orientation, or worldview that, despite its claims to the contrary, is capable of contributing to, sustaining and even entrenching global poverty, environmental devastation and widespread violence. They forget or ignore the role played by people's deepest longings, dreams and commitments—and how these profound aspirations become inscribed in the dynamic forces, interactional patterns and institutions of contemporary Western society. Assessments usually miss altogether what goes on at the deepest level in people's hearts and minds, what engages and moves them, what captures their imaginations, fills their hearts and satisfies their expectations. . . . In our view, neglecting this dimension deeply hampers the ability to break through the solution deadlock and find responsible solutions to the world's most complex, pressing problems. (26)

3. In *Graven Ideologies* (Downer's Grove, Illinois: Inter Varsity Press, 2002), philosopher Bruce Ellis Benson, like Goudzwaard, Vander Vennen, and Van Heemst, explores the ways in which ideologies become idolatries, exercising godlike powers over their followers.
4. For more on the concept of redemptive violence, see chapter 7 of Alan Mann and Steve Chalke's *The Lost Message of Jesus* (Grand Rapids: Zondervan, 2003); chapter 2 of Walter Wink's *The Powers That Be* (New York: Doubleday, 1998); and chapter 17 of *The Secret Message of Jesus* (Nashville: Nelson, 2006).
5. One might ask why I didn't choose a megastorm for the dominant metaphor in this book instead of suicide machine. The storm image works very well, I think, but storms are forces of nature, inherently beyond our control or responsibility. The global problems we face, in contrast, are largely human-made—like a machine, hence my preference for the mechanical metaphor.

CHAPTER 10: HOW MUCH MORE IRONIC

1. Of course, there are many modern Western nonreligious ontologies and framing stories too, plus Eastern ontologies and framing stories—both religious and irreligious.
2. This reflects a Calvinistic, evangelical, Protestant version of the message. The popular Roman Catholic version might say, "You must believe in the teachings of the church and follow its instructions, especially those regarding mortal sins and sacraments." The popular mainline or liberal Protestant version is sometimes vague and difficult to pin down, but one version of it might be summarized in its most dilute form as, "God is nice and wants you to be nice too."
3. This experience of transformation is, in my view, related to what Jesus means by "the kingdom of God."
4. For a solid analysis of the conventional view by a world-class scholar, see the work of Bishop N. T. Wright. For example, in a recent article (available at http://www.fulcrum-anglican.org.uk/news/2007/20070423wright.cfm?doc=205), Wright reflects on what I am calling the conventional view: "I am forced to conclude that there is a substantial swathe of contemporary evangelicalism which actually doesn't know what the gospels themselves are there for, and would rather elevate 'Paul' (inverted commas, because it is their reading of Paul, rather than the real thing, that they elevate) and treat Matthew, Mark, Luke and John as mere repositories of Jesus' stories from which certain doctrinal

and theological nuggets may be collected." (This critique resonates with my upcoming discussion of "junk DNA" in chapter 12.) Wright goes on to debunk the conventional idea that "Paul's epistles give us 'the gospel' while 'the Gospels' simply give us stories about Jesus." The conventional approach has led to "the marginalization of the four gospels as serious theological documents within Western Christianity, not least modern evangelicalism."

By contrast, if we situate Jesus first and foremost in the four Gospels and in the larger biblical narrative as "the emerging view" seeks to do, Wright claims that "what many have seen (and dismissed!) as the mere 'political' or 'historical' reasons for Jesus' death—Pilate's duplicitous vacillation, the Chief Priest's cynical scheming, and so on—are themselves part of the 'theological' interpretation of the cross offered by the evangelists."

Many notable defenders of the conventional view, Wright laments, show too little "evidence that they are really trying to hear what I and others are saying, but are instead simply waving us away" with various forms of dismissal and attempts to discredit. As a result, their critique of the emerging view, "shows every sign of the postmodern malaise of a failure to *think*, to read texts, to do business with what people actually write and say rather than (as is so much easier!) with the political labeling and dismissal of people on the basis of either flimsy evidence or 'guilt by association.'" (Some readers will detect some irony around Wright's use of the word *postmodern*, because several of the critics to which he refers have been outspoken opponents of the postmodern turn.)

Noting the "horrified" and "shrill" reaction of these critics to people like Steve Chalke (and myself) who have tried to articulate the emerging view, Wright asks whether this reaction may in fact be "not so much against what is said about the atonement, but against the idea, which is powerfully present in the gospels, that God's kingdom is coming, with Jesus, 'on earth as in heaven,' and that if this is so we must rethink several cherished assumptions within the western tradition as a whole." Their shrill tone, he goes on to suggest, may in fact have a political dimension, betraying "a fear that if we took [the four Gospels] seriously we might have to admit that Jesus of Nazareth has a claim on our political life as well as our spiritual life and 'eternal destiny.'" Obviously, that "claim on our political life" is crucial to the two essential questions at the heart of this book.

Wright calls for people on all sides of these controversies to follow the Berean pattern of Acts 17, where we go back to the Scriptures with an open mind "instead of 'knowing' in advance what scripture is going to say, ought to say, could not possibly say, or must really have said. . . ." This return to the Bible, and especially to the too-often marginalized parts of the New Testament that precede the Epistle to the Romans, is exactly what I am encouraging in this book, and in this chapter in particular.

5. This emerging view is deeply resonant with the Anabaptist and Eastern Orthodox views, so it is better understood as the recovery of ancient understandings rather than the creation of innovative ones. It is also more engaged than the conventional view with recent scholarship regarding "the historical Jesus," so is in this way an integration of something old with something new. Thanks to Frederica Matthewes-Green for the terms *infraction* and *infection*, and her insights into Eastern Orthodoxy (personal conversation).

6. This reproductive pressure helps explain the great appeal of celibacy in the early Christian movement. Celibacy wasn't simply a privation: instead, it represented liberation from an oppressive Roman system that valued a woman for her ovaries and little more. In contrast, a celibate woman in the Christian community was valued for her virtue, her piety, even her mind and work. Yale scholar Dale Martin explores this important theme in an unpublished article, "The Meaning of Sex," and in his book, *Sex and the Single Savior* (Louisville: Westminster John Knox, 2006). See especially his reflections on the second-century document *The Acts of Paul and Thecla*. In our culture, of course, we have made great progress: we value a woman for her breasts and vagina in

addition to her ovaries, and we also appreciate her taxable earning potential, upon which we have come to depend to maintain our standard of living. (Irony intended.)

CHAPTER 11: SWITCHING JIGSAW LIDS

1. The precursors of the Zealots, also known as the "Fourth Philosophy," probably arose right around the time of Jesus' birth. Zealots would routinely plan and execute assassinations of Roman officials and Jewish collaborators. The Zealots successfully mobilized an armed revolt against Rome in AD 67 and controlled Jerusalem until they were brutally crushed in AD 70. The Zealots were finally wiped out by the Romans in AD 73, at Masada. The historian Josephus (18.1.6) said the Zealots "agree in all other things with the Pharisaic notions; but they have an inviolable attachment to liberty, and say that God is to be their only Ruler and Lord."

2. The Pharisees emerged in the second century before Christ. They had joined forces with the Maccabees in the struggle against the Syrian empire in 165 BC, so they had a history of resisting imperial narratives. Some—not all—Pharisees in Jesus's day were hypocritical, but those who survived the Roman invasion and destruction of the temple in AD 70 provided essential rich ethical and theological resources for modern synagogue-based Judaism.

3. The Sadducee party probably emerged during the Syrian occupation. They were more literalist and exacting in their reading and application of the Mosaic law than were the Pharisees, and held to the more conservative and traditional Jewish view that angels, demons, and resurrection were not real. They held that only the Torah (the first five books of the Bible) was inspired, which conveniently exempted them from the sometimes antiestablishment messages of the Hebrew prophets. The Herodians, as their name implies, supported Herod the Great and his successors, the Roman empire's Jewish puppet kings, believing that God would work "in the system," so to speak. Together, Sadducees and Herodians supported the imperial establishment and opposed any who would unsettle it.

4. The Essenes shared common roots with the Pharisees and had joined the heroic but unsuccessful Maccabean revolt against Syria (165–155 BC), but later separated from all other parties. Highly fatalistic, they felt that the entire contemporary Jewish culture was doomed and so sought to establish a communal counterculture of highly committed and pious separatists.

5. For US readers, I highly recommend Ziauddin Sardar, Merryl Wyn Davies, *Why Do People Hate America?* (New York: Disinformation Co., 2002) and Richard A. Horsley, *Jesus and Empire* (Minneapolis: Fortress, 2003), especially the epilogue: "Christian Empire and American Empire." Also, Caryle Murphy's *Passion for Islam* (New York: Scribner, 2002) and Reza Aslan's *No god but God* (New York: Random House, 2005) can give US readers a needed window into the global Islamic revival.

6. Some will object to the word "better" in this sentence. If by "better" we mean "more urgently needed at this time in history than the conventional view," I would stick with "better." I do not mean "only," believing as I do that Jesus is too deep and complex a figure to be seen from one angle only.

7. Activist and master communicator Steve Chalke also uses this puzzle lid image in *The Lost Message of Jesus* (Grand Rapids: Zondervan, 2003). For more on Steve's work, see www.oasistrust.org.

8. Jesus's healings of paralysis would have a similarly revealing interpretation.

CHAPTER 12: NO JUNK DNA

1. Recalling the puzzle lid image found later in this chapter, "filler" passages or "junk revelation" would appear as extra puzzle pieces that don't match with the picture on the lid.

2. Regarding the meaning of the phrase *eternal life*, in Matthew, Mark, and Luke, Jesus' message is clearly centered in the phrase *kingdom of God* or *kingdom of heaven*. John, however, uses the term only three times; his Jesus focuses instead on the terms *life*, *eternal life*, and *life to the full*. Does John's Jesus have a different message from the other Gospel writers? Does their Jesus proclaim the gospel of the kingdom of God coming into this world, and John's Jesus proclaims the gospel of eternal life in heaven after death? The fact that the two terms are used interchangeably here in Mark 10 is significant. As I propose in note 6, Chapter 14, the term *zoien aonian*, literally *life of the ages*, means *life the way God wants it to be*, or *life when God's will is done on earth as in heaven*, or *life in the kingdom of God*. Interestingly, when John's Jesus defines eternal life (John 17:3), he doesn't define it in terms of heaven after death, but in terms of knowing God—being in an interactive, interpersonal relationship with God, which is the essence of life in the kingdom of God, both in this life and beyond it. For more on this subject, see N. T. Wright, *Mark for Everyone* (Westminster John Knox, 2004), 134–35, and *The Secret Message of Jesus* (Thomas Nelson, 2006).

3. Andrew Perriman's *The Coming of the Son of Man* (Carlisle, England: Paternoster, 2005), and his website (www.opensourcetheology.org) explore this theme in a most thorough and convincing way, as does the work of Max and Tim King (presence.tv).

4. I might add that the phrase *son of man* could be poetically interpreted as follows: *son* means *next generation* or *new generation*, and *man* means *humanity*. So *son of man* would mean *new generation of humanity*, or perhaps even *new kind of humanity* or *new stage in the development of humanity*. The term would resonate with Paul's terms *Second Adam* and *new humanity* (Romans 5:12–6:7; Ephesians 4:22–24; Colossians 3:9).

5. This understanding is in no way in conflict with belief in Jesus' divinity, a belief I myself hold and cherish. But it raises the uncomfortable question as to why many people who firmly uphold Jesus' divinity seem unable or unwilling to stand up against imperial claims made by their government. One would think that divinity trumps governmental authority, but the linking of "God and country" in so many quarters might suggest that we would rather locate Jesus' ultimate authority at a safe distance, in heaven with God, rather than here in history with us. For more on this, see my postings on the God's Politics blog (beliefnet.com/blogs/godspolitics).

6. This understanding helps explain why the early Christians would be persecuted as they were: their loyalty to Jesus as Lord ("KURIOS IESOUS") made it impossible to say the contemporary "pledge of allegiance"—"KURIOS KAISAR."

7. See Richard Horsley, *Jesus and Empire* (Fortress, 2003), 100ff.

CHAPTER 14: OR SO IT APPEARED

1. This is in no way to deny the importance of those doctrinal considerations, but only to say that they wouldn't have been on Peter's mind at that moment, at that point in the unfolding story.

2. City gates, in the walled cities of the ancient world, were the places official business was transacted, hence their association with power centers or authority structures. And hell was frequently used as a metaphor for evil. "The gates of hell" will not prevail against their joint project, Jesus says, using a phrase that could aptly be paraphrased "the authority structures and control centers of evil." If Jesus and his disciples are indeed standing by the cliff face, the statement takes on even richer meaning, because the opening at the base of the cliff, from which an underground spring flowed into the light, was known as the gates of hades, or the gates of the underworld. The use of this Greek word, *hades*, rather than a more Jewish word like *gehenna* or *abbadon*, would be significant. Jesus would be saying that all that flows from the dark spirituality and violent regimes of their oppressors would not defeat their mission. More, he would be saying that their mission would actually overcome these powers. The scene is quite

remarkable, with far-reaching resonances, which may explain Jesus' twenty-five-mile trip and six to eight days spent there.

3. I believe Peter was right: I believe Jesus was the Christ, the son of the living God. But Peter apparently was wrong about what those terms meant. They didn't mean a violent and coercive leader who would conquer through domination; they meant a leader who would be victorious through being defeated, who would demonstrate power through vulnerability, and who would establish a kingdom not of violent conquest but of faith, hope, and love. In the shadow of Caesarea Philippi and the springs of the underworld, Jesus accepts the title of liberating king—but it's clear that his type of liberation is radically unexpected, and its resources spring from a higher source.

4. One reason for John's avoidance of kingdom language may relate to timing. Scholars agree that it was written later than the other three Gospels, likely decades after AD 67–70. With the fall of Jerusalem, in a sense, the old world, the old age—Jewish life as the Jews had known it for centuries—was over. A new situation called for new language, for a translation of old terms into new. Another reason may have been audience. If John were writing, for example, for a multicultural Christian community in Alexandria, Egypt, home of famous libraries and a center for cosmopolitan intellectual life, the tight Jewish milieu of AD 30–33 in which various imperial narratives competed for Jewish confidence would have been distant and somewhat hard to relate to. A new audience in a new historical setting would require a new translation of the original message into new terms in their frame of reference—terms like *logos* and *life*, for example.

5. "Eternal life" is a common but unfortunate translation, in my opinion, of the Greek term *zoein aionian*. "Life of the ages" or "life on a higher plane" would be a better rendering of this important term, which contrasts with "life in this present age," or "life in the current regime." Rendering it as "life of the ages" would help people avoid the common and erroneous equation of the term with "life after death" or "life in an eternal timeless state beyond creation and history." See Chapter 12, note 2.

6. These important words spoken to Pilate continue echoing strongly among the early followers of Jesus, decades later: "Although we live in the world, we do not wage war as the world does" (2 Corinthians 10:3). We do not fight with fleshly weapons against flesh and blood—as if human beings were our enemies. No, we struggle against dark spiritual forces that are described as thoughts, arguments, pretensions, faulty reasoning. And we do not use the kinds of physical weapons used by typical kingdoms—swords, spears, or shields (Ephesians 6:10–18). Instead, we engage the falsehood and deception so prevalent in the world with "unarmed" truth, prayer, justice, alertness, peace, faith.

CHAPTER 15: PEACE THROUGH DOMINATION

1. John Meachum, review of Garry Wills's *What Jesus Meant* (New York: Viking, 2006).

2. Gary Wills, *What Jesus Meant,* quoted in *New York Times* (March 12, 2006), available online. (New York: Viking, 2006).

3. My Catholic and Eastern Orthodox friends would add another intermediate step: before applying Jesus' words today, we need to see how the church's scholars, especially in the early centuries, interpreted and applied them. I would certainly agree that we would be foolish to ignore their insights, but I wouldn't want to subordinate or limit the Gospels themselves to the interpretations of Christians, whether ancient or contemporary, and neither, I think, would my Catholic or Orthodox friends.

4. They continue, "That direction urgently calls all of us—citizens, governments, decision-makers—to embrace a life-sustaining peace-building vision or paradigm . . . it serves to integrate development and peace initiatives . . . at both policy and practice levels." See *Hope in Troubled Times: A New Vision for Confronting Global Crises* (Grand Rapids: Baker, 2007), 196.

5. Bishop N. T. Wright says "good news" was "a regular technical term, referring to the announcement of a great victory, or to the birth, or accession, of an emperor. (The first and third of these could of course be easily combined, if someone became emperor by means of a great military victory.) The coming of a new ruler meant the promise of peace, a new start for the world" (N.T. Wright, *What Saint Paul Really Said*, (Grand Rapids: Eerdmans, 1997) 43.

6. From John Dominic Crossan's *God and Empire: Jesus Against Rome Then and Now* (HarperSanFrancisco, 2007), as yet unpublished. Thanks to Dominic for early access to this important manuscript.

7. John Dominic Crossan, *God and Empire: Jesus Against Rome Then and Now* (HarperSanFrancisco, 2007), 148.

8. The stunning work of Michael Vlahos on narrative and war should not be missed in this regard, especially by readers in the USA. See, for example, http://www.amconmag.com/2007/2007_02_12/feature.html or http://www.huffingtonpost.com/michael-vlahos/will-we-fight-iran_b_16919.html.

9. N. T. Wright, *The Challenge of Jesus*, (Downer's Grove: Intervarsity, 1999), 43ff.

10. Some will be quick to note that Jesus also used strong language of exclusion—being thrust into "outer darkness," for example, where there is "weeping and gnashing of teeth." But in an irony that is so powerful it can hardly be overstated, Jesus applies that language to the typically exclusive (religious scholars, Pharisees, etc.), and asserts that the typically excluded (prostitutes, sinners, even Gentiles) will be included before them (Matthew 23:13; Luke 13:28–30; Luke 4:24-27). Clearly, Jesus is deconstructing the dominant system of exclusion—not fortifying it. For more on this subject, see *The Secret Message of Jesus* (Nashville: W Publishing, 2006), chapter 18, and *The Last Word and the Word After That* (San Francisco: Jossey-Bass, 2004).

11. Those who are concerned about the exclusively male imagery of fatherhood certainly have a valid concern that I have addressed elsewhere. See *A Search for What Makes Sense* (formerly *Finding Faith*) (Grand Rapids: Zondervan, 2007) 144–163. See also *A Generous Orthodoxy* (Grand Rapids: Zondervan, 2004) 82–85.

12. Francois Fenelon seemed to grasp this when he said, "All wars are civil wars, because all men are brothers. Each one owes infinitely more to the human race than to the particular country in which he was born." Available at thinkexist.com.

13. Of many wonderful explorations of Saint Francis, two of my favorites are chapter 11 of Leonardo Boff's *Cry of the Earth, Cry of the Poor* (Mary Knoll, NY: Orbis, 1997), 216 and Ian Morgan Cron's *Chasing Francis* (Colorado Springs: NavPress, 2006).

14. Arnold Toynbee (quoted by Leonardo Boff in *Cry of the Earth, Cry of the Poor*) observed that "in order to keep the biosphere habitable for two thousand more years, we and our descendants" must choose between the way of Francis and the way of his father. For more of Toynbee on St. Francis see ntgcc.org/35.htm.

CHAPTER 16: OCCUPYING REGIME, EQUITY GAP, EXCREMENT FACTORY

1. These words from John Stott strike an excellent balance: "Of course the announcement of God's kingdom was the very heart of the message of Jesus, and to Jewish audiences steeped in the messianic expectation the apostles continued to proclaim it. But already in the New Testament the good news was expressed in other terms. In John's Gospel the emphasis is on eternal life rather than on the kingdom, and to Gentiles Paul preferred to proclaim Jesus as Lord and Savior. Yet all these are different ways of saying the same thing. If we are to preach the gospel faithfully, we must declare that through the death and resurrection of Jesus a new era dawned and a new life became possible. But we may speak of this new life in terms of God's kingdom or Christ's lordship or salvation or eternal life or in other ways. It is certainly not essential to refer explicitly to the kingdom; indeed in countries which are not monarchies but republics kingdom

language sounds distinctly odd. There is an urgent need today for creative Christian thinkers who will be utterly loyal to the essentials of the biblical gospel, but who will express it in fresh ways appropriate to every culture. To this task the Incarnation commits us. In order to communicate with us, the Eternal Word became flesh. He entered our world and lived our life. We, too, if we are to reach others who are alienated from God and from the gospel, will have to enter their cultural worlds, in particular their thought worlds. Only so can we hope to share good news with them in terms which they can grasp." Available at www.intervarsity.org/ism/article/1952.

2. For more on Martin Luther King's term "a beloved community" see thekingcenter.org/prog/bc/.

3. David Korten says, "The outcome will depend in large measure on the prevailing stories that shape our understanding . . . Perhaps the most difficult and yet essential aspect of this work is to change our stories" *The Great Turning* (Washington DC: Berrett Koehler, 2006), 20.

4. Ibid., 237.

5. Ibid., 261.

CHAPTER 17: HOW DIFFERENT IT WOULD BE

1. Dislocated from creation in this way, Boff says, "The human being—called to be Earth's guardian angel and watchful tiller—may be Earth's Satan. Humans have shown that they can commit not only homicide and ethnocide, but biocide and geocide as well" (*Cry of the Earth, Cry of the Poor* [Mary Knoll, NY: Orbis, 1997], xi).

2. Desmond Morris' 1967 bombshell *The Naked Ape* (New York: McGraw-Hill) can in this way be seen as a secular attempt to deconstruct human's separation from creation and reconnect humanity with creation.

3. Economist Herman Daly expanded on this thought as follows: "A person is worth many sparrows, but for that statement to mean anything a sparrow's worth cannot be zero. All living things have both instrumental value for other living things and intrinsic value by virtue of their own sentience and capacity to enjoy their own lives" (*Beyond Growth: The Economics of Sustainable Development* [Boston: Beacon Press, 1996], 215). On the value of things in themselves, apart from their utility to humans, Robert Farrar Capon writes, "The world exists, not for what it means but for what it is. The purpose of mushrooms is to be mushrooms; wine is in order to be wine. Things are precious before they are contributory. . . . Creation is God's living room, the place where He sits down and relishes the exquisite state of His decoration. . . . God made the world out of joy; He didn't need it; He just thought it was a good thing" (Selected from *The Supper of the Lamb* [New York: Modern Library, 2002]).

4. To better understand the connection between human beings and the rest of creation, consider this thought experiment involving a woman named Maria whose life, you believe, has real value. You must acknowledge that Maria can't live without her 130-pound body, and she can last only a few minutes without air. So, if you want to say Maria's life has value, and if that involves Maria having permission to live for one more year, you have to extend that value to all 130 pounds of Maria's body plus a large volume of air—enough cubic meters for her to breathe for a year. Additionally, she can live for only a few days without water, so along with her 130-pound body and the cubic meters of air she needs, you need to picture a large volume of clean, fresh water. Without it, there will be no Maria. Then she needs some food. How many acres of wheat, corn, fruit, and vegetables are needed to provide food for Maria for one year? (We would have to add extra acres of grass and gallons of water to sustain livestock too, unless Maria happens to be a vegetarian.) Without these huge volumes of air, water, and land for plants (and animals), there simply is no Maria, and there is no you either. But we've still grossly underestimated Maria's connection to the environment, because

every day she not only takes in air, water, and food, but she also produces carbon dioxide, urine, and feces. Those wastes need to be processed and made either harmless or helpful to the environment, which requires still more land, water, and air for filtration, decomposition, and reconstitution into harmless or useful by-products—by various bacteria, chemical reactions, and plants. Otherwise, Maria will foul up the environment day by day with her wastes as she uses up its resources day by day. That level of personal waste production would be demanding enough, but in addition, as a modern Western person, Maria drives a car, heats and air conditions her home, uses electronic devices (from laptop computers to popcorn poppers), and in many other ways she both demands resources and produces wastes, all of which need to be donated and then reabsorbed by the land, water, and air around her. So Maria's footprint on the planet—the volume of land, air, and water her daily existence requires—is not a small one. So if you say her life has value, you have to value a large amount of land, water, and air, along with a host of plants, animals, and bacteria; otherwise, there will be no Maria to value. You can't have one without the other.

Now if you say that all human beings have a value equal to Maria's, you need to multiply the figures required for her solitary existence by more than six billion. It makes little sense, then, to speak of human life having value without also valuing a huge volume of air and water, along with vast acreage for plants and animals.

5. Herman Daly, *Beyond Growth: The Economics of Sustainable Development* (Boston: Beacon Press, 1996), 215. Reprinted by permission of Beacon Press, Boston.

CHAPTER 18: WHICH JESUS?

1. Wendell Berry, *What Are People For?* (New York: Farrar, Straus, and Giroux, 1990), 95–96.

2. I think Leonardo Boff is right when he says that Romanticism "is a product of modern subjectivity. The feelings of the self are projected onto the world . . . the self remains in its own universe . . . enclosed in its own stirrings" ([Mary Knoll, NY: *Cry of the Earth*, 1997], 213). That is far different from the alternative vision I'm trying to articulate here, in which (again quoting Boff) "the self is called to rise above itself, to open the closed circle, and to become kin with things, so as to sing jointly the hymn of praise to the Creator."

3. Considering that every molecule in your body came from food, and that all food ultimately came from plants, and those plants drew their nourishment and substance from soil, we are very literally organized dirt, created from "the dust of the ground" (Genesis 2:7).

4. One recalls the assessment of C. S. Lewis in *Mere Christianity* (San Francisco: Harper San Francisco, 2001) regarding people who take biblical imagery literally rather than literarily: "If they cannot understand books written for grown-ups, they should not talk about them" (137).

5. From a sermon called "Remaining Awake Through a Great Revolution" quoted in *God and Empire* by John Dominic Crossan (Harper San Francisco, 2007).

6. Mohandas Gandhi said, "The difference between what we do and what we are capable of doing would suffice to solve most of the world's problems." Available at brainquote.com.

CHAPTER 19: JOINING THE PEACE INSURGENCY

1. edition.cnn.com/transcripts/0410/24/le.02.html.

2. Sam Harris, *The End of Faith* (New York: Norton, 2005).

3. Sam Harris, *Letter to a Christian Nation* (New York: Knopf, 2006).

4. With the exception of this sentence and a few others, I have avoided using the generalized abstraction "Christianity" in these pages, except where quoting others who

use it. Instead, realizing that such a wide range of beliefs and practices are included within the term *Christianity*, I have tried to find more specific and concrete terms when possible. I have done the same with the terms *Islam* and *Judaism*.

5. These quotes are from an interview with Harris available at Salon.com, by Steve Paulson, 7 July 2006. This article first appeared at www.salon.com. It and others like it can be found in Salon's archives. Reprinted with permission.

6. Dwight L. Moody said, "I don't find anyplace where God says that the world is to grow better and better. . . . I look upon this world as a wrecked vessel. God has given me a lifeboat and said to me, 'Moody, save all you can.'" For more information on Moody see abcorg/moody.htm. A similar complacency could result from a religious belief that guaranteed an age of peace and harmony. *If a good outcome is destined to happen whatever we do, why work and sacrifice for it?* This is why I am suspicious of fatalistic or deterministic eschatologies. See *The Secret Message of Jesus*, chapter 19, and the previous chapter.

7. These quotes are from an interview with Harris available at Salon.com, by Steve Paulson, 7 July 2006.

8. Thomas Paine, *Age of Reason*. For more on Thomas Paine, see awitness.org/essays/thomas_paine.html. See also *Thomas Paine: Collected Writings* (New York: Library of America, 1995).

9. These quotes are from an interview with Harris available at Salon.com, by Steve Paulson, 7 July 2006. Dominic Crossan expresses similar frustration regarding the Apocalypse in the New Testament (see Revelation 19). There he sees a violent, retributive Jesus returning on a white horse to do battle—the opposite of the peaceful, donkey-riding Jesus presented in the Gospels (*God and Empire*, Harper San Francisco, 2007, 191ff). As I explained in Chapter 18, I read a pivotal passage in the Apocalypse (19:15ff.) differently from him. But the violent, vindictive reading is so common that until it is more widely corrected and rejected, I am sympathetic with Crossan's frustration, just as I am with Harris'.

10. This reassessment is occurring along several different lines, led by diverse scholars including Walter Brueggemann, Marcus Borg, Miroslav Volf, Dominic Crossan, Diana Butler-Bass, N. T. Wright, Steve Chalke, Tony Campolo, Joan Chittister, Jim Wallis, Shane Claiborne, Richard Rohr, Rene Padilla, Samuel Escobar, Ched Meyer, Mary Kate Morse, and others. This reassessment is, in many ways, a rediscovery of the Jesus of the sixteenth century Radical Reformation.

11. Grant LeMarquand, available at tesm.edu/articles/lemaruand-canaanite-woman. Thanks to Brian Walsh for introducing me to Grant's work.

12. Many have noticed the apparent contradiction in the Deuteronomy passage. If the Jews indeed were commanded to destroy the people totally, why would they have to be warned not to intermarry with them? Dead people can't intermarry! These intra-textual tensions provide biblical evidence against overly literalistic readings of the biblical text.

13. *God and Empire* (Harper San Francisco, 2007), Chapter 1.

14. Interestingly, in his December 12, 2006, departing address, retiring United Nations Secretary-General Kofi Annan rejected domination as a response to terrorism: "Against such threats as these, no nation can make itself secure by seeking supremacy over all others." Instead, in an application of Jesus' "golden rule" to international relations, he said that each nation increases its own security by safeguarding the security of its neighbors.

CHAPTER 20: WHOSE SIDE ARE WE ON?

1. Unless otherwise noted, data in this chapter is drawn from *Hope in Troubled Times: A New Vision for Confronting Global Crises* (Baker, 2007).

2. It would be unfair to suggest that all military spending is used to produce weapons. For

example, the military may respond to a humanitarian crisis like a hurricane, earthquake, or tsunami. And some military (or security-system) investments in research and development have resulted in important new communications breakthroughs with great peacetime value—such as some communications satellites and the Internet. Intelligence expenditures can be used to avoid war, not just wage it. And of course, military budgets also include large sums for the college education of military personnel and the health care of veterans (Keith Kranker, personal communication). However, these peaceful investments in no way account for the vast increases in military spending in recent decades.

3. Henry Kissinger, *The White House Years* (Boston: Little Brown, 1979), 217.

4. Military analyst William Arkin described in a May 2002 *defense* planning document "no target on the planet or in space would be immune to American *attack*" (emphasis added; also see Noam Chomsky, bostonreview.net/BR28.5/chomsky.html). This kind of omnipresent "defense by attack" rivals the "strategic sufficiency" of MAD for creatively deceptive military doublespeak.

5. According to James Sterngold, more than 5,000 warheads stood ready as of February 13, 2007. In the Moscow Treaty of 2002, the United States agreed to decrease its deployed arsenal to 2,200 by 2012. Even so, no US administration has yet Committed Itself to a Policy of Disarmament. ("Los Alamos Scientist Criticizes federal approach to arsenal," available at sfgate.com/cgi-bin/article.cgi?f=/c/a/2007/02/13/mngi1o3n0g1.dtl.)

6. Quoted in *Hope in Troubled Times* pp.110, 223 (note 30). For more information on this subject, see globalsecurity.org/wmd/library/report/crs/rl31623.pdf.

7. See globalsecurity.org/wmd/library/report/crs/rl31623.pdf.

8. William Fulbright, *The Price of Empire* (New York: Pantheon, 1989), 137.

9. Quoted by Jack Nelson Pallmeyer, "By the Sword," *The Other Side*, November/December 2002, 25. For analysis of Keenan's words, see swans.com/library/art11/ga192.html.

10. Take the year 2004, for example. Of 202 possible countries in the world (some would say there were only 199 because of the disputed independence of some nations), the United States had troops stationed in 163. That means that over 80 percent of the world's nations were now within the borders of the US concern . . . without even considering the territory covered by US economic interests.

11. From *Social Holiness*, unpublished manuscript.

12. Cornel West relates imperial ambitions with a kind of hyperactive masculinity: "The second prevailing dogma of our time is aggressive militarism. . . . It green-lights political elites to sacrifice US soldiers—who are disproportionately working class and youth of color—in adventurous crusades. This dogma posits military might as salvific in a world in which he who has the most and biggest weapons is the most moral and masculine, hence worthy of policing others." *Democracy Matters* (New York: Penguin, 2004), 5.

13. From *The Great Turning* (Washington DC: Berrett-Koehler, 2006).

14. Joseph Shumpeter, speaking about the Roman Empire in "Imperialism and Social Classes," said, "There was no corner of the known world where some interest [of the Roman Empire] was not alleged to be in danger or under actual attack. If the interest were not Roman, they were those of Rome's allies, and if Rome had no allies, then allies would be invented" (quoted by the editors, "US Imperial Ambitions and Iraq," *Monthly Review*, December 2002, 4). The similarities to the stated US National Security Strategy are haunting, as reflected in this quote from Edward Walker Jr., former deputy assistant secretary of state for Near Eastern affairs: "The president doesn't see any difference between American interests and Israeli interests with regard to the Middle East now" (from Sojo.net, 18 August 2006).

15. The National Security Strategy of the United States, available at www.us.gov.

16. In terms of percentage of GNP, the United States ranks twenty-first globally, giving 0.068 percent in aid. In comparison, Denmark gives at 1.04 percent, or fifteen times the rate of the US.
17. National Defense University, "Shock and Awe: Achieving Rapid Dominance," available at www.dodccrp.org.
18. *War Is a Force That Gives Us Meaning* (New York: Public Affairs, 2002), 14.
19. See wikipedia.org/wiki/clausewitz.
20. Carl von Clausewitz, *On War*, Michael Howard and Peter Paret, trs. (NY: Knopf, 1993), 731.
21. In the words of former Senator William Fulbright, "We continue to conduct our international relations in the same old way, by the same rules of crisis management, balance of power, arms races, and confrontation that always in the past—not sometimes but always—have sooner or later culminated in war. We still base our policies on Clausewitz's formula, that war is an extension of politics, carried out 'by other means,' and not on President Kennedy's proposition, expressed in his inaugural address in 1961, that war 'can no longer serve to settle disputes' because if we do not put an end to it, it will put an end to us. Everything has indeed changed, and we readily acknowledge it— but not to the point that it has significantly changed our manner of thinking" (*The Price of Empire* [Pantheon, 1989], 224).
22. Victor Frankl said, "Since Auschwitz we know what man is capable of. And since Hiroshima we know what is at stake." See books.google.com/books?isbn=155028259.
23. Available at brainquotes.com/quotes/d/dwightei136350.html.
24. Dietrich Bonhoeffer expressed a similar sentiment as he saw his nation, Germany, developing violent and imperial aspirations. He spoke of "our terrible alternative"—to wish and work for his own nation's defeat so that civilization could survive. See wagingpeace.org/articles/2006/0204_argo_bonhoeffersmessage.htm.
25. First drafts of this chapter and the next few chapters were written during the Israeli invasion of Lebanon in 2006, which was heavily supported by the US government, itself at war in Iraq and Afghanistan. This may explain some of the added emotion, intensity, and perhaps discouragement you'll find as you read.

CHAPTER 21: LAYERS AND LAYERS MORE

1. From *Voltaires' Bastards*, 82, quoted in *Hope in Troubled Times: A New Vision for Confronting Global Crises* (Grand Rapids: Baker, 2007), 178–9.
2. usinfo.state.gov/usa/infousa/politics/pres/fpolicy.htm.
3. See controlarms.org/the_issues/armsindustry.htm.
4. *Hope in Troubled Times* (Grand Rapids: Baker), 179.
5. Archbishop Desmond Tutu, commondreams.org/views06/0913-22.htm.
6. From Chris Hedges, *War Is a Force That Gives Us Meaning* (New York: PublicAffairs, 2002), 13. Additional page numbers will be quoted in the text.
7. Chris Hedges, *War Is a Force That Gives Us Meaning*, 10.
8. Ibid., 35.
9. Here's a sampling of Hedge's descriptions of war, in *War Is a Force That Gives Us Meaning*:

> Many of us, restless and unfulfilled, see no supreme worth in our lives. We want more out of life. And war, at least, gives us a sense that we can rise above our smallness and divisiveness. (7)

> The eruption of conflict instantly reduces the headache and trivia of daily life. The communal march against an enemy generates a warm, unfamiliar bond with our neighbors, our community, our nation, wiping out

unsettling undercurrents of alienation and dislocation. War, in times of malaise and desperation, is a potent distraction. (9)

Patriotism, often a thinly veiled form of collective self-worship, celebrates our goodness, our ideals, our mercy and bemoans the perfidiousness of those who hate us. . . . Such acceptance of nationalist self-glorification, turns many into silent accomplices. (10, 54)

Armed movements seek divine sanction and the messianic certitude of absolute truth. They do not need to get this from religions as we usually think of religion, but a type of religion: Patriotism provides the blessing. Soldiers want at least the consolation of knowing that they risk being blown up by the land mines for a greater glory, for a New World. (14)

The enemy is dehumanized; the universe starkly divided between the forces of light and the forces of darkness. The cause is celebrated, often in overt religious forms, as a manifestation of divine or historical will. (63)

However much soldiers regret killing once it is finished, however much they spend their lives trying to cope with the experience, the act itself, fueled by fear, excitement, the pull of the crowd, and the god-like exhilaration of destroying, is often thrilling. (171)

[The myth of war] . . . allows us to believe we have achieved our place in human society because of a long chain of heroic endeavors, rather than accept the sad reality that we stumble along a dimly lit corridor of disasters. It disguises our powerlessness. It hides form view our own impotence and the ordinariness of our own leaders. (23)

10. Shakespeare, *Coriolanus*, ACT IV, scene V.
11. Chris Hedges, *War Is a Force That Gives Us Meaning*, 21.
12. Ibid., 22–23.
13. Ibid., 67.
14. Ibid., 59.

CHAPTER 22: JOINING WARRIORS ANONYMOUS

1. See *Hope in Troubled Times* (Grand Rapids: Baker, 2007), pp. 192–199.
2. Chris Hedges, *War Is a Force That Gives Us Meaning* (New York: PublicAffairs, 2002), 158, 161.
3. It is interesting to note that many Christians in the United States have been energized to put the Ten Commandments in schools, courthouses, and other public buildings. One wonders why they haven't instead sought to put the Beatitudes in public places. One also wonders what the response might have been if Christians sought to promote peacemaking through the Beatitudes rather than moralism through the Ten Commandments. Perhaps these well-meaning activists have never understood Jesus' words about the "righteousness" of the kingdom of God surpassing that of the Pharisees and religious scholars (Matthew 5:20).
4. Many English Bibles use the word *righteousness* instead of *justice*, but I believe that *justice* is the better rendering. The former word suggests private religiosity, but the Greek word (*dikaios*) does not carry this connotation.
5. It is instructive to read Matthew's version of this material in relation to Luke's version (6:32), where Jesus describes God as "kind to the ungrateful and wicked," and then

calls his followers to "be merciful" (or compassionate) "just as your Father in heaven is merciful." Here, "be perfect" is translated to "be compassionate"—suggesting that God's perfection is, unlike that of the religious leaders of his day, a kind and compassionate perfection. By linking God's perfection with God's "promiscuous" compassion (not discriminating against the ungrateful and wicked), Jesus radically disposes his followers against the us-them thinking required to wage war, and he disposes them toward the kind of compassion that wages peace. To use the clever term of my friend David Anderson, Jesus teaches us to pre-empt racism with gracism (Downer's Grove IVP, 2007).

6. See Borg and Crossan, *The Last Week* (Harper San Francisco, 2006).
7. "Patriotism Is Not Enough," *Sojourners*, January–February, 2003, sojo.net.
8. Thanks to Nancy Murphy for this beautiful turn of phrase. For more about Nancy, see Northwestfamilylife.org.
9. See Nationalreview.com/coulter/coulter.shtml.
10. http://edition.cnn.com/TRANSCRIPTS/0410/24/le.01.html.
11. Peter's rash use of violence (John 17:10) shows how easily and pathetically he, like the pundit and the preacher and the rest of us, could fall short of his actual identity and high vocation.
12. Dr. Martin Luther King, *Strength to Love*, (New York: HarperCollins, 1963).

CHAPTER 23: CAPITALISM AS GOD

1. Herman Daly, *Beyond Growth: The Economics of Sustainable Development* (Boston: Beacon Press, 1996), 10.
2. See marxists.org/archive/marx/works/1847/poverty-philosophy/ch02.htm.
3. All references to Thomas Beaudoin in this chapter are from ptsem.edu/iym/lectures/2001/Beaudoin-after.pdf and highbeam.com/doc/1G1-93610958.html.
4. On advertising, one thinks of G. K. Chesterton's quip: "It is really not so repulsive to see the poor asking for money as to see the rich asking for more money. And advertisement is the rich asking for more money" (*The New Jerusalem*, Lenox, Mass: HardPress, 2006).
5. See ptsem.edu/iym/lectures/2001/Beaudoin-after.pdf and highbeam.com/doc/1G1-93610958.html.
6. Ibid.
7. Ibid.
8. Cornell West, *Democracy Matters* (New York: Penguin, 2004).
9. Thomas Beaudoin wrote: "The people had been seduced by a kind of progress that becomes a mania, an 'ideological pathology,' as some anthropologists call it." For more on this, see Roland Wright, *A Short History of Progress* (Toronto: House of Anansi Press, 2004), 61; also see Jared Diamond, *Collapse: How Societies Choose to Fail or Succeed* (New York: Penguin, 2005), 79–119.
10. *Hope in Troubled Times: A New Vision for Confronting Global Crises* (Grand Rapids: Baker, 2007), 28.
11. Daly (Boston: Beacon, 1996), 95.
12. Joel Bakan. *The Corporation*. DVD. Directed by Mark Achbar and Jennifer Abbot (New York: Zeitgeist Films, 2003).
13. Andrew Carnegie, *The Gospel of Wealth*. See planetpapers.com/assets/41.php for information on Carnegie. And for the 1889 essay that includes this quote see alpha.furman.edu/~benson/does/carnegie.htm.
14. Joel Bakan, writer of *The Corporation*, from credits, liner notes.
15. For debate on sweatshop wages, see www.independent.org/publications/working_papers/article.asp?id=1369.

16. The Great Law of Peace, from the Constitution of the Haudenosaunee (Iroquois) Nation, provides a striking alternative: "Look and listen for the welfare of the whole people and have always in view not only the present but also the coming generations."

17. Thomas Beaudoin quotes William Finnegan in this regard, speaking of the "savage tension between postindustrial capitalism's imperatives and the claims of family and community." See ptsem.edu/iym/lectures/2001/Beaudoin-after.pdf and highbeam.com/doc/1G1-93610958.html.

18. Joel Bakan. *The Corporation.* DVD. Directed by Mark Achbar and Jennifer Abbot (New York: Zeitgeist Films, 2003).

CHAPTER 24: OBLIGATIONS TO NONEXISTENT FUTURE PEOPLE

1. Joel Bakan. *The Corporation.* DVD. Directed by Mark Achbar and Jennifer Abbot (New York: Zeitgeist Films, 2003). Robert Monks, a corporate governance adviser, said it like this: "It was more or less as if we created a doom machine. In our search for wealth and for prosperity, we created something that was going to destroy us."

2. Ibid.

3. Ibid.

4. Paul Hawken, *The Ecology of Commerce* (New York: Collins, 1994).

5. Joel Bakan. *The Corporation.* DVD. Directed by Mark Achbar and Jennifer Abbot (New York: Zeitgeist Films, 2003). This phrase, "doing no harm," is probably the most interesting part of "the prayer of Jabez," which became widely known because of a book by the same title. Perhaps a sign of the book's unintentional affinity with theocapitalism, this line of the prayer drew minimal attention in comparison to the expansion of one's personal borders and success.

6. David Rischard, *High Noon* (New York: Basic, 2003), 34.

7. worldwatch.org.

8. Herman Daly, *Beyond Growth* (Boston: Beacon, 1996), 7.

9. Ibid., 221.

10. Ibid., 157.

11. Herman Daly, *Beyond Growth* (Boston: Beacon, 1996), 7.

12. Ibid., 8.

13. Herman Daly, *Beyond Growth* (Boston: Beacon, 1996), 221.

14. Since 1995, Anderson has led Interface, the world's largest commercial carpeting producer, to reduce its ecological footprint by one-third, and the corporation has committed itself to a goal of having an ecological footprint of zero by 2020. He provides a prime example of a trend that we can hope and encourage to grow in the years ahead: of corporations—communities of people who work together—striving for more than shareholder profit, but for the common social and ecological good.

CHAPTER 25: QUICK BLISS THROUGH FOOTWEAR, PALATE GREASE, AND SKIN PAINT

1. Thanks to Rene Padilla for his theological reflections on economics and personal communication.

2. Interestingly, it is also Paul who preserves for us a saying of Jesus unrecorded in the Gospel accounts, but utterly consistent with them. It also has to do with money and is recorded by Luke in the book of Acts: "It is more blessed to give than to receive" (20:35).

3. Galatians 2:10 reflects the continuing emphasis of the early leaders of the Christian movement regarding generosity to the poor.

4. Again, in my understanding, eternal life doesn't simply refer to heaven after death, but rather to life in the kingdom of God that begins in this world. Similarly hell doesn't mean literal postmortem flames, but rather the experience of having God judge one's

self-centered way of life as wrong, destructive, misguided, and a tragic, missed opportunity.

5. Herman Daly, *Beyond Growth* (Boston: Beacon) pp. 9, 3, 13.

6. For more on sustainability and the triple bottom line, see solsustainability.org.

7. David Korten, *The Great Turning*, 299.

8. David Myers, "The Secret to Happiness," www.yesmagazine.org, summer 2004. Interestingly, during the same period, we also doubled our teen suicide and divorce rates.

9. See www.psychologicalscience.org/pdf/pspi/pspi5_1.pdf and www.northwestwatch.org/scorecard/ for more on these studies.

10. Josef Pieper, *Happiness and Contemplation* (South Bend, Indiana: St. Augustine's Press, 1998).

11. I don't mean to deny the validity of pleasure to be had through a good pair of shoes, good and convenient food, or (I would imagine) quality skin-care products. As creatures with feet, taste buds, and skin, we can gratefully enjoy these products as gifts. My intention is to identify the danger of pursuing an unattainable abstraction under the cover of a good, attainable product.

12. I will explore the practice of spiritual disciplines, including fasting, in my upcoming book, *Finding Our Way Again*, (Thomas Nelson, 2008).

13. Many of Jesus's interactions regarding food have a similarly fascinating depth to them in this context, from his discussions on "defiling" foods (Mark 7:20) to his command to his disciples to go out on a preaching mission without bringing bread (Mark 6:8). Most significantly, we could consider the Eucharist in this light, with Jesus offering himself as our food and drink.

14. Herman Daly says, "The technical problems involved in achieving sustainability are not that difficult. The hard problem is overcoming our addiction to growth as the favored way to assert our creative power. . . . " (Daly, *Beyond Growth*. Boston: Beacon, 224)

CHAPTER 26: COLLABORATION FOR CO-LIBERATION

1. See Richard Horsley's *Jesus and Empire* (Minneapolis: Angsburg Fortress, 2002), especially chapter 2.

2. As mentioned in chapter 22, note 3, most English Bibles translate this as "hunger and thirst for righteousness." "Righteousness" to the average reader today means "religiosity" or "religious scrupulosity," a far cry for the social implications of the word *justice*. I see the common English translation as an unintentional (I hope) avoidance of the clear meaning of the text—a blessing pronounced on those who desire justice. This meaning becomes unavoidable when, in verse 12, he alludes to the prophets—who were persecuted not simply for religious scrupulosity, but for demanding justice for the poor, the widow, the orphan, and the oppressed.

3. Rene Padilla, personal communication, August 2006.

4. A frequently quoted critique of trickle-down theory runs like this: *it is like feeding horses premium quality oats so that hungry sparrows can avoid starvation by feasting on their manure.*

5. Zaccheus's willingness to give away half of his possessions contrasts with Jesus' call to the rich young ruler in the previous chapter to give away all his possessions. The contrast suggests that the point is not what percentage of one's wealth is given away (50 percent versus 100 percent), but whether one is willing to defect from the system of exploitation associated with the Roman Empire.

6. Herman Daly, *Beyond Growth* (Boston: Beacon), 164.

7. Brainyquote.com/quotes/b/bono129987.html.

CHAPTER 27: ON THE SIDE OF THE REBEL JESUS

1. Jackson Browne, "The Rebel Jesus."

2. Cornell West, 3–4.
3. See cipa-apex.org/toomuch/articlenew2006/June26a.html. See also oneworld.net/article/view/144146/1/3319. See also mondediplo.com/1998/11/01leader.
4. *Awakening Hope* (Grand Rapids: Baker, 2007) 20–1.
5. Jeffrey Sachs, "The End of Poverty," (*Time,* 14 March 2005, 33). It is not easy to define either poverty or "extreme poverty." As Aseem Shrivastava explains (*Sojourners,* February 2007, 7), economists speak of two levels of poverty. Those in extreme poverty live on $1 or less per day, and those in "normal" poverty live on less than $2 per day. However, it's clear that a dollar goes further in some places than others, because living expenses are higher in some places than others. So economists also speak of the Purchasing Power Parity Index (PPPI). Taking the PPPI into account, we would say that in India, the $1/day of extreme poverty actually equals 20 cents of US purchasing power. With 80 percent of Indians surviving on less than $2.15, we would say that using the PPPI, 800 million people live in poverty, on 40 cents or less daily in US terms. And 35 percent of Indians, or 350 million people, live in extreme poverty, on 20 cents a day or less in actual US terms. Globally, 2.7 billion people live without adequate nutrition in "normal" poverty, according to official estimates. But when we take PPPI adjustments into consideration, the figure may actually be 3 or 4 billion, 50 to 60 percent of our world's population.
6. www.newint.org/issue/keynote.htm.
7. David Korten, *The Great Turning* (San Francisco, CA: Berrett-Koehler Publishers, Inc., 2006), 67. All rights reserved. www.bkconnection.com
8. Ibid., 181.
9. Ibid.
10. J. F. Rischard, *High Noon* (New York: Basic, 2003), 31.
11. (Daley, 203; Korten, 181).
12. Cornell West, 204.

CHAPTER 28: BEYOND BLAME AND SHAME
1. Dr. David Anderson, *Gracism* (Downer's Grove: IVP, 2007).
2. "Social Holiness," unpublished manuscript. Clinker cites Wesley's response to the contemporary claim that slavery was an economic necessity (a claim that is echoed in various defenses of today's growing global equity gap): "Better is honest poverty than all the riches brought in by tears, sweat and blood of our fellow creatures." And responding to so-called "pious" slaveholders, Wesley showed remarkable sensitivity to systemic injustice: "It is your money that pays the merchant, and through him the captain and the African butchers. You therefore are guilty, yea, principally guilty, of all these frauds, robberies and murders. You are the spring that puts all the rest in motion; they would not stir a step without you; therefore the blood of all these . . . lies upon your head."
3. Ibid.
4. Ibid.
5. David Lowes Watson, "Proclaiming Christ in All His Offices: Priest, Prophet, and Potentate," and M. Douglas Meeks, ed., *The Portion of the Poor* (Nashville: Kingswood Books, 1995), 122–23, 17. Used by permission.
6. Walter Rauschenbusch, *A Theology for the Social Gospel,* (Louisville: Westminster John Knox, 1997).
7. Quoted in Duane Clinker's "Social Holiness," unpublished manuscript.
8. Eldin Villafane, quoting Steven Charles Mott, concludes, "Our spirituality, and the very gospel that we preach, needs to be as big and ubiquitous as sin and evil. We will falter in our spirituality and thus grieve the Spirit if 'our struggle with evil' does not 'correspond to the geography of evil.'" *Seek the Peace of the City: Reflections on Urban Ministry* (Grand Rapids: Eerdmans, 1995), 22.

9. My friend Dwight Friesen makes a similar point using almost opposite language. He says that our conventional gospel is too big, meaning it deals with cosmic issues of sin and atonement, but doesn't deal with a little girl crying in a little village because she has had too little food. The incarnation represents God becoming small, moving into our neighborhood, and having time for little people in great pain.

10. David Korten *The Great Turning* (Washington DC: Berrett-Koehler, 1996), 289.

11. Quoted in Duane Clinker's "Social Holiness" unpublished manuscript.

12. J. F. Rischard, *High Noon* (New York: Basic, 2003).

13. Sojourners/Call to Renewal (sojo.net) and emergentvillage.com are trying to assist churches in the pursuit of justice.

CHAPTER 29: A NEW KIND OF QUESTION

1. Kofi Annan, un.org/news/ossg/sg/stories/articlefull.asp?TID=12&type=article.

2. Jeffrey D. Sachs, "A Rich Nation, A Poor Continent," *New York Times*, July 9, 2003. For a critical response to the work of Jeffrey Sachs, see William Easterly's *White Man's Burden* (New York: Penguin, 2007). www.earthinstitute.Columbia.edu/about/director/pubs/nyt070903.pdf.

3. Ibid.

4. From Nikki van der Gaag, "Poverty: Challenging the Myths," *New Internationalist*, Number 310, 222. newint.org/issue310/keynote.htm.

5. The total cost of the war was predicted to reach $1.2 trillion before the troop surge was instituted. Jim Wallis (sojo.net, January 2007) quotes a column in *The New York Times* by David Leonhardt on what this amount means:

> The way to come to grips with $1.2 trillion is to forget about the number itself and think instead about what you could buy with the money. When you do that, a trillion stops sounding anything like millions or billions.
>
> For starters, $1.2 trillion would pay for an unprecedented public health campaign—a doubling of cancer research funding, treatment for every American whose diabetes or heart disease is now going unmanaged and a global immunization campaign to save millions of children's lives.
>
> Combined, the cost of running those programs for a decade wouldn't use up even half our money pot. So we could then turn to poverty and education, starting with universal preschool for every 3- and 4-year-old child across the country. The city of New Orleans could also receive a huge increase in reconstruction funds.
>
> The final big chunk of the money could go to national security. The recommendations of the 9/11 Commission that have not been put in place—better baggage and cargo screening, stronger measures against nuclear proliferation—could be enacted. Financing for the war in Afghanistan could be increased to beat back the Taliban's recent gains, and a peacekeeping force could put a stop to the genocide in Darfur.

All that would be one way to spend $1.2 trillion. Here would be another:

The war in Iraq.

6. From the World Alliance of Reformed Churches Taskforce Report 2004, at the Accra Meeting of General Council.

7. John Stott, *Culture and the Bible* (Downers Grove: InterVarsity, 1981), 36, also available online at www.intervarsity.org/ism/article/1952.

8. See, for example, tradeasone.org, the Heifer Project, Opportunity International, Integra Ventures.

ott's seminal booklet *Culture and the Bible* (Downers Grove: InterVarsity, 1981) is out f print, but it is available in its entirety online at www.intervarsity.org/ism/article/1952.

10. Great Law of Peace of the Iroquois Nation, indigenouspeople.net/iroqcon.htm.

11. This concern for future generations must bring together both "left" and "right" in pursuit of a new moral center. For example, in spite of calling himself a "Christian conservative" and an "avid indoorsman," Rod Dreher, in a *USA Today* article (4/23/2006), argued that ecological conservation and political conservatism should go together because both call us to self-discipline on behalf of our children:

> Russell Kirk and Richard Weaver, two founding fathers of modern American conservatism, hated the way industrial capitalism saw nature as merely a thing to be exploited. Weaver observed that we moderns "have allowed ourselves to be blinded by the insolence of material success [and] the animal desire to consume." He saw this as alienating us from nature and the foundations of a sustainable conservative order. Kirk wrote: "In America, especially, we live beyond our means by consuming the portion of posterity, insatiably devouring minerals and forests and the very soil, lowering the water table, to gratify the appetites of the present tenants of the country." He demanded that Americans act with more self-discipline to honor "the future partners in our contract with eternal society."

12. J. Richard Middleton and Brian J. Walsh *Truth Is Stranger Than It Used to Be* (Downers Grove: InterVarsity, 1995), 192. www.ivpress.com

13. This selection comes from a handout by Josh Kaufman-Horner, who edited the text for inclusive language. For more on Josh's work to advance Dr. King's dream, see eucharism.org.

14. I recently heard these words of encouragement from congresswoman Nancy Pelosi: "Where is hope to be found? Right where it has always been: between faith and love." (Comments at Sojourners Pentecost gathering, June 6, 2007, Washington, DC.)

CHAPTER 30: ORGANIZED RELIGION OR RELIGION ORGANIZING FOR THE COMMON GOOD?

1. Ziauddin Sardar and Merryl Wyn Davies, *Why Do People Hate America?* (New York: Disinformation Company, 2002), 195–96. Sardar's indictment of America resonates with a similar indictment made by the prophet Isaiah: "Woe to you who add house to house and join field to field till no space is left and you live alone in the land" (5:8). This aggressive prosperity project, Isaiah says, will fail: "Surely the great houses will become desolate, the fine mansions left without occupants" (5:9). The aggressive and dominant will experience only reducing returns on investment (5:10) in spite of their frantic activity and cultural sophistication (5:11–12), "because they have no regard for the deeds of the LORD, no respect for the work of his hands." Their dominance will end "for lack of understanding" (13–20).

2. My personal proposal: that we create an international fair trade seal (like the Good Housekeeping Seal of Approval) that could rate any product or service based on the ethics of its production. This seal would help people who want to engage in ethical buying to compare products. A level-one product, for example, would be produced by employees who made an international minimum wage or above, using ecologically sustainable means. Level two might indicate 15 percent above international minimum wage, ecological sustainability, and at least 50 percent recyclability. Level three might indicated 15 percent above international minimum wage, ecological sustainability, 75 percent recyclability, and transportation costs less than 20 percent of product price, and so on.

3. Herman Daly, *Beyond Growth* (Boston: Beacon), 61, 3. Daly adds: "Is it better or worse for the South if the North continues to grow in its own resource use? The standard answer is that it is better because growth for the North increases markets for Southern exports, as well as funds for aid and investment by the North in the South. The alternative view is that Northern growth makes things worse by preempting the remaining resources and ecological space needed to support economic growth in the South up to a sufficient level, and that it also increases global inequality and world political tensions. This view urges continued development in the north, but not growth. These two answers to the basic question cannot both be right." (67).

4. Economist Gary Becker and others have shown that when families move out of poverty, they predictably have fewer children. This might seem paradoxical, since wealthier families could afford more children. But in poor societies, children are an economic asset: they can work in the fields and care for their parents in old age, while in wealthier societies, children are (in economic terms) an expense, especially in terms of education, health care, and either lost income (for the stay-at-home parent) or child daycare (Keith Kranker, personal communication).

5. Herman Daly, *Beyond Growth* (Boston: Beacon). In Daly's own words: "Some years ago I advocated a minimum and a maximum income as part of the institutional basis appropriate to steady-state economy. The minimum income, of course, has a great deal of political support . . . the notion of a maximum income has none. . . . It would clearly be unjust for 99% of the limited total product to go to only one person. I conclude, therefore, that there must implicitly be some maximum personal income. . . . No one is arguing for an invidious, forced equality. A factor of ten in inequality would be justified by real differences in effort and diligence, and would provide sufficient incentive to call forth those qualities. To be conservative make it a factor of twenty. But bonds of community break at or before a factor of one hundred" (202, 203).

6. Consider the analysis of Amy Chua, quoted in *World on Fire: How Exporting Free Market and Democracy Breeds Ethnic Hatred and Global Instability* (NY: Anchor, 2003): "In the numerous countries around the world that have pervasive poverty and a market-dominant minority, democracy and markets—at least in the form in which they are currently being promoted—can proceed only in deep tension with each other. In such conditions, the combined pursuit of free markets and democratization has repeatedly catalyzed ethnic conflict in highly predictable ways, with catastrophic consequences, including genocidal violence and the subversion of markets and democracy themselves. This has been the sobering lesson of globalization over the last twenty years. . . . Rather than reinforcing the market's liberalizing wealth-producing effects, the sudden political empowerment of a poor, frustrated 'indigenous' majority often leads to powerful ethno-nationalist, anti-market pressures. And if these pressures, as Rwanda, Indonesia, and the former Yugoslavia vividly show, are more likely to lead to confiscation and ethnic killing than to the widespread peace and prosperity that proponents of free market democracy envision." [Quoted in *Awakening Hope*, later released as *Hope in Troubled Times: A New Vision for Confronting Global Crises* (Baker, 2007)].

7. David Korten, *The Great Turning* (Washington DC: Berrett-Koehler, 2006), 15.

8. Jim Garrison, quoted in David Korten, *The Great Turning* (Berrett-Koehler, 2004), 193–94.

9. William Fulbright, Arkansas Senator from 1945–1974, and long-term chair of the Senate Foreign Relations Committee, anticipated the need for these kinds of network organizations in the 1980s, describing them as "joint ventures": "Joint ventures, aside from their intrinsic value, have the added, perhaps greater value of alleviating mistrust. Men and women who work together to solve a problem or reach a common goal often develop a sense of comradeship and trust; they become humanized in each other's eyes" *The Price of Empire* (New York: Pantheon, 1989), 230.

CHAPTER 31: THE MOST RADICAL THING WE CAN DO

1. The resonance between this sentence and Paul's words in Romans 1:20 is intentional.
2. In contrast to this stance of the early churches, Walter Wink observes, "The failure of churches to continue Jesus' struggle to overcome domination is one of the most damning apostasies in history. With some thrilling exceptions, the churches of the world have never decided that domination is wrong" (*The Powers That Be* [New York: Doubleday, 1998], 11).

CHAPTER 32: AN UNFOLDING, EMERGENT, SPIRALING PROCESS

1. Shane Claiborne celebrates the here-ness of the kingdom in his beautiful book *The Irresistible Revolution: Living As an Ordinary Radical* (Grand Rapids: Zondervan, 2006): "Some of us have worked on Wall Street, and some of us have slept on Wall Street. We are a community of struggle. Some of us are rich people trying to escape our loneliness. Some of us are poor folks trying to escape the cold. Some of us are addicted to drugs and others are addicted to money. We are a broken people who need each other and God, for we have come to recognize the mess that we have created of our world and how deeply we suffer from the mess. Now we are working to give birth to a new society within the shell of the old. Another world is possible. Another world is necessary. Another world is already here" (188).
2. Clare Graves at claregraves.com.
3. *George Soros on Globalization* (New York: Public Affairs, 2005).
4. On thinking straight, Albert Einstein had this to say in 1945: "Now everything has changed except our manner of thinking. Thus we are drifting towards a catastrophe beyond comparison. We shall require a substantially new manner of thinking if mankind is to survive. (quoted in Fulbright, *The Price of Empire* [New York: Pantheon, 1989]). The different kind of thinking he called for, I imagine, was at least in part thinking infused with hope.

CHAPTER 34: MOVING MOUNTAINS

1. The concept of "eternity," meaning a timeless state, never occurs in the Bible. It is an import, I suggest, from another framing story, and its popularity among many Christians suggests the degree to which the popular "Christian" story is funded by resources from outside the biblical narrative.
2. See note 3, chapter 12.
3. I hope to more fully explore this call to action in a future book.
4. Many of these faith communities avoid the term *church* because the term is so associated with co-opted religious institutions. For more on these emerging faith communities in the United States, see emergentvillage.com, with links to other global networks. See also Ryan Bolger and Eddie Gibbs, *Emerging Churches* (Grand Rapids: Baker, 2006).
5. See Diana Butler-Bass, *Christianity for the Rest of Us* (San Francisco: Harper San Francisco, 2006), and see also the justice churches network, sojo.net.
6. In a sermon on 2 Corinthians 12:9, Dietrich Bonhoeffer spoke of the need for more public action against injustice: "Christianity stands or falls with its revolutionary protest against violence, arbitrariness and pride of power and with its plea for the weak. Christians are doing too little to make these points clear rather than too much. Christendom adjusts itself far too easily to the worship of power. Christians should give more offense, shock the world far more, than they are doing now. Christians should take a stronger stand in favor of the weak rather than considering first the possible right of the strong." members.tripod.com/~lutheran-peace/bonhoeffer24quotes.htm.

Uncovering the Truth that Could Change Everything

The *Secret* Message *of* Jesus

UNCOVERING THE TRUTH
THAT COULD CHANGE EVERYTHING

Brian D. McLaren

Author of A NEW KIND of CHRISTIAN

Now including a bonus chapter and discussion guide

In *The Secret Message of Jesus*, Brian McLaren leads readers on a journey as groundbreaking as it is life-changing.

The quest: Find the essential message of Jesus' life—even it overturns conventional ideas, priorities, and practices.

⁌ Available Now in Paperback ⁍